ADOBE INDESIGN
f/x & Design

Elaine Betts

CORIOLIS

The Coriolis Group, LLC
14455 N. Hayden Road, Suite 220
Scottsdale, Arizona 85260

480/483-0192
FAX 480/483-0193
http://www.coriolis.com

Library of Congress Card Number: 99-049156

President, CEO
Keith Weiskamp

Publisher
Steve Sayre

Acquisitions Editor
Mariann Hansen Barsolo

Marketing Specialist
Beth Kohler

Project Editor
Melissa D. Olson

Technical Reviewer
Rick LePage

Production Coordinator
Meg E. Turecek

Cover Design
Jody Winkler
additional art provided by Brandon Riza

Layout Design
April Nielsen

CD-ROM Developer
Robert Clarfield

Printed in the United States of America
10 9 8 7 6 5 4 3 2 1

Other Titles For The Creative Professional

To the finest, most supportive, most generous offspring a mother could ever hope for—Kristin and Eric Rivedal, and Eric's SO, Sue.
—Elaine Betts

ABOUT THE AUTHOR

Elaine Betts writes primarily computer books, and she is a certified technical trainer who teaches a variety of software applications. She is the coauthor of *QuarkXPress 4 In Depth* (Coriolis), the *ACT! 4 Bible* (IDG Books), and documentation for HindSight, Ltd. She has contributed to MS Office 97 and 2000 books and training materials. For the past 14 years, she's worked as a photography and film stylist, specializing in off-figure garments, linens, sets, and food. She welcomes email comments and questions at **e@ebetts.com**.

ACKNOWLEDGMENTS

What wordsmith exists in a vacuum? Without you, dear reader, I have no reason to write, no ear to hear my voice. I thank you for filling my life with purpose.

My name would not be on this book without Mariann Barsolo, whose faith in me and gentle guidance are endless. Despite her wearing two hats throughout most of this book, acquisitions editor and project editor, the second pairing of Betts and Barsolo was even better than the first, and I thought the first was perfect.

All errors and misstatements in this book are mine, and mine alone, but there were lots more before Rick LePage combed through the content for technical flubs and offered kindly corrections and great suggestions that improved the book immensely.

To the people at The Coriolis Group, kudos and gratitude: Margaret Berson, the copyeditor who hated my use of "may" and "since," but always managed to make sense when I didn't; Robert Clarfield, who slaved to make the best CD possible; and Melissa Olson, the kind of project editor every writer yearns for.

Thanks to those who shared their expertise with me: John Pelaez of Spectrographics; Daira Dundov of Cies-Sexton Visual; Tim Meehan, the script writer who spent longer than anyone should ever have learning VB; the Adobe staff who went many extra miles to help me: Brian Wiffin, Raine Bergstrom, Tim Cole, Carlos Palacian, and Bill Eisley; and all those beta testers who freely shared experiences, expertise, insights, and smoothed the learning curve.

I owe a special debt of gratitude and love to my friend, Susan Chandler Foster, who encouraged me to finally buy a home to live in and work on this book, and whose departed spirit is, even now, smiling at me and saying, "You can do it." I did, Susan, house and book.

My special thanks go to Dave Kottler, chief-in-charge-of-everything at APEX Communications, for generously providing his files for projects in this book, for letting me take liberties with those files, and for making me feel important.

—*Elaine Betts*

CONTENTS AT A GLANCE

TABLE OF CONTENTS

Chapter 4
Mastering Document Pages   67

PART II
DELVE DEEPER INTO INDESIGN

Chapter 7
Features To Spice Up And Speed Up Production   141

Chapter 8
Color Management   169

Chapter 11
Putting Your Publication To Bed   247

INTRODUCTION

Adobe InDesign is the centerpiece among many applications contributing to professional publications, such as magazines, newspapers, advertising pieces, and catalogs. In a world that has had little, if any, serious competition to date for creating and publishing high-end publications, InDesign offers alternatives and innovations sure to be embraced by many publishers, graphic artists, and designers.

About This Book

This book isn't meant to cover every single element of Adobe InDesign in minute detail. Rather, it is an overview of InDesign tools with a select body of information about specific features and behaviors that are unique to InDesign. It is meant as a quick learning tool for those with experience in using other desktop publishing (DTP) and graphic applications.

I assumed that most folks using this book want to get up to speed with InDesign. There is no discussion of elementary skills required to use the application or your computer. I've concentrated on specific skills and InDesign features that let you hit the ground running with this revolutionary, new desktop publishing application.

Comparisons To Other DTP Programs

In some places, I've referred to other applications by name, citing how things are done in an existing application compared to the way that InDesign handles the same task or skill. The other applications I've mentioned are Illustrator, Photoshop, QuarkXPress, and, in rare instances, CorelDRAW, so you can relate your real-world experience to your new bank of information.

Structure Of This Book

Naturally, every author hopes that his or her book will be so compelling that readers open the front cover and can't put it down, but I know how I use a reference book. I sometimes skip around, targeting only the information I need right away to complete the job at hand. I presume you are no different, so I've made it as easy as possible to open the book anywhere and find what you need. I recommend that you try to restrict your jumping about to a minimum, because some projects rely on earlier files you create and skills previously introduced.

There are plenty of figures to give you visual guidance as you learn, and the color InDesign Studio in the center of the book refers to projects you work on throughout the book. Careful indexing leads you to the information you want, in whatever order you prefer.

Discussion Of Concepts And Tools

The first two chapters address InDesign's basic concepts and tools. These discussions lay the groundwork for projects and act as a quick reference guide to speed you through the bumps in your learning curve. Throughout, I introduce concepts, list tools, or explain procedures, emphasizing those things that InDesign handles differently from other DTP and graphic applications. I suggest that you read the first two chapters before launching into the project chapters.

Hands-On Projects

Starting with Chapter 3, you'll find that each chapter covers concepts, tools, and procedures that lead to hands-on projects, some of which are highly structured in step-by-step format, while others test your learning by providing little more than a list of specifications. Where I found the subject particularly interesting or useful, I suggested free-form practice projects with no specifications. These projects are meant to further reinforce the skills you've practiced in structured projects. The goal of all projects is not to create great art, but to learn InDesign quickly and painlessly.

Minimum Hardware Requirements

Yes, it's possible to work with InDesign using computers with less than the stated hardware requirements, but, trust me, you'll find it frustrating. Processing speed is sorely impeded, and, often, screen redraw infuriatingly slow. Stick to the following minimum requirements, and you'll have a good experience with InDesign.

Macintosh Requirements

- PowerPC 603e processor or greater

- Mac OS 8.5 or later

- A hard disk with at least 120MB of free space

- At least 48MB of random access memory (RAM)

- A CD-ROM drive

- Monitor resolution of 800 by 600 pixels

- Adobe PostScript Level 2 (or higher) printer

For the best performance, Adobe Systems recommends the following hardware and software:

- PowerPC G3 processor

- 64MB or more of RAM

- High-resolution 24-bit screen display

Windows Requirements

- Pentium II Intel processor

- Windows 98, Windows NT 4 Workstation with Service Pack 3, or later

- A hard disk with at least 75MB of free space

- At least 48MB of random access memory (RAM)

- A CD-ROM drive

- 256-color (8-bit) display card

- For PostScript printing devices, Adobe PostScript Level 2 (or higher) printer driver

Note: Some non-PostScript printers are supported on the PC platform.

For the best performance, Adobe Systems recommends:

- Pentium II 300Mhz or faster Intel processor

- 64MB or more of RAM

- High-resolution (24-bit Super VGA or greater) video display card

- Adobe PostScript Level 2 (or higher) printer

Note: Keep in mind that, during installation, you must upgrade your Postscript driver to 4.3, which doesn't support Level 1 devices.

Both Mac and Windows users will find an Internet connection desirable in order to log-on to the Adobe site for discussion forums relating to InDesign.

Maximizing This Book And CD-ROM

Experienced designers and students with a background in using other graphic and desktop publishing applications who define their level of usage as intermediate to expert will reap the most benefit from using this book. It addresses both Macintosh and Windows users.

Preparing To Use The CD-ROM Project Files

Certain files must be copied from the CD-ROM accompanying this book to your hard drive. Other files can be used directly from the CD, although it's not recommended.

Note: There are system limitations to the number of fonts you can use at any given time in both PC and Mac systems. You can use a font utility, such as Suitcase, to activate or deactivate fonts on the fly (available at **www.extensis. com/suitcase/index.html**).

Installing Fonts

Throughout this book you'll find instructions to install fonts before beginning to work on projects. As much as I hoped to include all the fonts used in the project files, I am unable to do so because of copyright restrictions. Adobe kindly granted permission to provide Macintosh users with their screen fonts, but, because of the way PCs handle fonts, there are no fonts included for Windows users. (For a complete list of fonts used, refer to the readme file on the CD-ROM that accompanies this book.)

Rest assured that the absence of PC fonts has no effect on the usefulness of the project files. InDesign automatically substitutes fonts in the publications from among the fonts you have installed and activated on your computer. Irrespective of the fonts displayed in the files, each project can be successfully completed.

On either platform, an alert will warn you about missing fonts and list the names of the missing fonts. When InDesign substitutes missing fonts with a default font, all attributes applied to type set in the original font, such as tracking, horizontal and vertical scaling, color, and so on, are retained. In rare instances, text may reflow when it's set in a substitute font.

In the publication files, type set in a substitute font is typically highlighted in pink on screen. To identify the original fonts, click the Type tool on text set in a substituted font. The name of the original font appears surrounded by brackets in the Character palette. To eliminate the pink highlight applied to substituted fonts:

1. Choose File|Preferences|Composition.

2. Deselect Highlight Substituted Fonts.

You need to have sufficient hard drive space available to install the fonts required for projects throughout the book.

You also need enough hard disk space to copy at least the InDesign publication files to your computer.

Graphic Files

It is possible to leave publication graphic files stored on the CD-ROM or on a network, but you'll soon discover that access is slower. I suggest that you have enough hard disk space to copy the image files to your hard drive.

Relink Graphic Files To Project Publications

You might need to relink graphic files in publications you copy to your hard drive.

Use the Links palette (it opens automatically when you open files that need relinking), and highlight all the graphics listed in the palette.

1. Click the Relink button at the bottom of the Links palette.

2. Locate the folder containing the graphic files listed in the Links palette.

3. Click the Open button to re-establish the proxy graphics in the publication to the original graphic files in the folder.

Contents, Structure, And Use Of The CD-ROM

The CD-ROM accompanying this book contains InDesign publication files, Macintosh screen fonts, and text and graphic files required to properly display the InDesign publications. All the files necessary for any given project are nested inside a platform-specific folder labeled Mac or Win.

In most instances, graphic files have been saved in low-resolution formats suitable for on-screen display. The project files are not meant for high-resolution printed output.

In addition, the CD contains scripts to be used with InDesign as is or modified to suit your needs.

All of the APEX Communication files and accompanying images are copyright protected. You may freely use them in conjunction with this book for learning InDesign, but you may not use them for any other purpose.

Contributors

The majority of project files used in this book were contributed by Dave Kottler, designer par excellence, and founder of APEX Communications. Not only did he contribute his files, but he gave me license to change them. Working with Dave's designs spared me endless hours in preparing projects, and the projects should give you the pleasure of working with professional quality designs. Throughout the book, there is more information about Dave's professional history and some of his client's files that you will use. If you want to send Dave an email, his address is **APXcom@aol.com**.

Script Contributor

Adobe clearly wants you to customize the behaviors of InDesign to make your workflow efficient and productive. Because no application can meet the needs of all users, InDesign is scriptable, and you, as a user, will want to learn about scripting in order to customize InDesign tasks to meet your own unique set of tasks.

Scripting differs from plug-in technology. Plug-ins are designed to address global needs, and scripting meets the specific needs of your workflow. Tim Meehan used elementary scripts as the basis for demystifying scripting and teaching you how to create your own scripts. Even if you never wanted to learn a programming language, you'll find this information enlightening and easy to apply to your own needs. You can contact Tim at **t.meehan@att.net**.

More InDesign Information

As of August 30, 1999, release day for InDesign, there is already an excellent, highly active email discussion forum at **www.blueworld.com/ blueworld/lists/indesign.html**. Anyone may join.

You'll receive many messages, most of which are informative, and you can add your own observations and queries to the pile. I've found this very helpful. Often, someone from Adobe, including Product Manager David Evans, is the person who replies to questions in this forum, so the information is reliable.

A Small Disclaimer

Please, let me remind you that this book was written while I used various generations of beta software. The program changed, even as I wrote, and you might find some minor differences in the final release version, although the Coriolis team and I have made every effort to avert that possibility.

It is the policy of the Coriolis Group to make available any critical corrections or files that were overlooked during production of this book via their Web site at **www.coriolis.com**. You may also contact me, Elaine Betts, directly with any questions, observations, or comments via email at **e@ebetts.com**. Be sure to include the words, "InD fx and design reader," in the Subject line to expedite a reply.

Moving On

Welcome to Adobe InDesign and to the fastest learning tool available. In the first chapter, you'll find an overview of InDesign, why it's special, and how it can increase your production efficiency. There is also a brief, introductory comparison of InDesign to other DTP applications.

PART I

GETTING
UP TO
SPEED WITH
INDESIGN

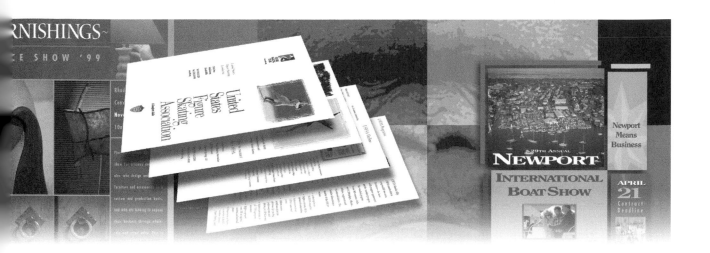

A BRAVE NEW
DTP WORLD

Scan the vistas that InDesign opens to print and on-screen designers. Discover its integrated workflow and accessibility to developers, and see how it stacks up in comparison to other DTP applications.

Skills Covered In This Chapter

- Prepare to use the Adobe workflow effectively

- Assess InDesign's features

- Learn about InDesign's scriptability

During the 15 years from 1984 to 1999, a revolutionary concept, desktop publishing, evolved and expanded to touch every aspect of visual communication. The computerized tools of desktop publishing remained few, but they bore such promise and smoothed so many production paths that even applications that were less than perfect won our hearts.

Some applications attempted to be all things to all users. Others narrowed their focus to graphics or page design. Often these improvements came at the price of a daunting learning curve. Finally, an application called InDesign steps beyond all that to meet the sophisticated requirements of graphics and publishing, both electronic and print.

Why InDesign Is The Hot Choice

If you've been in the graphics and publishing business for any stretch of time at all, you've no doubt used a desktop publishing program of some sort. Because Adobe's InDesign is brand new, there must be some reason you're reading this book! Either you're the voraciously curious sort with book budget dollars to burn, or, like many others, you were vaguely unhappy with other desktop publishing applications and bought InDesign with a list of wishes. You yearn to learn that those wishes have been fulfilled by InDesign.

Analysis Of The DTP Industry

Every publication, regardless of its destination and purpose, is a multifaceted production. Visual components, text, and page geometry combine to make a powerful statement. Each element adds to the strength of the statement, but is fraught with an equal potential for disaster. The more that tools of publishing are made readily accessible to large numbers of people, the greater the potential for creative use of those tools, and the more likely you are to encounter problems, particularly with output.

The dramas of missing printer fonts, graphics that won't print because they've been manipulated in the page layout or saved in a volatile format, quirky text flow, and myriad other output bugaboos are eliminated when completed files are converted to PDF. Adobe, with the release of Acrobat 4, has resolved many of those dilemmas. Version 4 embeds the CMS data, giving you more reliable color printout, and the problem with fuzzy EPS graphics in version 3 has gone away, to name but two improvements.

Using a feature preprogrammed into InDesign, documents can be converted to PDF without purchasing an additional application. The original InDesign file remains intact, fully editable, and ready to be converted again to any format other than InDesign's. The PDF version is editable up to a point, ready for proof printing or final output with as little room for error as is presently possible in the world of printed material. PDF is probably the most revolutionary development since the inception of desktop publishing.

InDesign's Concept

My first question was, "Why does Adobe want another desktop publishing application?" Face it. It has two already: PageMaker and FrameMaker, and Illustrator has lots of desktop publishing capabilities. What's up?

The official Adobe word is: "...PageMaker continues to enjoy high demand among business customers, particularly on the Windows platform. These customers want more professional-looking output than entry-level desktop publishing tools can provide, and they view PageMaker as the natural next step." Hmmm. What's this really saying?

The company PR continues, "Adobe Systems plans to continue developing, marketing and supporting PageMaker as a page-layout program with professional-level features for business publishers." Reading between the lines, I presume they are positioning PageMaker to meet demands from big businesses who must produce all manner of publications using a work force that isn't necessarily trained in the visual arts or page layout design. PageMaker now comes with lots of predesigned templates and less challenging, albeit less rich, layout capabilities.

So where's InDesign going? "Adobe InDesign is more than just a new page-layout program. It's a key component in an integrated, business solution" (at this point I had to jerk myself up by the collar to keep from snoring) "that includes Acrobat and its composite PDF workflow, PostScript, Illustrator, and Photoshop." And this brought me to full attention: "Together these Adobe programs deliver the best solution for the future of professional publishing because of their tight integration, powerful productivity and design tools, and high-quality output...." I might add that the Adobe product support has consistently been prompt, courteous, and thorough!

So, now I see the point.

Building Professional Print Publications

InDesign belongs in the hands of design professionals who want to create high-end output from the ground up. All design decisions are left to the user. The program provides all the bells and whistles required for sophisticated publications and varied visual design plus the advantage of a familiar interface to expedite production.

Create your own templates, work with eccentric paper sizes, and manipulate every object or frame on the pages you design. Edit, tweak, and finesse the contents of any frame. The sky, good taste, and your budgets are the limit.

Compatibility Features

If you've ever used Adobe Illustrator or Photoshop, you're already familiar with the ways and means of InDesign. Open all three, and you'll find the on-screen differences so slight as to be insignificant. The screen components are essentially the same: palettes, a document window, and menus. InDesign has colored margin lines, and Illustrator and Photoshop documents don't. All three applications can combine text and graphics. InDesign *concentrates* on page geometry, however, allowing the graphics and text imported to or created in layouts to be handled in the most creative manner.

Each application, however, has a particular capability it performs best. It's hard to top Photoshop for manipulating scanned images. Illustrator is tops at line art. InDesign's strengths lie in the complexities of page layout design, text, and page geometry. For years I've taught graphics software classes and faced the question, "But why buy two or three programs when one can do it all?" and my response is, "Well, I can take a telephone and make it into a planter, but neither the plant nor the caller is completely happy."

No application, regardless of how powerful, can be all things to all users. Creators of software try valiantly to meet the greatest number of needs expressed by their users, but some needs are esoteric and not economically feasible to program into the application. Those familiar with other Adobe products know that a host of plug-in developers provided customizing solutions for Illustrator and Photoshop users. Now many of those same vendors, and some new ones, are working feverishly to gratify the demands for specialized ways of using InDesign features.

Familiar Interface

Opening InDesign is a bit like going to your favorite hangout with a bunch of colleagues. Not much changes from the last time you were together. Everything's familiar and comfortable.

InDesign's tool palettes look and work almost identically to those in other Adobe software. The keyboard shortcuts are the same as the ones you've learned for Illustrator and Photoshop. If you learned QuarkXPress keyboard shortcuts before getting InDesign, you can activate the familiar set of QuarkXPress shortcuts so thoughtfully provided under the InDesign File menu (see Figure 1.1).

Everything on an InDesign page is an object, and all objects can be modified. Some objects are frames for holding text or graphics. Other objects are the familiar geometric shapes and lines you've worked with in Illustrator and Photoshop: rectangles, ellipses, polygons, and so on. Even the Selection

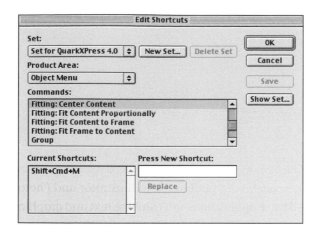

Figure 1.1

A complete set of keyboard shortcuts from QuarkXPress that perform the same action for InDesign is made accessible through this dialog box (for instance, centering a graphic file in a frame is Command+Shift+M on the Mac, and Ctrl+Shift+M in Windows).

tool and Direct Selection tool look the same and perform the same tasks across all three programs (see Figure 1.2). For that matter, InDesign's selection tools are even located at the top of the Tool palette as they are in Illustrator's Tool palettes. It's just darned hard to get lost in or overwhelmed by InDesign, no matter what desktop publishing history you're coming from.

File Conversions

Adobe promises that InDesign can directly open files created in other applications, specifically PageMaker 6.5 and QuarkXPress 3.3x and 4.x. Taking very little on faith, I had to try this. Sure enough, my XPress files opened perfectly, and my PageMaker 6.0 files didn't. When they say 6.5, that's what they mean.

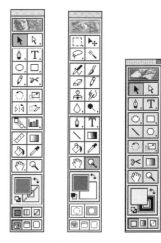

Figure 1.2

One glance at the tool palettes in (from left) Illustrator, Photoshop, and InDesign is all it takes to know that the Adobe environment is being more and more standardized so you can work faster.

Opening QuarkXPress documents requires absolutely no effort and produces exactly the same document on screen and from a printer or press as the original application that created it. There is one huge caveat, though. QuarkXPress documents created with third-party QuarkXTensions are dicey. Sometimes the XTensions cause problems, and sometimes they don't.

If you're the creator of the original QuarkXPress document, you'll know what XTensions you have and activated as you worked. In that case, the best solution for reliable conversion is to open QuarkXPress, deactivate third-party XTensions, open the file, and resave it with no possible connection to those XTensions. That should make conversion seamless.

If, on the other hand, you didn't create the QuarkXPress document, you're in for a trying session. Try opening and saving it in your own version of QuarkXPress with no third-party XTensions. If that fails, I fear you'll have to do as I did in a few instances, re-create the file in InDesign. It's not an overwhelming task, just tiresome.

When I encountered a QuarkXPress document that wouldn't convert, I just opened both applications and used the Measurements Palette and dialog boxes to assure that the re-do was accurate. The best part about this trial is that you learn oceans about InDesign and see first-hand the advantages available to you that the other application lacks.

Formats other than QuarkXPress 3.3.x or 4.x and PageMaker 6.5 need a plug-in to directly open these documents in InDesign. As of this writing, no information is available about third-party plug-ins, but stay tuned to the Adobe Web site for the latest announcements. It's early in the development stage of this program, so things appear daily that enrich the new program. Adobe's InDesign Web pages seem to change before your very eyes, so you can be certain you're getting the latest breaking news from the Adobe Web site at **www.adobe.com/prodindex/indesign/**.

Functionality

The joy of InDesign's new features rests in their versatility. I'm certainly not being paid by the Adobe Public Relations Department to ballyhoo and carry on about how grand these features are. For me, it's simply a matter of comparing all the programs I've used and taught over the past 10 or 15 years, and assessing their abilities in comparison to InDesign. In some cases I actually opened the programs simultaneously on screen.

There is little, if anything, that other desktop publishing applications can do that InDesign can't, and plenty of things InDesign does that other page layout applications don't, such as converting documents to PDF and automatically converting any frame of any shape to a Bézier polygon, to name but two. It's largely a matter of your comfort zone and the degree of efficiency and integration you want in your work life.

There are plenty of folks who think Microsoft has gone over the top trying to be all things to all people, and there is a bit of that aura surrounding Adobe's approach to graphics and page layout. What I also see is that Adobe programs increasingly address the competition, offering equal or greater power in a more friendly and familiar interface.

In a nutshell, Adobe's goal is to help you create polished, professional-level publications and avoid as many pitfalls as possible with solidly integrated applications. That's not such a bad idea.

Color Models

When it comes to color, you name it, you can do it with InDesign. Black and white, grayscale, halftones, four color, spot colors, standardized colors, custom color, on-screen colors, all are available to use singly or, where appropriate, in combination in any publication. You can work in any one of three color spaces, RGB, CMYK, or LAB.

Workflow And Production

Isn't it always the way? Seemingly straightforward words are the most misleading. In relation to InDesign, these two words—workflow and production—have many interpretations. *Workflow* can refer to the development of content for an InDesign document or for the manner in which you prepare that document for output. *Production* can refer to task management decisions you must make before starting to design a publication or to the steps leading to producing the final output. With that crystal clear (not one bit!), you can wander down the slippery slope of ambiguity in document creation.

Developing Publications In Multiple Applications

It's becoming all but impossible to think of desktop publishing in terms of one application. More often than not, at the level you are accustomed to producing desktop publishing documents, a number of persons using a variety of applications contribute to the end result. Photographers use one set of tools to prepare their images for a page layout document, illustrators often prefer a different set of capabilities found in other applications, and copy writers use yet another collection of applications for developing the word content of page layout documents. The larger the number of contributors to a publication, the more chance for problems with the workflow.

Determining who must sign off each contribution is essential. Working backward from a deadline can be helpful for establishing a timeline for each submission. If you use this method to determine your schedule, double the logical time required for every contributed component. That way you should have about half as many crises as you otherwise encounter. If it can go wrong, it will, so prepare. Come in ahead of schedule and under budget, and I guarantee you'll have more work than you ever hoped for.

Input And Output Dictate Workflow

InDesign readily imports documents created in other Adobe products, and it has filters that open the gates for documents created in WordPerfect, Microsoft Word, and Microsoft Works. The imported text documents retain most of their character, paragraph, and style attributes. ASCII text documents, such as email and Notepad or SimpleText documents, are also welcomed to InDesign. Entering, importing, and formatting text are discussed in Chapter 5.

Some of the components easily accomplished in other Adobe applications, such as tables made with PageMaker's Table Editor, don't make the transition. In this case, the workaround is to save the table as an EPS and replace it in PageMaker before the conversion. Inelegant, but successful.

A vast array of applications can contribute visual components to InDesign layouts. Naturally, documents produced by any of Adobe's graphics applications are compatible, but other software can also join in the workflow. The determining factor for importing graphics is the format in which the graphic is saved. If an application can save the graphic file in a format compatible with InDesign, it doesn't matter which application you use to create the graphic. The graphic file formats are covered in Chapter 7.

The salient factor, in either a simple or a complex project, is what must be produced in which order. Your workflow for a periodical publication based on a well-honed template will be quite different from the workflow for a one-off document.

Finally, the output destination is critical in assessing your workflow. Documents headed for on-screen presentation require a completely different timeline than those going to an imagesetter, and those going to a service bureau need a different timeline than those going to an imagesetter. All of these factors help determine your workflow.

Adobe's Workflow

In trying to take some of the bumps out of the graphics professional's work life, Adobe has a collection of applications that work seamlessly together to make life in the fast lane much less complicated. Photoshop and Illustrator feed artwork into InDesign's page layout in their native format, and PressReady is the PostScript 3 proofing tool that provides interim color proofing on particular models of Hewlett-Packard, Canon, and Epson inkjet printers and simulates high-end web press output.

Finally, Acrobat converts completed or interim documents to a format that eliminates the typical printing hazards of missing fonts, fonts embedded in PostScript graphics, color shifts, erratic text reflow, and myriad other unwanted quirks that can arise when dealing with service bureaus and imagesetters.

Print Features In InDesign

Producing a publication is only the first step to communication. After all the design and layout is honed to a fine edge, somebody has to see it to accomplish its mission. InDesign provides everything you expect for web press or service bureau output, but it has new ways to give your clients a reliable proof print and to distribute final product to the masses.

PDF Conversion

Programmed into InDesign is a slimmed-down version of Acrobat with the same ability to convert your documents to Portable Document Format (PDF) files. The rumble is that PDF technology is dramatically changing the printing industry. Converted files allow simple editing, if necessary, while maintaining design integrity and consistent color conversion with the added benefit of file compression. The original file remains intact, so there's no loss if you need to make more dramatic revisions. Assembling everything that belongs to a publication for printing or display on screen—graphic files, fonts, and so on—becomes a non-issue with PDF.

In passing, it's interesting to note that Adobe is releasing two different versions of Acrobat 4, one for Windows and one for the Mac OS. The Windows version aims at business users, with email and Web integration. It provides for digital signatures. Using a utility in the Windows version (called Web Capture), you can convert existing HTML pages and Web sites into printable PDF files for annotation or viewing offline.

The Macintosh version targets the graphic arts and prepress community and includes support for Open Press Interface (OPI) 2.0.

Both versions handle last-minute editing of graphics and text as well as taking advantage of TrueType technology and PostScript 3's Smooth Shading for gradients. Acrobat 4 even converts duotone and Hexachrome images to a PostScript composite, though as of the first release, InDesign doesn't support Hexachrome.

Desktop Printer For Proofs

Face it, we all have clients because we specialize in something they don't have the time or expertise to do. We develop their suggestions, hopes, and needs into concrete designs and then show the clients a comp. (We all know that comps are approximations of what the final product will look like.) The clients look at it this way and that way and then launch into the things they like and the things they want changed. And back you go to the midnight oil and black coffee.

Unless your clients pop for a professional proof print, they never really know exactly how the final prints will look. Proof prints aren't cheap, but they're accurate.

Some clients can't or don't want to afford this added expense. InDesign lets you produce remarkably accurate inkjet proof prints at a fraction of the cost of imagesetter or offset press proof prints. That client who used to drive you nuts with nitpicking and revision after revision will suddenly become your most contented client because you can produce endless desktop proof prints at negligible cost using specific models of desktop printers. (There's more information about desktop proofing in Chapter 11.)

InDesign Documents On Screen

Anything that looks simple seldom is simple, especially when it comes to visual design. When you've finally gotten through the maze of meetings required to settle on a print document's design and content, you certainly don't want to spend untold hours revising it yet again so it can be used on screen.

InDesign allows you to conveniently export your document as an HTML document ready for the Web. You can maintain the positioning of objects on your pages, but some design elements, especially those relating to font manipulation, will be lost. (Exporting to HTML is discussed in Chapter 9.) While Adobe is working feverishly to make Web conversions more elegant and accurate, its stand is still that conversions don't replace a good HTML editor. That's probably the reason they acquired GoLive to plump out the suite of publishing applications.

XML And SVG

Extensible Markup Language (XML) started the ball rolling toward a standard vector data format for Web designs. Adobe, Sun Microsystems, IBM, and Netscape, in a cooperative effort, developed Precision Graphics Markup Language (PGML) to provide the professional quality typography that simple HTML tags can't accomplish. Granted, there are tags for determining font faces *if* viewers have those fonts loaded on the computer they're using to look at a site, but the limitations are such that few HTML-bound designers are ever really satisfied with the end result.

Scalable Vector Graphics (SVG) makes available to Web designers the same high-quality graphics, precise layout, and color use that print designers have always employed. With the adoption of SVG as an XML-compliant graphics standard, PGML opens the Web to a full selection of graphic options. Adobe plans to support the SVG standard in Illustrator, Acrobat, PressReady, GoLive, and possibly other Adobe software. Because InDesign works with these applications, there's every reason to believe that converting existing InDesign print documents to Web-ready documents will be accomplished with little if any loss of the original design.

Repurposing Documents

In almost every instance, you can use Acrobat to convert documents to a more versatile format for distribution and more stable print output, but what do you do when you want to use an existing InDesign document and its content for a different purpose, such as an intranet or the Web? InDesign allows you to save existing documents in HTML format for on-screen viewing. (For more information about HTML conversions, see Chapter 10.)

InDesign's Accessibility To Developers

Right out of the box InDesign has plug-ins. There are plug-ins for editing dictionaries, creating special effects in graphics, filters for importing files, plug-ins for manipulating text, and for gathering up your file components for output. Adobe's and third-parties' plug-ins expand the capabilities of InDesign. Developers have created and are busily producing specialized InDesign plug-in solutions for things like publishing databases, creating tables, managing ad layouts, and tracking advertisements.

So far, Em Software (**www.emsoftware.com**) has announced InDesign versions of InData and InCatalog, its database publishing plug-ins. InData automatically formats database or spreadsheet information for use in catalogs, directories, and other structured publications. InCatalog creates hot links between a product database and an InDesign document. Changes in either file automatically update in the other. ShadeTree Marketing (**www.bordersguys.com**) plans to offer an InDesign version of Fraemz, that lets you apply one of 404 high-resolution borders to text and picture frames in InDesign documents. Fraemz also includes drop shadows.

But wait! There's more than just plug-ins. InDesign is scriptable for the Macintosh using AppleScript, and for Windows using Visual Basic. Although not everyone is able or willing to learn these programming languages, major publications, such as newspapers, catalogs, book publishers, and others who need to repeat the same task again and again will find it worth the investment in hiring someone to create scripts specific to their needs. The CD-ROM accompanying this book contains some basic scripts for you to study and edit to your specific needs.

Comparing Competing Products

First, let's take a look at the things other Adobe page layout programs do well. FrameMaker is best suited to long documents with few artistic or graphic elements. For instance, government offices and software documentation writers love it. It's sometimes referred to as a technical writing tool. Someone establishes the templates for a huge volume of information, sets up the workflow, and then others fill up the frames with what they do best, writing. Every program has its kinks, and FrameMaker isn't immune. For instance, pasted Word text isn't directly editable. There are also quirks when converting FrameMaker documents to PDF files. (Clearly, FrameMaker hasn't always been an Adobe product.) It takes a lot of workarounds to fix either one of these problems. Although it's a powerful publishing tool, FrameMaker's emphasis isn't particularly artistic nor is its interface intuitive.

PageMaker, the original page layout program, still has a warm place in my heart. I cut my desktop publishing teeth on it back in the mid-eighties. But the underground tom-toms suggest that because its underlying structure was designed so long ago by Aldus (remember them?), it's not efficient to (or may be impossible to) reprogram PageMaker for today's highly demanding electronic and print publishing milieu. Adobe won't leave the installed base up in the air, though. PageMaker is still a good program that produces fine documents. It costs less than InDesign and is more likely to meet the needs of businesses and organizations with limited budgets that want to step up from cumbersome layouts created in word processors.

Now, moving on to the giant in the tower, QuarkXPress has, for years, been the only application that encompassed typographic excellence, artistic design elements, and the production needs of those creating complex publications. As time wore on, Quark improved and honed its features, but it always was and is a vessel for holding graphics produced primarily by Adobe software. Originally it also relied, for the most part, upon text produced by word processors, which was then refined after the text was imported into a layout. Despite QuarkXPress's vastly improved text entry capabilities over the years, the graphics continue to come from Adobe products, causing a brain shift from one environment to another. Now, with the advent of InDesign, all the layout sophistication and the parallel interface are conjoined in one suite of applications.

In addition, as of this writing, QuarkXPress 4.x doesn't have built-in PDF capabilities, though Callas Software has a PDF XTension. (Drop by **www.callassoftware.com** if you're interested.) The shift to PDF delivery methods in both printed and electronic output is probably the strongest argument for using InDesign as the foundation of complex publications because PDF conversion is already an integral, ready-to-use part of the program.

Moving On

In the coming chapter you'll become acquainted with the InDesign environment. Each of the screen components is briefly but concisely covered, and you'll learn about the features that make using InDesign more efficient.

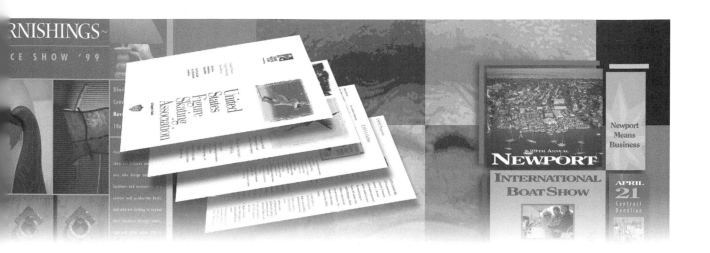

SURVEYING InDESIGN'S LANDSCAPE

The dawning of a new era in desktop publishing brings exciting new features and capabilities wrapped in the familiar look and feel of other Adobe product environments.

Skills Covered In This Chapter

- Investigate the InDesign environment

- Identify screen components

- Get an overview of this book's projects

You have experience in the desktop publishing industry. You've used page layout applications long enough to know your way around, and produced publications aplenty, but you've never worked with a program quite like InDesign. In this chapter, you'll learn the basic information needed to make use of InDesign's many capabilities. Use this chapter to quickly get up to speed, and as a reference when you work with things that are new or unfamiliar to you.

InDesign Environment

All right, I confess. Computers R My Life, so hardly anything is more exciting to me than opening a new program. The first thing I do is take a good look at what's on screen, then I cruise through all the menus and play with all the tools to see what they do.

As you might guess, opening InDesign for the first time was, for me, like going home for the holidays. It all looks and behaves with the familiarity of family. Because I've been using PageMaker, Photoshop, and Illustrator for many versions, past and present, the biggest surprise in InDesign was that there are no surprises! There are plenty of presents, though.

Pasteboard Work Area

Many graphic and desktop publishing applications have a pasteboard area—that place on screen outside a document page where you can store things that aren't yet positioned on a page and where you can extend objects beyond the page boundaries to create a bleed. InDesign handles the pasteboard differently from other DTP programs I've worked with.

PageMaker has one pasteboard that travels along to whatever page or spread you are viewing at the moment; thus objects on the pasteboard are always in the same relationship with every page. A rectangle on the pasteboard to the left of page 2 will be to the left of page 22. QuarkXPress has a global pasteboard that encompasses all pages and spreads. Objects on the pasteboard stay put. A rectangle to the left of page 2 appears only on the pasteboard beside page 2.

Each page or spread in InDesign has its own pasteboard. You may not realize this fact until you view an InDesign publication in a thumbnail-sized percentage view (see Figure 2.1). The effect is similar to the global pasteboard of QuarkXPress.

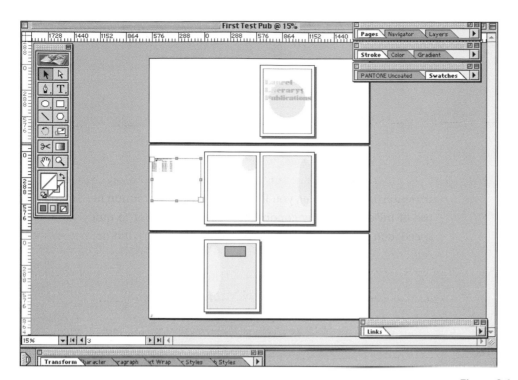

Figure 2.1
Simulate a thumbnail view by using a reduced percentage view.

Speaking of thumbnail views, InDesign doesn't have one. Your best option is to look at multiple pages at a small percentage view. You can reduce views as far as 5 percent and as large as 4,000 percent. Yes, that's four thousand percent. At that magnification, precision becomes a glowing reality, not a by-guess-and-by-golly proposition.

Pages And Page Parts

Rearranging pages in a publication involves dragging the page icons in the Pages palette to a new position. (The Pages palette is covered in a later section of this chapter.) That way no objects on the pages are disturbed. If you take a notion to drag one or more objects on a page to another page far removed, a reduced view works nicely. Using this method, the object simply moves from one page to another page. It's not automatically duplicated (see Figure 2.2). However, if you were to drag and drop the object from one InDesign document to another, then it would be duplicated rather than simply moved.

Island Spreads

Island Spreads are unique to InDesign. When you design spreads—two or more pages side by side that you want to be inseparable—you can select the spread pages in the Pages palette and use the pop-up menu at the top right of the palette to assign the Island Spread attribute. An Island Spread can't be joined to other pages. No matter whether you add pages to your document, remove pages, or move pages, the island spread remains as a unit. Up to 10 pages are permissible in Island Spreads.

DUPLICATE AN OBJECT AS YOU DRAG AND DROP

If you want to leave a duplicate of an object on one page within a document and have a copy on another page in the same document, press the Option key (Mac) or the Alt key (Windows) to make a copy of the object as you drag it to the new location within the document.

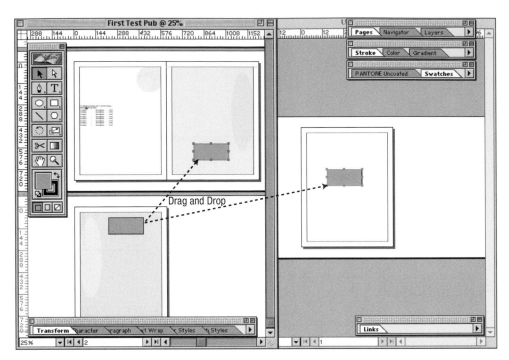

Figure 2.2

The method for dragging and dropping an object from page to page within a document and from one document to another is identical: Reduce the page view percentage, click the object, and drag and drop it where you want it.

If you prefer some flexibility in positioning pages within a spread or want to remove pages from a spread, forego or temporarily turn off the Island Spread attribute. Then you can drag one or more pages out of a spread until the black rectangle or vertical bar (displayed by the dragged page in the Pages palette) doesn't touch any existing pages, and drop the page in a new position on the Pages palette.

Objects On Pages

Everything you draw, type, or place on a page or the pasteboard is considered an object. Objects can be grouped so their relationships are maintained, and locked after positioning so that the object can't accidentally be moved. You can also create complex objects, such as a text box with a doughnut hole or a combination of shapes to create asymmetrical objects using Compound Paths found on the Object menu.

Watermarks

A watermark used to be something only paper manufacturers embedded in their best paper stock. Now it's often used by page layout artists as a design element. You can create a digital text watermark file of your own.

Most of the time, digital watermarks are a function of your printer's capability, and they are set from the Print dialog box. With InDesign, you can create the watermark as a master item or place it on a layer that holds only the watermark, and then you can display or hide the watermark at will (see Figure 2.3).

Figure 2.3
Use watermarks on shorter documents as a graphic element or as part of a corporate identity package you design.

Figure 2.4
Each export format has its particular niche.

Exporting Files

Any InDesign document can be exported in any of several formats. Select File|Export to open the Export dialog box and select from the Format menu at the lower right of the dialog box (see Figure 2.4). These formats include:

- *Adobe PDF (Portable Document Format)*—More and more, this is the format of choice for document delivery both on the Web and to print production. This conversion allows very limited editing of text and graphics, if necessary, just before printing or uploading. It retains all the refinements of your design and can even be printed from a desktop printer. Also, PDFs can be emailed for client approval, with no loss of fidelity, or viewed online, but only if the viewer has Adobe Acrobat. At this writing, Netscape Navigator 3 or later and Internet Explorer 4 or later support PDF reading within their browser windows. Because Acrobat Reader is a freebie download, available in multitudes of places on the Web, anyone who wants to view a PDF document offline can do so with a minimum of effort.

- *EPS (Encapsulated PostScript)*—Preferred by many service bureaus, this format preserves all your design work in a highly refined image of your document that alleviates the necessity for the service bureau to have even the software on which you created the document. The one drawback is your inability to edit an EPS file after exporting it. In some cases, that can be a blessing unto itself. No inept printer operator can botch up what you've done.

- *HTML (Hypertext Markup Language)*—If your destination for a file is the Web, you're well advised to plan and develop the document for on-screen viewing from the start. Simply converting documents intended for print output to HTML can give you major headaches. Because there are few text formatting tags in HTML, all your elaborate tweaking for the web press output is likely to be lost in transition. Colors you've created for CMYK, then converted to RGB lose their subtlety, and may take on a garish look.

- *Prepress File*—An alternative to the EPS export format, this format is device-independent and will print to just about any PostScript output device. The Prepress format is especially suitable for post-processing chores, such as trapping and the imposition of document pages.

InDesign Screen Components

Before launching into some spiffy projects that should help you learn more about using InDesign, it behooves me to do a brief tour of the basic screen components and what they do. Because it is my wont to begin with the menus when I'm getting acquainted with a program, the first thing you may want to do is open InDesign. That way I can keep the verbiage to a minimum while being sure you have everything at your fingertips.

If you haven't bought or installed InDesign yet, I'll try to provide enough screenshots to get you through this part with as little stress and mystery as possible.

1. Get yourself a refreshing drink.
2. Open your InDesign application.
3. Explore with me, proceeding from left to right in the menu bar.

Menus

You learn a lot about how the programmers of an application think, the sorts of organization they've established, and the capabilities of a program by looking at the listings in each menu. I'll start at the left and progress right across the main menu, touching upon everything, but elaborating on only those things that are different or particularly noteworthy in the following menus:

- File
- Edit
- Layout
- Type
- Object
- View

- Window

- Help

File

All File menus deal with generalities pertaining to the documents produced in a program. If you're familiar with other Adobe graphics programs, there are few surprises here. Admittedly, more things are listed in the InDesign File menu than in the purely graphics-oriented Adobe applications, but that's because it produces documents with multiple pages combining text and graphics in a wide variety of documents. The content of InDesign documents is often drawn from documents created in other applications. InDesign also has special needs for gathering up every component used in a document to print that document (see Figure 2.5).

Below the Place command, used for selecting and importing files, are the following items:

- *Links*—Just another way of opening the Links palette that shows the name and path of files you place in a document. There's more about the palettes later in this chapter.

- *Document Setup*—Relates to the way you want your document to look. It determines the Number Of Pages you want a document to have when you first open it. Choose to have Facing Pages and whether to apply a Master Text Frame to each page of the document. Document Setup also lets you determine the Page Size and Page Orientation (landscape or portrait).

- *Page Setup*—Relates to how the document is prepared for sending to a printing device. PCs and Macs handle the Page Setup in different ways. If you work with a Macintosh, use the Page Setup command in the File menu to establish which printer you want to use and output options. If you use a PC, use the Print command in the File menu to set these instructions and options. There is more about printers and printing in Chapter 11. In all other File menu listings, the Macintosh and PC versions are identical.

- *Preflight*—Relates to things you want to do before printing your document. In QuarkXPress, the Preflight checks are found under the Utilities menu. InDesign has Preflight in the File menu. It's a dialog box with several screens for checking Fonts, Links And Images, Colors And Inks, and Print Settings (see Figure 2.6).

- *Package*—This is the final step before sending your publication to press. It gathers everything needed, including the fonts used in your publication.

Figure 2.5

In addition to commands relating to the document as a whole, InDesign's File menu includes a list of recently opened documents and an entry for accessing Adobe's Web site.

Note: Document Setup and Page Setup both appear on the Macintosh version, but only Document Setup is listed on the File menu of the PC version.

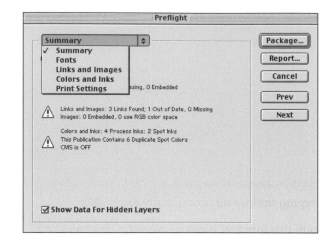

Figure 2.6
Each screen of the Preflight
dialog box gives feedback about
your document.

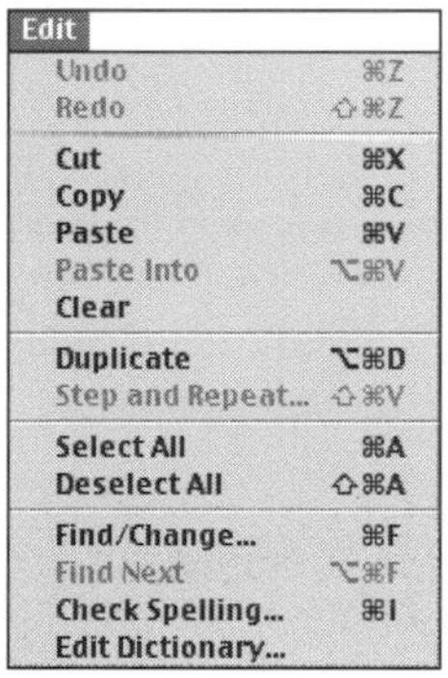

Figure 2.7
Observe that the key commands
to the right of most Edit menu
commands, and of other menus,
are identical to key commands
found in other Adobe software.

• *Edit Shortcuts*—Loads a set of Quark key commands that use the same keyboard shortcuts for identical actions performed in QuarkXPress and InDesign. The Quark key set doesn't override every InDesign keystroke, only those for actions that are the same in both programs.

Edit

No efficiency impediments here. The Edit menu is as familiar as a sunrise, with a few possible exceptions (see Figure 2.7):

• *Undo, Redo, Cut, Copy, and Paste*—Standard system functions in applications.

• *Paste Into*—Allows you to paste whatever is on the clipboard into a predefined selection shape on a page of your document. The pasted contents can be manipulated within the confines of the selection, so if you create a selection area with an irregular shape, and paste a rectangular photograph or drawing into the irregular selection, parts of the pasted rectangle are obscured. You can then use the Hand tool to move the pasted selection about until you reveal just exactly what you want to show in the irregular shape. Photoshop uses this command.

• *Clear*—Deletes without using the clipboard.

• *Duplicate*—Makes a copy of whatever is selected.

• *Step And Repeat*—Similar to Duplicate; however, rather than making only one copy of a selected object that is slightly offset, it makes a specified number of duplicates that you offset an exact distance either horizontally, vertically, or both.

• *Deselect All*—Ensures that nothing on a page is selected. You can then work globally with pages rather than within selected objects on the page. I have to confess I'm disappointed that Adobe didn't assign

Cmd+D or Ctrl+D for Deselect All. I've worked in Photoshop so long that it's an autonomic response, like breathing.

- *Find/Change*—Locates text strings with or without specific attributes based on criteria you establish. Change replaces part or all of a text string and/or attributes based on criteria you establish.

- *Find Next*—Continues searching for criteria established in the Find dialog box.

- *Check Spelling*—Saves embarrassment in the face of harried deadlines and mumble-finger typing that we all occasionally experience.

- *Edit Dictionary*—Though this function is not as powerful as some word processors' dictionary options, you can add or remove words in the InDesign dictionary. It's interesting to note that Adobe approaches changes to its dictionaries by maintaining a list of words you add and a list of words you remove. If you change your mind about a given word, you can either add it again or remove it again without laborious typing, just a shift from one list to the other.

InDesign ships with a dozen or so foreign-language and profession-specific dictionaries, such as medical and legal terms. My wish list begs for custom dictionaries to build from the ground up with client-specific terminology, but the Added Words and Removed Words will have to suffice. Who knows? I may grow to love this.

Layout

Arriving at the Layout menu, you definitely encounter some things unique to InDesign at the top of the menu. The rest of the commands listed are typical navigational aids and an alternative to using the Pages palette for working with pages in your document (see Figure 2.8):

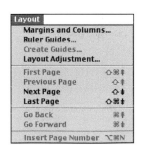

- *Margin And Columns*—Sets the width of each margin around the periphery of a page and sets the number of columns for individual pages in the dialog box that opens.

- *Ruler Guides*—This opens a dialog box where you enter a minimum view percentage at which the Guides show. At a lesser percentage than set, the View Threshold is exceeded, therefore those Ruler Guides don't show (see Figure 2.9).

Figure 2.8

Throughout the development of a publication you'll use this Layout menu often.

Figure 2.9

You have only two options in this Ruler Guides dialog box, but you'll find it helpful to set these specifications before using Create Guides or dragging Guides from the rulers.

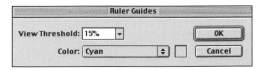

The Color option pop-up menu in the Ruler Guides dialog box offers an astonishing array of color options to set different colors for the guides at each View Threshold percentage. View Threshold in the Ruler Guides dialog box has the effect of displaying and hiding guides automatically at given percentage views, and the colors help identify guides set for specific threshold percentages.

If you set up a multitude of low percentage View Thresholds, but view your pages often at say, 50 percent and 100 percent magnification, you'll see every guide with a threshold of 100 percent or less. Though you can Hide Guides using the Window menu, you might prefer to set most of your guide thresholds at a percentage greater than 100 percent to eliminate that dreaded screen clutter except when you zoom in to position objects precisely or zoom out for an overview of pages. Each InDesign guide is just another object on a page. That means you can copy and paste them. When you do, the specified color and View Threshold is duplicated along with the guide.

- *Create Guides*—Lets you set up grids of guides in rows and/or columns. If you're not the math whiz kind of designer who sets every spec by the numbers, try choosing the number of columns or rows you want on a page, then apply one of the automatic fitting options: Fit Guides To Margins or Fit Guides To Page. If you goof, just click Remove Existing Ruler Guides and start over. Be advised, though, that this removes *all* ruler guides on the page, not just the ones you're previewing. It may be better to return to your document page and double-click on the guides you want removed.

- *Layout Adjustment*—This feature, introduced to the desktop publishing world by Adobe in PageMaker, allows you to swiftly make major changes in your layout designs. For instance, you can change a portrait layout to a landscape orientation, or even change the page dimensions, and InDesign automatically scales and repositions everything you designed to accommodate the new layout specifications without affecting the relationships of objects on the page (see Figure 2.10).

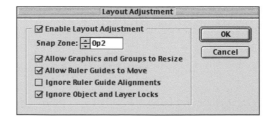

Figure 2.10

With Enable Layout Adjustment activated in the Layout Adjustment dialog box, you can select any or all of the options available.

First, you must click the Enable Layout Adjustment checkbox for flexibility in working with the graphics, guides, objects, and layers in your layout. Once this is activated, set the Snap Zone, the proximity at which objects snap to nearby guides, and choose from the other options according to your needs at the moment. The options are: Allow Graphics And Groups To Resize, Allow Ruler Guides To Move, Ignore Ruler Guide Alignment, and Ignore Object And Layer Locks. As you can see from the choices, Layout Adjustment gives you plenty of control.

Type

Moving on to the Type menu, you'll recognize every command, especially if you've ever worked with PageMaker. This menu might just as well have been called the "Text menu," but given Adobe's origins in the realm of type, it's only reasonable to call it the Type menu (see Figure 2.11):

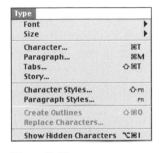

Figure 2.11

Type attributes and manipulation, Adobe's forte, are applied to text using commands in the Type menu to open palettes.

- *Font*—Applies a font to selected text using the pop-up menu associated with this menu item.

- *Size*—Sets the point size of fonts using the pop-up menu associated with this menu item.

- *Character*—Activates the Character palette displayed by default with the Paragraph and Transform palettes at the bottom of the InDesign window.

- *Paragraph*—Activates the Paragraph palette. (More about these palettes follows in this chapter.)

Note: Without a table-making plug-in, tabs are the only way of accomplishing tables, ersatz though they be.

- *Tabs*—Opens the Tabs palette, which is resizable, and displays a ruler for setting tabs in paragraphs. This palette is accessible only from the Type menu.

- *Story*—Opens a palette available only from the Type menu for adjusting the Story Direction, the flow of text in a Horizontal or Vertical direction, and for selecting Optical Margin Alignment. You can establish an Optical Margin that positions punctuation and edges of wide characters, or the entire left margin of the story (see Figure 2.12).

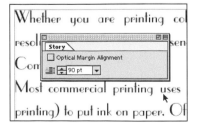 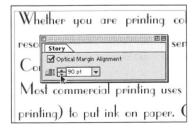

Figure 2.12

These figures show the before and after appearance of a story with Optical Margin Alignment of 90 points for 14-point type.

Note: If you're familiar with and loved the Story Editor in PageMaker, get out the crying towel. It's gone.

Typically, you set a point value equal to the font size, but your design sense is the final determinant. Set a point value between 0.1 and 1296 points for Optical Margin Alignment. If you push the point setting high enough, text reflows to the next line, but, depending on your font and size, a low setting adjusts the subtle but seeming misalignment of initial caps, such as a W, with the margin. Negative values for Optical Margin Alignment are not an option (see Figure 2.13).

Figure 2.13
Without Optical Margin Align-ment activated, the initial W appears to be inset. With a 12-point Optical Margin Alignment for 12-point type, the problem is cured.

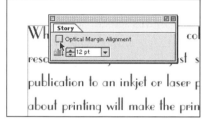 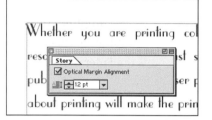

Note: The on-screen view is, at best, an approximation of what you'll get in a printed version of your document. Different output devices affect text flow, no matter how carefully you align story mar-gins. Only by converting document pages to PDF or EPS files can you set text flow in stone.

- *Character Styles*—Opens the Character Styles palette. The best part about InDesign's implementation is the centralized access to every attribute you ever wanted to apply (see Figure 2.14) The New Character Style dialog box, accessed by selecting New Style, has the following options:

  - *Basic Character Formats*—Gives you the Font, Size, Kerning, Case, Leading, Tracking, and Position options. This screen also has checkboxes for Underline, Strikethrough, Ligatures, Old Style, and No Break.

  - *Advanced Character Formats*—Covers the Horizontal Scale, Vertical Scale, Baseline Shift, and Skew of characters. This screen also lets you identify the Language characters are set in, and that covers a long list of Occidental languages plus Medical and Legal. (I always suspected that doctors and lawyers spoke another language.)

  - *Character Color*—Assigns any color you have already placed into the Swatches palette. Set a Tint percentage and stroke Weight

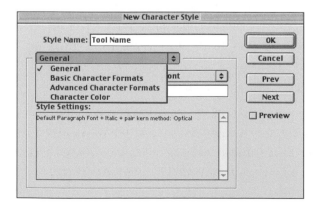

Figure 2.14
Use the pop-up menu to access each of the attribute screens, or leaf through the screens using the Prev and Next buttons to the right of the Character dialog box.

with accompanying checkboxes for designating Overprint Fill and Overprint Stroke.

- *Paragraph Styles*—Opens the Paragraph Styles palette. Self-explanatory to most page layout mavens, this palette has a pop-up menu for defining styles, revising existing styles, loading styles from other InDesign documents, and, blissfully, selecting all unused styles so they can be deleted. The Paragraph Style dialog box, accessed by selecting New Style, has *11* different screens to define a style's parameters:

  - *General*—Paragraph attributes appear in this screen. Set what the paragraph is Based On, what the Next Style will be when you press the Enter or Return key, or a Shortcut key for applying the paragraph style. In the lower portion of the screen, a Style Settings box shows the choices you make for the style.

  - *Indents And Spacing*—Define paragraph Alignment, Left Indent, First Line Indent, Right Indent, Space Before, Space After, and whether to Align To Baseline Grid in this screen.

  - *Drop Caps*—Make the usual decisions here about how many letters to drop and how many lines to drop them, but the most interesting part of this screen is the option for using Adobe's new Multi-line or Single-line Composer.

    Typographers take note: InDesign handles line composition for you in single lines or over multiple lines of text. Both work in conjunction with the hyphenation and justification tables. Multi-line Composer automatically adjusts spacing for optimal line breaks, assessing all lines in the paragraph to balance the spacing and line color. Single-line Composer only considers a line by itself.

  - *Justification*—This screen has options for Auto Leading, Word Spacing, Letter Spacing and...what's this? Glyph Scaling? According to a highly reliable source (an Adobe techie), Glyph Scaling is "...a parameter that allows degrees of horizontal scaling to be used in addition to word and letter spacing when justifying a line to a set width." He continues, "To be used with extreme discretion (in most cases, not at all) as it distorts the font." In other words, now that you know, use it with caution and practice.

  - *Tabs, Hyphenation, and Keep Options*—Tabs and Hyphenation need no explanation, but Keep Options on this screen may flummox you for a second. Keep Options are decisions to keep paragraphs and lines within a paragraph together. For some obscure reason,

---

GET THE MOST OUT OF MULTI-LINE COMPOSER

For the greatest flexibility when using Multi-line Composer, set up your Preferences on a document-by-document basis. Select File|Preferences| Composition, and choose the number of lines to Look Ahead, a number for alternatives in the Consider Up To box, and what you want highlighted when Multi-line Composer assesses the text: Keep Violations (keep lines together, and so on), H&J Violations, and Substitute Fonts.

the option for starting a paragraph Anywhere, In Next Columns, and On Next Page are also found in this screen of the Paragraph style dialog box.

- *Paragraph Rules*—No, that's not graffiti scrawled on some wall. It's the lines above or below a paragraph. InDesign's options cover Weight, Color, Width, Offset, Left Indent, and Right Indent.

- *Basic Character Formats, Advanced Character Formats, and Character Color*—The remaining screens address Basic Character Formats, Advanced Character Formats, and Character Color within paragraphs, just as they were handled in the Character Styles dialog box.

- *Create Outlines*—The function of this screen parallels the QuarkXPress command to Convert Text To Box and Illustrator's Convert To Outlines. After selected text is converted, you can place a graphics file inside the outline or apply a Gradient, Fill, or Stroke to the text. The converted text remains as a unified collection of objects, but you can reshape individual letters because every letter becomes an editable object made up of Bézier curves and lines—AKA: a path (see Figure 2.15).

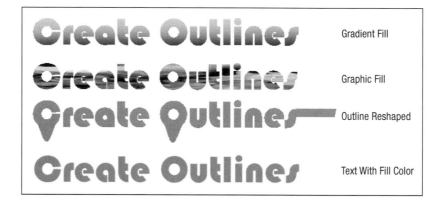

Figure 2.15
Only the lowermost text in this figure is not converted to outlines, and that text has a Fill color applied.

Gradient Fill

Graphic Fill

Outline Reshaped

Text With Fill Color

- *Insert Character*—Handles those special symbols, such as a copyright or trademark symbol. If you use Microsoft Word, the Insert Character dialog box will be old hat. Select the special character set of any font installed on your computer, and choose the symbol you want inserted.

- *Show/Hide Hidden Characters*—Toggles to display or conceal the paragraph, space, and tab indicators on screen.

Object

Here we are at the Object menu dealing with all objects created on pages. In some other page layout applications, these controls are scattered all over the place, but InDesign puts them in one menu (see Figure 2.16):

- *Arrange*—With this menu item's pop-up menu, you can move selected objects within the stacking order on a layer. It's good to remember that objects automatically stack in the order they're created. That is, the first object created is the farthest down in a stack. This is a good place to mention that InDesign can also create layers for pages. Layers are covered in greater detail later in the "Palettes" section of this chapter. For now, suffice it to say that layers differ from stacks of objects. You can stack objects on a layer, and use Arrange to change the stacking order without affecting layers.

- *Group*—Combines separate object so that the objects can be moved as a unit while maintaining their relationship to one another within the group.

- *Ungroup*—Disconnects grouped objects to revise or move objects independently.

- *Lock Position*—Prevents unwanted moving of objects.

- *Unlock Position*—Allows you to change your mind and move objects.

- *Text Frame Options*—Opens a feature-packed dialog box for establishing attributes in text frames. Set the Number or Width of columns, and the Size Of The Gutter between columns. If you prefer, you can have Fixed Column Width. Inset Spacing determines how far from the edge of a text frame the text inside the frame stops flowing and wraps to create another line of text.

The First Baseline Offset options are Ascent, Cap Height, and Leading. Dramatic text effects are possible depending on which of these you choose. Ascent uses the font's highest ascender, whether that ascender is on the baseline or not. Cap Height uses the height of the highest cap in the line, setting the top of the capital at the top of the text box. Leading uses the leading value you choose to set the text, and the text can rise above the boundaries of the text frame. For example, if you use a base leading of 14 points and have a 24-point cap at the beginning of the line, the cap will be partially above the frame.

The standard leading is 120 percent of the font size. Figuring out that 10-point type is standardized on 12 points of leading is easy enough, but calculating the proper ratio of type to leading in other font sizes isn't easy or intuitive. But designers will design, and you can override Auto Leading at any time by selecting a set leading in the Preferences dialog box.

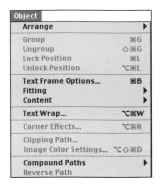

Figure 2.16

After you create objects on pages, the tweak-and-revise necessities are readily available in the Object menu.

Finally, you can opt to Ignore Text Wrap. More about text wrapping is forthcoming in short order. It's another of the Object menu commands.

- *Fitting*—Yea! No secret key combination required. No third-party plug-in, either. InDesign has programmed commands in the Object menu that Fit Content To Frame, Fit Frame To Content, and in either case, use Fit Content Proportionally to undo a fit choice that doesn't work for you.

  Content assigns the kind of things that go into a frame, graphic, or text. As in other page layout programs, graphic frames display a non-printing X to help you recognize both the kind of frame it is and that it's empty. If you're indecisive or need some flexibility, create a frame and select Unassigned. This might be a frame within a two-column story that could, from issue to issue of a publication, hold either text or a graphic, but is always the same size and in the same position on the page.

- *Text Wrap*—Opens a palette for setting parameters determining the way text wraps around a frame overlapping or stacked on top of a text frame. The choices are: No Text Wrap; Wrap Around Bounding Box (the overlapping or embedded frame); Wrap Around Object Shape (a drawn object); Jump Object, which leaves open space with no text on both sides of the object; or Jump To Next Column. Individually set the top, bottom left, and right offset distance, or, if you want text to wrap *inside* an object, click the Invert checkbox.

- *Corner Effects*—Brings up a dialog box with interesting effects for frames. Each effect applied overlays the contents of the frame, be it text or a graphic. Experimentation is your best bet here. For fun, create a frame, fill it with any color you like, and play. Your choices are Fancy, Bevel, Inset, Inverse Rounded, and Rounded. Each takes up a greater or lesser amount of the frame corners based upon the Size you set. Be sure to activate the Preview checkbox as you play so you can see how each choice looks applied to the frame. You'll be astounded when you discover what the frame with Corner Effects applied really looks like after it's deselected.

- *Clipping Path*—A complex and powerful command to mask part of an imported graphic. If you position a graphic with a clipping path inside a text box, you can cause text to flow around the shape created by the clipping path. In QuarkXPress, the Runaround option, Image, results in essentially the same effect. In Photoshop and Illustrator you can create clipping paths and import them to InDesign (see Figure 2.17).

With the Clipping Path dialog box open, you set Threshold, the amount of difference between tone values to include inside the clipping path selection; Tolerance, how precisely the final clipping path follows the selection made by Threshold; and whether to Invert the selection, Include Inside Edges of elements that meet Threshold and Tolerance criteria within the image, or Use High Resolution Image rather than the usual low resolution proxy on screen.

Figure 2.17
Here is an example of InDesign's Clipping Path with all the Bézier curve anchor points selected.

- *Image Color Settings*—Some advance planning is required before you use the dialog box that opens when you select this command from the Object menu. Either as part of your Application Preferences, which apply to all new InDesign documents, or, if turned off, as part of the Preferences for a specific document.

  In Chapter 9 you'll find much more information about color and color management. For now, suffice it to say that the way to make color management revisions on an image-by-image basis is available here.

- *Compound Paths*—With multiple objects in close proximity to one another, select this menu item to combine the objects and devise unique negative and positive spaces in one single object, as in hole-in-a-donut, for instance. Create some objects, position them atop one another, select all the objects, and choose Make from the Compound Paths pop-up menu. You've created a compound path (see Figure 2.18).

Figure 2.18
These before-and-after views of two objects converted to a single Compound Path help you understand the negative/positive results of combining shapes.

Having created a single Compound Path, you can then make the shape a graphic element on its own; fill it with text, color, or a graphic; and wrap text inside or outside the shape. The really good part about compound paths is that they're not a forever thing. You can select the compound path object and choose Compound Paths|Release, and you're back where you started, with multiple objects.

- *Reverse Path*—Applies only to straight paths you create. Open paths are considered directional based upon the initial point created, not the location on the page of the first point, left to right. QuarkXPress, you may be aware, operates on the theory that everything begins on the left and proceeds right, no matter which way you draw or position things. Not so InDesign.

If you need an arrow pointing a particular direction, and the arrow head winds up on the wrong end, use Reverse Path to correct the problem. Only situations involving open paths with directional designs—up, down, left, or right—show any change when you use this command.

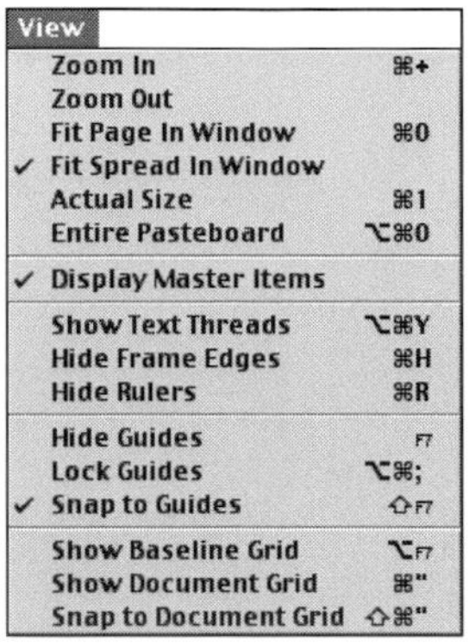

View

If you understand that the menu name, View, refers to the way things look on screen, you've got the whole concept of the View menu (see Figure 2.19). The View menu includes the following:

- Zoom In

- Zoom Out

- Fit Page In Window

- Fit Spread In Window

- Actual Size

All of the preceding menu items seem clear and comprehensible without further explanation. Each provides a way of viewing your InDesign document.

- *Entire Pasteboard*—Another way of viewing your InDesign document. Each spread has its own pasteboard, so the Entire Pasteboard option reduces the percentage view to show the entire width and height of at least one pasteboard, no matter what size monitor you have.

- *Display Master Items*—Reveals or conceals things designed on the Master pages. It shows or hides Master page components across all pages of a selected spread, but not on spreads that aren't selected in the Pages palette.

- *Show/Hide Text Threads*—Displays/conceals the invisible connections between text frames holding portions of the same story...as in "continued on page 4." Directional arrows temporarily display in each connected text frame indicating which way text is flowing.

- *Show/Hide Frame Edges*—Displays/conceals the on-screen perimeter of all frames. Hide Frame Edges is useful for assessing all or part of pages without annoying lines around every frame.

- *Show/Hide Rulers*—Toggles to reveal or conceal the rulers on screen.

Figure 2.19

Many of the commands shown on the View menu have keyboard shortcuts because these commands are used constantly during document layout.

- *Show/Hide Guides*—Toggles to reveal or conceal all the guides.

- *Lock Guides*—Activate this menu item so you can't accidentally reposition guides. As you'll soon see, guides can be numerous, and they can be displayed only at certain percentage views.

- *Snap To Guides*—This can be activated to facilitate accurate placement of objects within the guides, or turned off for manual positioning that is unaffected by the magnetic pull of your guides.

- *Show Baseline Grid*—Displays text frame-related horizontal grid lines.

- *Show Document Grid*—Displays grid lines vertically and horizontally that cover the entire pasteboard and document pages.

- *Snap To Document Grid*—When activated, this causes objects you move to jump into alignment with the gridlines set for the document as the object is moved within a set distance from any of the gridlines. That distance is established in the Preferences.

Window

The top two sections and the bottom two sections of the Window menu have to do with things other than palettes. A palette, you know, is just another kind of window. The top three menu commands, New Window, Cascade, and Tile, refer to document window management. The bottom two sections change as you use the program. The Libraries command has a pop-up menu that grows to include newly created Libraries, and the very bottom section of the Window menu displays the names of any and all currently open documents (see Figure 2.20).

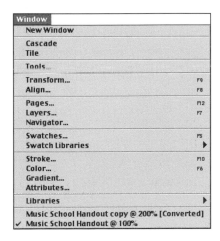

Figure 2.20
Documents listed at the bottom of the Window menu may vary from those listed in the File menu because the File menu displays recently opened documents and whether any of those listed are currently closed or not, whereas the Window menu displays only the names of documents open at the moment.

A fast cruise down the list of palettes (because they're covered fully later in this chapter) reveals: Tools, Transform, Align, Pages, Layers, Navigator, and Swatches. Wait! Let's not be too hasty here. The Swatches palette shows the colors and gradients you've already chosen for your document, but what about Swatch Libraries?

InDesign comes with a complete collection of standardized spot colors and both Macintosh and Windows system color swatches, plus Web swatches for on-screen documents. Use Other Library, located in the pop-up menu of Swatch Libraries, to add Illustrator swatches to the list.

And on we go, down the list of palettes in the Window menu: Stroke, Color, Gradient, Attributes. Lest you think I'm dismissing these too lightly, there's plenty more coming about each of these palettes a little later in this chapter.

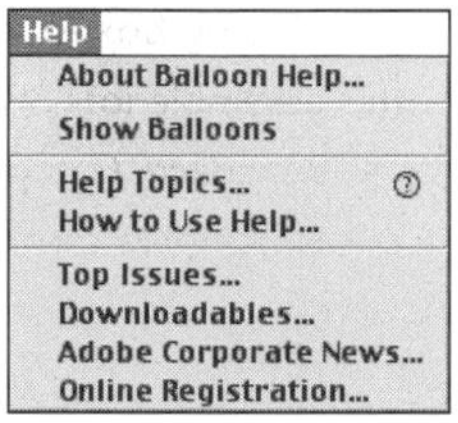

Help

A small difference appears in the Help menu between platforms. The Macintosh Help menu lists About Balloon Help first followed by Show Balloons, whereas the PC Help menu has About InDesign first on the list. Every other listing is parallel between platforms (see Figure 2.21):

- *Help Topics*—Opens a comprehensive volume of linked information covering just about anything you can think up. There are basic instructions for using the application components, tools, window, and very helpful explanations of color theory, information about printers, and some background information. Frankly, I am biased toward InDesign Help files. I love 'em. I wander through them, just as some folks wander on the World Wide Web, as the time disappears.

Speaking of the Web, the next section of listings in the Help menu all relate in one way or another to things on the Web:

- *Top Issues*—Opens Acrobat Reader (if you have it installed) for reading documents about what's hot, not, and whatnot. If you don't have Acrobat Reader, use your installer CD to put it on your hard drive. It's very useful.

- *Downloadables*—Opens a dialog box showing items available online for downloading. There's a description and download options as well as View Options that let you choose to see only new files available or all the available files. You can ponder the Adobe Corporate News, use Online Registration, or follow Adobe Recommended Links and InDesign Recommended Links.

So, the tour of the menus concludes. Kindly take your drink containers to the kitchen and check the overhead bins for belongings. We hope you enjoy your time in the Palettes section, and thank you for choosing Adobe InDesign.

Figure 2.21

Often more quickly accessible than the user guides shipped with your InDesign application, the Help Topics are thorough and easy to understand.

Palettes

Lots of programs use palettes these days. Word processors have palettes. Page layout programs have palettes. They're everywhere, and for good reason. Palettes are easy to use and have a lot of options in a little space, in many cases eliminating the need to pull down a menu to open a dialog box.

There are 18 InDesign palettes to make getting work out the door more efficient. The screen can become pretty cluttered, but you don't have to work in clutter. There's no need to open every palette available. Those familiar with other Adobe software know that you can open and group the palettes you use the most into a single palette. It's simply a matter of dragging each palette by its title tab and dropping the palette on top of another palette until you've organized a compact group of palettes that meets your work needs. To activate one of the palettes in a group, click on its name tab.

You will have occasion to single out a palette when you perform specific tasks, like creating and selecting colors to add to the Swatches for a document. Just drag the palette out of the group. When you don't need a palette and it's in your way, close it.

As with the menus, I'll touch briefly on palettes that most intermediate and advanced users know, and I'll elaborate on palettes that might be a bit different, or brand new, in InDesign. Nearly every palette has a pop-up menu of options accessed by clicking the arrow in the far upper-right corner of the palette. The options are directly related to the other options available in the palette, and need few explanations. Some are shortcuts, others are additional attributes to choose, and sometimes there are things you can do that apply to the palette itself, so I'll skip those and trust you to look them over. Some pop-up menus have listings found nowhere else. Those I'll discuss.

First, some generalities about palettes:

- Every palette has icons and Tool Tips to identify what each icon does.

- By default, Tool Tips are turned on, but you can turn them off in the General Preferences dialog box.

- All palettes can be used grouped or separately. Click the tab of a grouped palette to activate it.

- The most commonly used palettes are available through the Window menu.

Tools

The Tools palette opens automatically when you open InDesign, and looks very much like other Adobe tool palettes. It's the one palette you'll probably always keep open. It's central to everything you do with InDesign. As

WHAT DO THOSE THREE DOTS MEAN?

Here's a tidbit of information that even some expert users haven't thought about. An ellipsis after a menu listing indicates that a dialog box or palette opens when you select that command. You may never look at a menu the way same again. Dialog boxes and palettes assemble lots of options in a little space. Can you imagine how long menus would be without them?

AUTOMATIC PALETTE TOGGLING

Several of the default palette groups, such as the Transform/ Character/Paragraph palette, automatically activate the palette associated with the tool you choose and what you have selected on the page of your document. For instance, when you click the Type tool inside a text frame, the Paragraph palette is automatically activated and placed on the top of the group.

Figure 2.22
Adobe maintains consistent arrangement of tools on the Tools palette in all of its graphics programs to avoid confusion as you switch between several open Adobe applications.

BOUNDING BOXES ABOUND

Everything you draw, be it a shape or a frame, has a rectangular bounding box regardless of the shape of the object. The bounding box has eight handles for resizing the object (irrespective of its shape) and defines the farthest reaches of the object. There's no adding or removing handles to a bounding box, but every drawn object is a Bézier curve with anchor points. Each anchor point has control handles to manipulate the line segment between points. Ultimately, the collection of anchor points and line segments is called a *path*. Paths can be open or closed. For instance, a line is an open path, and a rectangle is a closed path.

a matter of fact, the Tools palette has no Close box. What's more, you can't add the Tools palette to a group.

Every tool on the palette is identical to tools found in the Illustrator, Photoshop, and PageMaker Tools palettes, though each of these programs has a slightly different assortment of tools (see Figure 2.22).

Tools are meant for teamwork. Use one tool to create things, and another tool to edit, move, or enhance what you've created.

InDesign's collection of tools includes, starting at the top of the palette, and moving from left to right:

- *Selection tool*—Activates and moves objects on pages.

- *Direct Selection tool*—Activates and works with anchor points on objects and the content of objects.

- *Pen tool, Add Anchor Point tool, Delete Anchor Point tool, and Convert Direction Point tool*—The Pen tool creates Bézier anchor points joined by curved and straight line segments that make up a path. Other Pen tools in the pop-up menu are used to manipulate a path after it's drawn.

- *Type tool and Vertical Type tool*—The Type tool defines the insertion point for entering text, and can be used to draw text frames, which then have the cursor blinking at the upper-left corner of the frame. Whenever you manipulate, edit, or enter text, this tool must be selected. The Vertical Type tool automatically reorients the text insertion point horizontally and to the right. Words you type flow from the upper-right corner of a text frame filling the frame top to bottom and wraps to fill the frame right to left. If this orientation doesn't suit your purposes, you can use the Rotate tool to revolve the frame and achieve the text flow direction you want.

- *Ellipse tool and Ellipse Frame tool*—The Ellipse tool draws rounded shapes. Use the Ellipse tool pop-up menu to access the Ellipse Frame tool and create rounded frames that can be set from the Object menu to hold text or graphics or be unassigned a content.

- *Rectangle tool and Rectangle Frame tool*—Draws rectangular shapes or rectangular frames that can contain text or a graphic or be unassigned using the Object menu.

- *Line tool*—Draws lines of any length at any angle. There is no pop-up alternative tool with the Line tool. Any line can be manipulated using either its bounding box or the anchor point at each end of the line. An InDesign line is just another Bézier path.

- *Polygon tool and Polygon Frame tool*—This Polygon tool set is vastly different from the Polygon tool in QuarkXPress. Adobe's Polygon tools automatically create a hexagon, but you can add and remove anchor points using the Pen tools, and make whatever shape you prefer. That, in my opinion, is much better than being restricted to the predefined polygons some other page layout applications offer.

- *Rotate tool*—Allows you to revolve any object clockwise or counterclockwise around a reference point set in the Transform palette. The pivot point for rotating an object is determined by clicking one of the reference points in the proxy icon at the left of the Transform palette.

- *Scale tool and Shear tool*—Both scaling and shearing use the reference point set in the Transform palette proxy. To scale objects proportionately, drag one of the corner handles of the bounding box surrounding any object. To scale an object horizontally or vertically, use a handle along the side of the bounding box.

- *Scissors tool*—Cuts through a path. All closed objects have a path around the perimeter. A line of any description, straight, squiggled, or curved, is a path unto itself—an open path. If you cut a closed path, thus converting it to an open path, two anchor points, one on top of the other, are added at the spot where you click the Scissors tool. You can then reposition the newly created anchor points using the Direct Selection tool mentioned earlier in this discussion of the Tools palette.

- *Gradient tool*—Used to define the direction of a gradient fill in an object after an object is filled with a gradient. Select an object, fill it with a gradient you created and then use the Gradient tool to click and drag across the filled object in any direction. The gradient fill flows in the direction you drag the Gradient tool.

- *Hand tool*—Moves the contents of the main InDesign window in any direction. Temporarily activate the Hand tool by pressing the spacebar when using any tool but the Type tool.

- *Zoom tool*—Increases the viewing percentage of the main InDesign window. Decrease the percentage view by holding down the Option or Alt key as you use the Zoom tool. Zoom to a specific part of your screen by drawing a box with the Zoom tool to enclose the area of the page you want to see at a greater magnification.

SYMBIOTIC RELATIONSHIPS

No single tool does it all. For instance, with either the Ellipse tools or the Rectangle tools, you need to click on the page and drag to create shapes. Hold down the Shift key to constrain the shape to perfect symmetry. With a shape drawn, you can use the Selection tool to drag the shape into place, or the Transform palette to precisely size and position the object you've created. Or you might prefer to use guides and the snap-to feature for positioning. And that's just the beginning.

ZOOM TRICKS

Similar to Illustrator and Photoshop, you can Zoom your document view to 100 percent by double-clicking the Hand tool. Zoom your document to fit the window by double-clicking the Zoom tool.

DRAG AND DROP COLORS AND GRADIENTS

Instantly change the color you want to apply. Drag a predefined color or gradient from the Swatches palette and drop it on either the Fill or Stroke icon in the Tools palette or in the Colors palette. Not only is this fast, it's fun to watch.

- *Fill and Stroke*—Located at the lower portion of the Tools palette, the icons for Fill and Stroke toggle the colors assigned to Fill and Stroke by clicking the arrows at the upper-right corner of the icon box. These apply color preselected from the Swatches palette (they remove color, too) to either Fill or Stroke of an object. The tiny icons in the lower-left corner of the Fill and Stroke area reset the colors to the default black and white, just as they do in Photoshop. (The default colors can be changed. Refer to Chapter 9.)

Use the buttons along the bottom edge of the Tools palette to Apply Color, Apply Gradient—also preselected from the Swatches palette—or use Apply None to remove a fill or gradient. Fill or Stroke is applied according to which icon is uppermost in the Tool palette (see Figure 2.23).

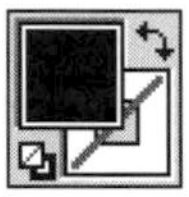

Figure 2.23
In this figure, the Fill icon is uppermost, and any color selected in the Swatches palette will be applied as fill to a selected object.

That wraps it up for the Tools palette. Now on to other palettes.

Transform

The Transform palette is another palette you're very likely to keep open. If you dutifully read the preceding section about the Tools palette (you are reading every word, aren't you?), it's clear that the Transform palette works in conjunction with the tools, and it is used for setting objects' attributes, position, size, angle of orientation, shear, scale, and point of reference (see Figure 2.24).

Figure 2.24
Position objects with pinpoint accuracy using the Transform palette.

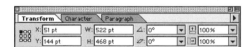

Unlike QuarkXPress, with InDesign all life does not begin at the upper-left corner of the bounding box or shape. Presuming you have InDesign open and are reading while looking at the screen, create a test object on the page of a new document. Leave the object selected. Glance at the Transform palette with particular attention to the dimensions in the various measurements boxes. Now, click on one of the squares in the Reference Point proxy icon. Click on a different square. Ah ha! Some of the measurements change because the reference point for measuring changed. With that little insight, everything else in the Transform palette becomes crystal clear. Be sure to set the reference point for an object, and then have at it.

Character

To use the Character palette you must have the Text tool activated. Obviously you must also have some text highlighted or the insertion point blinking inside a text frame (see Figure 2.25).

Figure 2.25
The Character palette automatically pops to the foreground of a group of palettes the moment you use the Text tool to click in or highlight text.

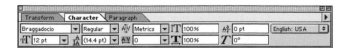

Everything on this palette is straightforward. Choose a font; set a font size; assign any attribute, such as Regular, Bold, and so on; set the leading, tracking, and kerning; and adjust the font scale horizontally and/or vertically. Apply a Baseline Shift, or force an italic face to a greater or lesser angle of tilt.

If the icons on the Character palette don't give you sufficient guidance, hover your cursor over an icon to reveal its Tool Tip. Tool Tips tell you the name of each icon, but not what it does. Most are easy to understand. There's no Tool Tip for the pop-up menu at the far right, but I'll let you in on it: That pop-up menu's for identifying the language of highlighted words, so words in a language different from the rest of the text can be handled differently by spell checking and hyphenation.

Paragraph

The Paragraph palette handles things such as paragraph alignment, inset from the left and right edges of the text frame, the distance for a first line indent, and how much space is before and after a paragraph. Assign drop cap specifications from this palette, as well (see Figure 2.26).

The checkbox at the far right turns automatic hyphenation on or off.

Oh, you're wondering about those two icons beneath the Right Indent option? Those lock or unlock *all* the text in a text frame to the baseline grid. Don't overlook the Paragraph palette pop-up menu. It's rich with options.

Character Styles And Paragraph Styles

Because the Character Styles and Paragraph Styles palettes are identical in every respect, save the specific text they affect, I'll pair them for this discussion. Paragraph styles apply globally to a paragraph, but character styles can be applied within a paragraph without affecting the global formatting of the paragraph. A few minutes spent setting up attributes in the dialog boxes rewards you tenfold in efficiency after you place or enter text (see Figure 2.27).

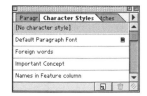 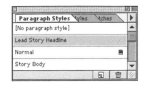

Look to the Type menu for the Character Styles or the Paragraph Styles palettes and use the pop-up menu of the palette to define a New Paragraph or New Character Style. Because Character Styles apply only to selected words or letters, and affect only the Basic and Advanced Character Formats

Figure 2.26

Any attributes you assign in the Paragraph palette apply only to the paragraph in which your cursor is located, or to all selected paragraphs.

Figure 2.27

Both the Character Styles palette and the Paragraph Styles palette have choices on their pop-up menus for loading saved sets of styles.

and Character Color, the choices are fewer than the choices available for defining a New Paragraph Style that involves Indents And Spacing, Drop Caps And Composer settings (referring to those wonderful Single-line and Multi-line Composers), Tabs, Hyphenation, Paragraph Rules, and the like. Once you've established a style, apply it by selecting the text and then clicking the style in the palette.

If you've used styles, you know that changing the definition of a style after it's applied to text in your document automatically updates every instance where the style is applied. Now, what could be more efficient than that?

Story

The Story palette handles text flow direction within a text frame (horizontal or vertical), Optical Margin Alignment, and nothing more. (There is more about Optical Margin Alignment in the "Menus" section of this chapter.)

Tabs

Tiny as it is, the Tabs palette is ideal for setting up tabbed text for tables. Word processors often have automatic table-building features, but I've never seen a page layout program that does. That falls to third-party developers, or, in the case of PageMaker, Adobe purchased and now ships a table maker with the program (see Figure 2.28).

Figure 2.28

Even if you reorient text flow in the Story palette, you can resize the Tabs palette to the width of the text in which you're setting tabs.

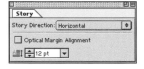
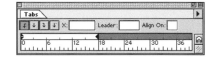

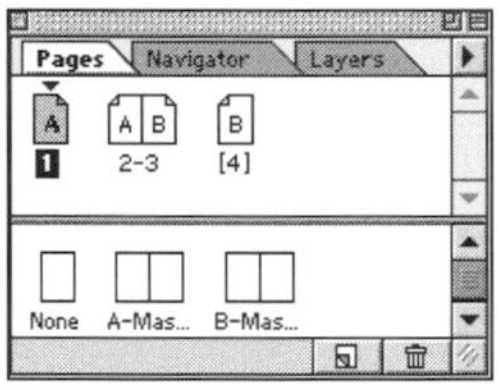

Figure 2.29

Be sure to investigate the pop-up menu in the upper-right corner of the Pages palette.

Pages

Attention QuarkXPress users. InDesign's Pages palette reversed the position of Master pages and document pages from the way you're accustomed to seeing them. Master pages are at the bottom of the palette, and document pages are at the top (see Figure 2.29).

Every new document has, by default, a blank Master page and one document page, with icons representing both of these appearing in the Pages palette. Typically you'll design Master pages first, and then apply the Masters to document pages.

To add pages to your document, drag a Master page to the top of the palette and drop it into position. The palette is resizable, and you can jump to a particular page on screen by clicking on the document page icon on the Pages palette.

Icons at the bottom of the Pages palette let you create a new page or delete selected pages.

Layers

Oh, jubilation! Layers just like Adobe graphics programs you know and love! Beware of InDesign's difference in working with layers. Each and every layer spans the entire set of publication pages. You can put anything you want on any layer, and stack the layers in any order by dragging them about on the Layers palette. In the Layers palette, the active layer is highlighted (see Figure 2.30).

Though I haven't touched on the pop-up menus in the palettes discussed so far, it's important to go through those options for the Layers palette because you'll use them extensively. The functions on the Layers palette pop-up menu, as with all palettes' pop-up options, are available no other place in the program:

- *New Layer*—Creates a new, document-pervasive layer.

- *Delete Layer "name"*—Purges an entire layer, across all pages of the document.

- *Layer Options For "name"*—Opens a small dialog box for assigning an identifying color to each layer. This is particularly helpful when you work with many layers. Every object on each layer has the same color assigned to the bounding boxes of objects on the layer, so you can immediately identify which layer an object is on when Show Frame Edges is activated.

Also available in the Layer Options dialog box are checkboxes that, when activated, Show Layer, Lock Layer, Show Guides, and Lock Guides for the layer. Show Guides and Lock Guides are straightforward, and apply to only one layer. To display or unlock a single layer's guides, you must return to the Layer Options dialog box.

Show Layer and Lock Layer are trickier functions. The selection you make in the Layer Options dialog box affects the options available on the Layers palette pop-up menu. If, for instance, you choose to hide a layer by deselecting the Show Layer checkbox in the Layer Options dialog box, the next function on the pop-up menu toggles to Show All Layers, so you can override the hide option you chose without returning to the Layer Options dialog box. In fact, the Show Layer checkbox is automatically reselected in the Layer Options in this case.

The same toggling occurs if you choose Lock Layer in the Layer Options dialog box. The pop-up menu function displays Unlock All Layers. If the layer is not locked, the pop-up menu function is Lock Others.

Although this all sounds confusing, it's perfectly logical and simple to use in actual practice. You'll find that this toggling of functions works

Figure 2.30
Use the Layers palette to create different versions of the same page for client approval, or for making it easier to edit objects that would otherwise be buried beneath other objects.

as an efficiency mechanism for performing tasks you use a zillion times as you work with layers. What's more, most of these items are easily achieved by clicking in appropriate places on the Layers palette.

- *Paste Remembers Layers*—This option could cause some consternation if you don't understand what it does. It has flummoxed me more than once. When Paste Remembers Layers is activated, if you copy something to the clipboard, then paste the clipboard contents back into your publication, it may not be immediately evident, but the clipboard contents are pasted on the same layer you copied it from; otherwise, it's pasted into the currently active layer.

- *Merge Layers*—This has the same effect as using a hot iron to fuse two pieces of clear plastic. Everything on the merged layers becomes part of a single layer. Layers must be contiguous in the Layers palette to merge them. To select the layers you want merged, hold down the Shift key as you click on the layers. When layers are merged, the resulting single layer assumes the name and Layer Options of the topmost layer you merged.

- *Delete Unused Layers*—Removing layers reduces file size. The more layers in a document, the larger the file size. The larger the file size, the longer it takes to print.

Now a few generalities about the Layers palette:

- The eye icon indicates that a layer is visible.

- The pencil with a red slash indicates a layer is locked.

- By default, each layer is assigned a color, and given the name Layer with a numeral. All bounding boxes on that layer appear in the color assigned to the layer.

- Rename a layer by double-clicking on the layer name in the palette.

- Rearrange layers on a page by dragging a layer to a new position.

- A small box at the far right of a layer's name indicates something on that layer is selected.

Navigator

I know people using other Adobe graphics programs who would rather fight than give up the Navigator palette. In that one place you can tell which part of a page or spread you are viewing on screen. You can view all the pages in a spread, and zoom in or zoom out using a slider on the palette or the icon to the right of the slider. Toggle between the previous magnification and the present magnification by clicking the icons at either side of the slider (see Figure 2.31).

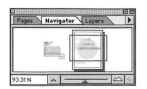

Figure 2.31
In the heat of production, the Navigator palette saves having to scroll about to view parts of your document pages.

You can jump from viewing one page in a spread to viewing another just by clicking the page icon in the Navigator palette. Or drag the red rectangle that indicates the part of a page you see on screen to a new position on the page icon of the palette, and you immediately are viewing that portion of the page on screen. Save worlds of time moving about your document in the Navigator palette, and never wonder which page of the document or what part of that page you are looking at on screen, even at huge magnification.

Stroke

The Stroke palette sets the Weight of a stroke, but also allows you to design your own stroke. You can spend hours playing with the Type of stroke, solid or dashed, and then choosing one of the many Start and End options for dashes within a stroke (see Figure 2.32).

Apply the Cap and Join options in conjunction with the Miter Limit to adjust the way corners of rectangles and polygons meet. If you choose a Dashed Type stroke, you can set the length of each dash in any or all of the three dash boxes and the length of gaps in any of the three gap boxes. That ought to keep you busy for a while. And we haven't even gotten to Color yet. That comes next.

Figure 2.32
Use a simple solid or dashed stroke, or design your own strokes in the Stroke palette.

Color

There are three color spaces to use, LAB, CMYK, and RGB. Select the one you want for your document from the pop-up menu at the right of the Color palette. There's plenty of information about these color spaces in Chapter 9. For now, let's keep it simple. Predefine colors in the Swatches palette, and then, in the Color palette, adjust the percentage of that color you want printed for a selected object's fill and/or stroke (see Figure 2.33).

Use the slider to select a color value, type in a value, or click in the Tint Ramp at the bottom of the dialog box to choose the value you want.

Figure 2.33
The tiny rectangle at the right side of the Tint Ramp at the bottom of the Color palette is actually a mini-button for applying 0%.

Gradient

Gradients rely on several palettes to develop and a tool to apply transitional colors. The Swatches palette pop-up menu has the choice New Gradient. With this choice, you establish the colors used in the gradient. The Color palette determines the tint of colors you use, and the Gradient palette is for establishing the transition points of colors within the gradient you predesigned in the Swatches palette (see Figure 2.34).

The Gradient tool determines the directional flow of gradients applied to objects. This is old hat to Illustrator and Photoshop users, but may be a whole new world for QuarkXPress users, the land of two-color gradients and seven preset gradient options. If you're working in this palette and don't see the Type, Location, or Angle of a gradient in the palette, use the pop-up menu to display these options. Add colors to a gradient by clicking at the bottom of the gradient ramp to add a square, and then choose a

Figure 2.34
The number of colors in a gradient determines how many diamonds and squares appear along the top of the gradient ramp in the Gradient palette. The diamond icons above the ramp are for adjusting the midpoint between two colors, and the boxes underneath the ramp are for the colors in the gradient.

color for that square. You can adjust the transition point between colors by positioning the diamonds above and the squares below the gradient ramp.

Attributes

This is a simple palette with only two options, one for Overprint Fill and one for Overprint Stroke (see Figure 2.35).

These choices are based upon the kinds of inks you are using and the colors of your fill and stroke. But that's for a later discussion.

Figure 2.35
Though the options in the Attributes palette are simple, your choice can make a big difference in the way your print job turns out.

Swatches

Store all the colors you want to use in your document in the Swatches palette. This is the starting point for applying color to objects in your publication. Other palettes make adjustments to these foundational colors, but you need to have the color here before you can use it throughout your document (see Figure 2.36).

In the pop-up menu at the right of the Swatches palette, you can choose to create a New Color Swatch, a New Tint Swatch, or a New Gradient Swatch. You can also Duplicate Swatch, Delete Swatch, and, mercifully, Select All Unused swatches to decide if you want to delete them or use them later in the design phase.

Figure 2.36
The Swatches palette stores the colors you expect to use throughout your publication.

Text Wrap

The Text Wrap palette, you may recall from the earlier section covering menus, is opened from the Object menu. That makes sense if you remember that you're wrapping text around an object (see Figure 2.37).

Click on one of the wrap icons and set the distance from the object you want text to wrap on the top, bottom, left, and right of the object. It's as simple as that. Of course, you must have the object selected first.

Figure 2.37
Icons along the top of the Text Wrap palette are for choosing the way you want text to wrap around objects.

Align

Consistent with the Align palette in Illustrator, InDesign's Align palette has icons for aligning and distributing objects (see Figure 2.38).

Naturally, you must first select the objects to align, and then use one or more of the icons to achieve the arrangement you want. If you don't see the option you want, choose Options in the Align palette pop-up to expand the palette.

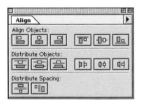

Links

This palette has all the information about source documents placed in your publication, and, because the Links palette is talking about files, you open the palette from the File menu (see Figure 2.39).

Figure 2.38
If you forget what each icon in the Align palette does (there are lots of them and no descriptive text below any of them), use the Tool Tips to remind you.

Every time you use Place in the File menu to import text or graphics, or cut and paste from another document into your InDesign document, the newly imported file is listed in the Links palette with its page location shown to the right of the file name. The letters PB indicate the file is placed on the Pasteboard. Double-click on a file listed there to open a dialog box showing all the pertinent information about the file (see Figure 2.40).

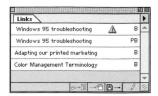

Figure 2.39
Each listing in the Links palette displays the path to the original file if you hover the cursor over the page reference to the right of the file.

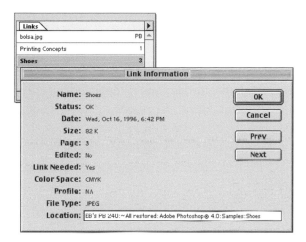

Figure 2.40
Peruse the information about each link at any time, but especially before packaging your document for handing off to the printer or service bureau.

The pop-up menu at the right of the Links palette has functions to work with your publication's source files:

- *Go To Link*—Locates and displays the imported file on a page of your publication.

- *Edit Original*—Opens the application that created the source file and displays the original file.

- *Update Link*—Lets you relocate a moved source file.

- *Embed*—Breaks any connection between a source file and the application that created the file.

- *Link Information*—Opens the Link Information dialog box that shows every bit of information relevant to you and to InDesign. It lists file name, file status, the date the file was created, and file size. It shows what page of your publication the file is placed on, whether it's been edited, and whether the link is needed (or the file is embedded). There is other pertinent information, depending on the kind of file it is, text or graphic.

There are also three sort choices in the Links palette: Sort By Status, Sort By Name, and Sort By Page.

Figure 2.41

The name of the loaded library file appears in the tab at the top of the Libraries palette.

Libraries

The content of each Libraries palette is a separate file created and saved under an identifying name. Any library can be opened at any time. As you develop a publication, you may want to create a library associated with a particular publication for storing an amazing array of reusable things related to InDesign (see Figure 2.41).

To add things to a library, simply drag what you want stored to the open Libraries palette, and a copy is placed in the library. By default the newly added item is named "Untitled." Now, double-click on the icon representing the added item to open the Item Information dialog box (see Figure 2.42).

The Creation Date you add an item is automatically entered in the dialog box along with the item's preview. You have the privilege of entering an Item Name and selecting the Object Type. If you look closely at Figure 2.42, you'll see that you can add Page Geometry to a library! In addition, you can add Images in various formats, a Page, or Text to a library. At the bottom of the dialog box, fill in a Description if you like. The description is a handy way to communicate specifics about an item to others who work at the same computer station or over a network.

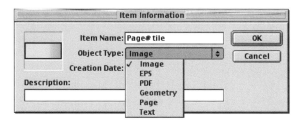

Figure 2.42

Icons representing added items in a library are ranked left to right in the Libraries palette.

With that, we've reached the end of our tour of the palettes. I hope the encapsulated overview reassures you that InDesign is simple to use, and full of old, familiar, and powerful new features that professional page layout designers have longed for.

Moving On

In the next chapter, you'll examine an existing InDesign document, establish preferences that suit your work style and publications, and start creating a catalog.

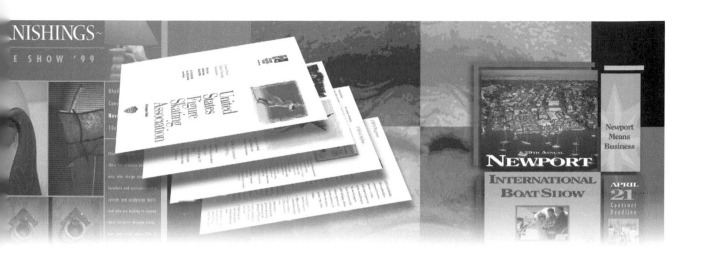

SET TO WORK

3

Look over an existing publication to see how it's put together, then set Preferences and get a feel for creating your own publications by replicating portions of the document you examined.

Skills Covered In This Chapter

- Navigate within a document

- Identify pages and Master pages

- Identify page components

- Set Preferences

- Start a new document

- Save a document

Since the High Renaissance, artists have honed their skills by replicating the works of the masters. It's a method that concentrates on techniques and tools of the medium and is every bit as useful in electronic media as in oil paints or marble. Before the artist begins, the artwork is studied from every angle, mentally disassembled, and the methods used to achieve various effects analyzed. Then tools and materials are assembled, and replication can begin. That's exactly the method I use in classes, and in some portions of this book.

In this chapter, you'll first examine a catalog publication, and then you'll set about replicating some of the catalog's pages in order to get up to speed with InDesign while creating a file of your own.

InDesign Document Makeup

Before you create your own InDesign document, you should examine one that has already been created. It may even prompt you to wonder how something was done, and then you can set about doing it yourself.

What's In An InDesign Document?

The first step in getting things going is to open InDesign and look at a catalog designed by Dave Kottler, art director and founder of APEX Communications. For a look at some of the pages from the catalog, flip to the color InDesign Studio.

Following the Renaissance model of learning, you'll spend some time looking over the catalog before you replicate it. Open the file **Turferct.indd** (see Figure 3.1).

Scroll through or use the upper portion of the Pages palette to look over each of the five pages in the file (see Figure 3.2).

Examine the ways that InDesign makes consistent page geometry easier. If the guides are not displayed, choose View|Show Guides. If the frame edges are hidden, choose Show Frame Edges from the View menu. The page margins

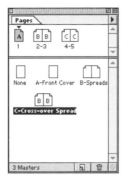

Figure 3.1

(Left) The Turfer catalog uses clean design and lifestyle and garment photographs to sell outdoor wear embroidered with logos of local teams throughout New England.

Figure 3.2

(Right) Click on the icons representing each page in the Pages palette to jump to viewing the publication's pages on screen.

are magenta (horizontal) and purple (vertical), but they appear along the edges of each page because the publication was set up with 0 margins.

Take a look at the Master pages by clicking on the Master page icons at the bottom of the Pages palette (see Figure 3.3).

Some Master pages have Master items, others have placeholder items, and still others have only guides. Some of the frames are filled with graphics and others hold text because these items will appear in every issue of the catalog (see Figure 3.4).

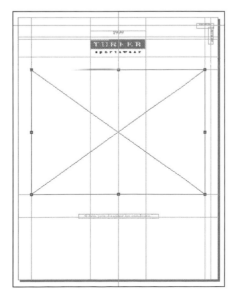

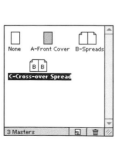

Figure 3.3

(Left) Notice that the lower-left corner of the Pages palette tells you how many Master pages are in this catalog.

Figure 3.4

(Right) An X in a frame indicates it is assigned as a graphic frame.

Figure 3.5

At this stage of development, there are only two layers in this publication, Master Guides Layer 1 and Photos. More layers can be added at any time.

Open the Layers palette using the Windows menu. Try hiding and showing the layers (see Figure 3.5). Keep in mind that every designer, and quite possibly every publication, may use a different system of organizing layers. This model is but one way. You should also try experimenting with zooming in and zooming out to see the entire pasteboard (see Figure 3.6).

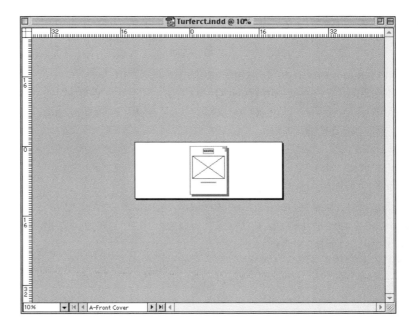

Figure 3.6

This view of the catalog front cover master page is at 10%, which is shown in the lower-left corner of the window.

The catalog Dave designed for Turfer Sportswear, a 30-year-old Rhode Island company, is an annual affair done in full color. The entire project, including design, photography, and printing, covers a time frame of almost six months, start to finish.

Before moving his design studio to Woodland Park, Colorado, Dave co-founded the third largest graphic design studio in Phoenix, Arizona, and built a client list that included The North Face, Teva Sport Sandals, and JanSport. Most of the project files used for this book are from Dave, which gives you an idea of the breadth of his skills and the variety of his client base.

Some QuarkXPress Caveats

The 20-page 1999 Turfer catalog was created in QuarkXPress 3.3.1, but it caused me a great deal of consternation when I tried to open it with InDesign. It simply wouldn't open. Every other QuarkXPress document I tried to open went as smoothly as Adobe promised, but not the Turfer catalog. I tried every trick I know—remove the pictures, check the fonts, look for and delete errant empty boxes, and replace frames around boxes that might be the problem. I even re-created the catalog on a new document in QuarkXPress, duplicating every box and all the text. I tried resaving the photographs in Photoshop in a different format. Nothing worked.

I finally called Dave and asked if he'd used any third-party XTensions, and sure enough, he had. Dave used QX Layers on the front cover, and QX Shadow throughout to create his drop shadows under garments. Be mighty circumspect before assuring a client or editor that converting those QuarkXPress documents will be a piece of cake. Ask the actual designer what XTensions, if any, were used.

QuarkXPress documents designed using third-party Extensions, especially the QX Tools set, are problematic. I know that Extensis is releasing InDesign plug-ins, but, as of this writing, there's no official word on which ones, nor whether Extensis plans to do something about the current dilemma in converting documents created using their Quark tools. My only alternative was to meticulously re-create Dave's QuarkXPress file using InDesign, and believe me, I learned a lot!

Navigating InDesign Documents

How do I navigate? Let me count the ways. There's the Layout menu command for going to the First Page, the Previous Page, the Next Page, or the Last Page, as well as their corresponding shortcut keystrokes (see Figure 3.7). You can also toggle between the last page you viewed and the current page you're viewing using the Layout menu commands Go Back and Go Forward. These, too, have shortcut keystrokes. Who wouldn't love this feature, especially if you're constantly working at a huge magnification and jumping from one object on a page to another or comparing things that are pages apart?

There are the ubiquitous scrollbars with their arrows for jumping from the first page to the last page, the next page, or the previous page. Or, if scrolling goes too fast for you to see something that's just barely out of view, press the spacebar to temporarily activate the Hand tool (while using any tool but the Type tool), and push the document page itself.

Probably the coolest way to get around a page or a spread is with the Navigator palette. This little pearl displays a red outline around the area of a page or spread that is displayed on screen (see Figure 3.8). Drag the red outline around on the icon of your page or on the pasteboard to quickly jump your document page to something you want to check out or work on.

Use the View menu commands to Zoom In or Zoom Out. These commands work on a sophisticated mathematical formula that sometimes doubles the magnification, and other times simply jumps to the nearest percentage. For example, zoom out while you're viewing something at 43%, and the percentage view zooms to 50%. Zoom in while viewing at 200%, and the new zoomed view is 400%. It beats me how they figured this out. Other commands and shortcut keystrokes in the View menu are also very helpful (see Figure 3.9).

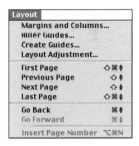

Figure 3.7

Leaving nothing to chance, available shortcut keys appear to the right of menu listings.

Figure 3.8
The magnification percentage is displayed in the lower-left corner of the Navigator palette, and to the right is a slider for increasing or decreasing the magnification.

Finally, there's the palette means of navigating. Double-click on an icon in the Pages palette to immediately display the page or spread on screen.

Should you lose track of what page you're viewing and how big the magnification is (it happens to me all the time at greater magnifications), glance down at the lower-left corner of the document window. And, while you're at it, check out the menu of preset view percentages attached to the magnification box (see Figure 3.10).

View	
Zoom In	⌘+
Zoom Out	⌘−
Fit Page In Window	⌘0
Fit Spread In Window	⌥⌘0
Actual Size	⌘1
Entire Pasteboard	⌥⇧⌘0
✓ Display Master Items	⌘Y
Show Text Threads	⌥⌘Y
Hide Frame Edges	⌘H
Hide Rulers	⌘R
Hide Guides	⌘;
Lock Guides	⌥⌘;
✓ Snap to Guides	⇧⌘;
Show Baseline Grid	⌥⌘"
Show Document Grid	⌘"
Snap to Document Grid	⇧⌘"

5%
12.5%
25%
50%
75%
100%
200%
400%
800%
1200%
1600%
2400%
3200%
4000%

Figure 3.9
(Left) The View menu's Fit Page In Window, Fit Spread In Window, Actual Size, and Entire Pasteboard are valuable navigation aids.

Figure 3.10
(Right) Open this percentage view by clicking the down arrow to the right of the current percentage view.

Identifying Pages And Page Components

As you scroll through the catalog file, you'll immediately notice that only 5 of the Turfer catalog's 20 pages are included. For learning purposes, that seemed to me to be enough. Look to the InDesign Studio for catalog examples.

Each page has guides for placement of photographs and text frames. Though you may not realize it at first, there are also layers throughout the catalog file. Open the Layers palette to see the layers (see Figure 3.11).

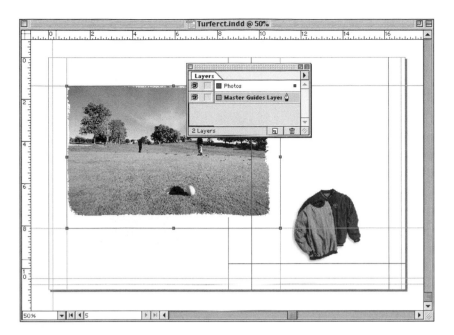

Figure 3.11
The Master Guides Layer 1,
like any layer in any publication,
can be hidden by clicking the
eye icon.

Dave made two versions of the catalog cover to present to the client. In QuarkXPress that required two different documents, but with InDesign and layers it's much easier and simpler to understand how the two choices would look in relation to the entire catalog. You simply have to hide one of the cover layers to see the difference a different cover makes.

Looking At The Master Pages And Spreads

In the lower portion of the Pages palette, click on the Front Cover Master to see how the page geometry was established. *Page geometry* is the overall appearance of a page, the design of the page based on placement of frames and graphic elements, enhancements such as borders and lines, and typography choices.

Take as much time as you like, cruising the pages, clicking on things, zooming in and zooming out. Try to determine what tools were used, and how they were used. If you're using the catalog file directly from this book's CD-ROM, you can't save any changes you might make to the file, so be fearless. If you've copied the file from the CD to your hard drive, and you accidentally move or delete something, use Undo to reverse the last thing you did, or choose Revert from the File menu to restore the file to its original condition. You'll use this file as a "go-by" or reference for projects, and you don't want anything changed before you've completed referring to the catalog. Of course, if you copied it from the CD, you have the original there and can copy it again.

Make InDesign Work Your Way

Before embarking on the layout and design of your catalog project, a little time in the Preferences should make it easier and save some time as you develop the catalog. Preferences control, among other things, the way images are displayed on screen, page numbering, what measurement units and increments of those units are displayed on the rulers, and how the Multi-line Composer works. You can also use Preferences to establish a document-wide grid for aligning guides and objects throughout the pages of the catalog.

Setting Preferences

You may already know, perhaps from working with QuarkXPress, that Preferences set with no document open are global preferences and apply to all documents you create after setting the Preferences. Documents created earlier are unaffected by changes made in a new set of global preferences.

Establish document-specific preferences by setting the Preferences screens with the document open. Document-specific preferences don't affect the global Preferences settings. In fact, a document's Preferences migrate along with the file wherever it's transferred—to a print house, another computer on your network, or onto an archival storage medium.

All seven screens of options for Macintosh and Windows Preferences are identical and are accessed individually using the File menu or by using the tabs along the top of the Preferences dialog box after it's open.

General Preferences Screen

The General Preferences screen determines whether you display low-resolution Proxy, Full Resolution, or Gray Out images, often called greeked images. Proxy images equate to FPO (For Position Only) images, and in most instances they are perfectly adequate for on-screen work. Full resolution images are really only effective on large, high-resolution monitors set to 1124×870 or higher. They also bulk up your publication file.

As you work with text in a document that has lots of placed images, you may find it easier to concentrate on the text manipulations if you temporarily turn off all image display by choosing Gray Out. This is a preference you definitely activate with a document open. It makes little sense to choose it for a global preference because you can't see images you place, and clicking on the grayed-out image doesn't display the image either (see Figure 3.12).

Text Preferences Screen

For the catalog there's no need to adjust the defaults set for character spacing: Superscript, Subscript, and Small Cap. By default, all three options under Type Options are selected, but you'll want to adjust one of these (the last one) because the catalog is to be professionally printed (see Figure 3.13).

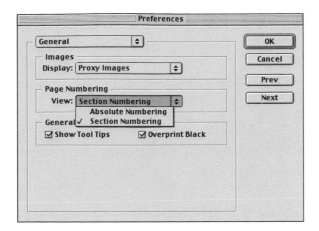

Figure 3.12

Beneath the Display pop-up menu in the General Preferences dialog box are two choices for Page Numbering View: Absolute Numbering or Section Numbering. You can also set preferences to Show Tool Tips and Overprint Black.

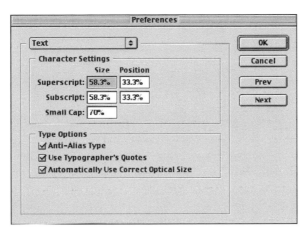

Figure 3.13

In most instances, you won't change these Character Settings in the Text Preferences, but you certainly could, for instance, in a template you plan to reuse for many issues, or as a design element for a client.

Final output destination dictates which Type Options you need to select. Anti-Alias Type creates a soft, transition pixel around the periphery of each letter, thus eliminating a hard-edged appearance to the type. For hard copy output, it's a must. However, if you're designing a Web-bound or on-screen document, antialiasing tends to make type look mushy.

Typographer's quotes, often called "curly quotes," are standard for indicating quoted text, but if you expect to deal more often in inch marks in a document, turn off this option and use the special character sets when you need to quote someone.

The final option concerns optical kerning, a feature that spaces letters and characters from different fonts, or in the same font but of different sizes, to a visually pleasing distance. In addition, or instead, you could manually adjust kerning to one-thousandth of an em on a case-by-case basis.

Composition Preferences Screen

Multi-line Composer settings determine the number of text lines to be considered in making decisions about line color and spacing. Line color, in this instance, isn't the color applied to a line you draw; it's the density of text along a line of type. If you're using a small font size in a text frame with many lines of text, you may want to consider more lines than the default, six. Reducing the number of alternatives to consider may cause Multi-line Composer to overlook choices that would improve the balance in lines of text. Both Look Ahead x Lines and Consider Up To x Alternatives must be between 3 and 30 (see Figure 3.14).

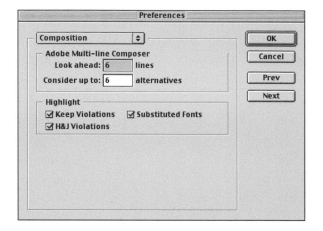

Figure 3.14
Even in documents with limited text, activating the Preferences in the Composition screen helps assure that your line color is balanced.

The Highlight area of the Composition Preferences screen is for on-screen proofing of adjustments made by Multi-line Composer. These options have no effect on output. They simply display using a highlight color where Multi-line Composer chose to override any of the options you set up as paragraph or paragraph style parameters. Keep Violations relates to instructions to Keep Lines Together or Keep With Next Paragraph. The H&J Violations setting uses the hyphenation and justification table applied to paragraphs or styles, and Substituted Fonts highlights instances where you may have substituted real italics and small caps built into a font for those that InDesign sets.

Measurement Units

Your choice of measurement Units & Increments is purely a matter of preference (see Figure 3.15). If you're more comfortable working with typesetters' units—picas or points—choose one of those. Or you may prefer to work with inches, either in the U.S. conventional 12 to the foot, or in decimal increments of 10 inches. You can also select millimeters, centimeters, ciceros, or a custom increment. Whatever you choose, that is the measurement displayed on the rulers, and, by default, in dialog boxes that rely on measurements. The Keyboard Increments setting determines the size of adjustments applied when you use a shortcut key combination. (Refer to the sidebar for "Typography Shortcuts" later in this chapter.)

As you work on a document, chances are very good that you'll use at least a couple of different measurement units and increments. Many designers

Note: Unlike with Photoshop 5, you can't change ruler increments by double-click

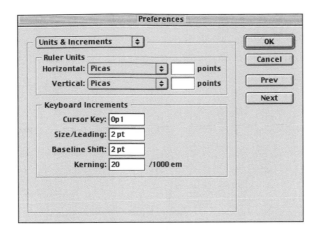

Figure 3.15
Select a unit of measure from the pop-up menu beside Horizontal and Vertical in the Units & Increments Preferences screen.

like to work with inches or centimeters for object placement on the page, but switch to points or picas for refining text. (Ciceros are not used in the U.S., but are used by some other countries.) Table 3.1 gives equivalencies of various typography measurements on a ruler; however, you can enter any unit of measurement in any dialog box.

Grids Preferences Screen

Grids create a graph-paper-like arrangement of nonprinting lines across your entire document. These grid lines affect other decisions you make in text frames based upon your preference for Baseline Grid and for aligning objects to the Document Grid (see Figure 3.16).

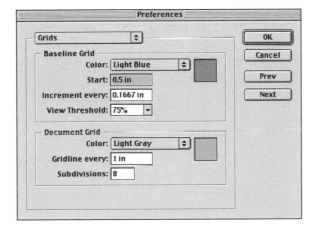

Figure 3.16
You can change the colors for grid lines by double-clicking on the color swatches in this Grid Preferences screen.

Table 3.1 Typography measurement equivalents.

Increment	Equivalent Picas	Equivalent Points	Equivalent Centimeters	Equivalent Inches
Inch	6 picas	72 points	2.54 centimeters	N/A
Decimal Inches	60 picas	720 points	254 centimeters	N/A
Cicero	6.9366 picas	83.2392 points	2.197 centimeters	0.86497 inches

Guides Preferences Screen

You'll return to this screen when you work with graphics in the catalog. At that point, you'll prefer to have the Guides In Back, but for openers, leave that unchecked (see Figure 3.17).

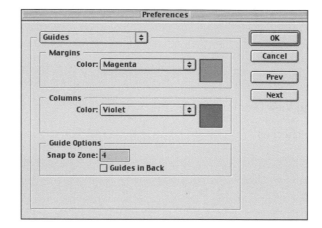

Figure 3.17

Look at the lower portion of the Guides Preferences dialog box for the checkbox that determines whether guides run on top of or beneath frames in the document or pasteboard.

Dictionary Preferences Screen

The choice you make in the Dictionary Preferences screen determines many things typographical, including hyphenation and spell checking. For this project, the language is American English (catalog) versus, say, UK English (catalogue) (see Figure 3.18).

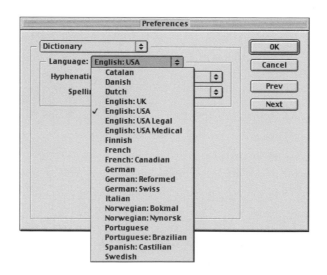

Figure 3.18

InDesign provides an international feast of dictionary choices.

That concludes the Preferences settings you'll need for the catalog, but you may want to take a break from reading to set up the Adobe Online Preferences. There's no need to save after setting Preferences unless you have set document-specific Preferences.

PROJECT Phase 1 Of Designing A Catalog: Setting Your Preferences

1. Close the Turfer Catalog file to set global Preferences.

2. Select File|Preferences|General to open the Preferences dialog box, or use the shortcut Cmd+K or Ctrl+K.

3. Set these General Preferences:

   - Images Display: Proxy Images

   - Page Numbering View: Section Numbering

   - Show Tool Tips: checked

   - Overprint Black: checked

4. For Text Preferences, leave all the Character Settings selected, but set the following Type Options:

   - Anti-Alias Type: checked

   - Use Typographer's Quotes: checked

   - Automatically Use Correct Optical Size: unchecked

5. In the Composition Preferences, leave the default settings in place:

   - Look Ahead: 6 lines

   - Consider Up To: 6 alternatives

   - Highlight options: all checked

6. For Units & Increments Preferences, set the following Ruler Units:

   - Horizontal: Inches

   - Vertical: Inches

   This can be changed at a later stage of developing the catalog.

7. In the Grids Preferences, leave the Baseline Grid color swatch, Start, and Increment Every settings as is, but enter these Grids Preferences:

   - View Threshold: 50% (This causes the Baseline Grid to show only at a magnification of 50% or more.)

   - Gridline Every: 12 in (12 inches)

   - Subdivisions: 10

8. In the Guide Options of the Guides Preferences, leave Snap Zone at 4 pixels, unless you have difficulty moving your mouse with precision. If that's the case, you may want to increase the snap distance slightly.

Note: The choice of units made in the Units & Increments screen appears by default in the Grids screen. You can type in any increment, regardless of the choice you made in Units & Increments, provided you also type in an abbreviation identifying the units.

9. In the Dictionary Preferences, be sure that you have the Language set to English USA.

Adobe Online Preferences

Having these Preferences set up makes signing on to the Adobe site for the latest upgrades and information a snap. Use the Setup button to start. Then follow the steps through the Assistant (Macintosh) or Wizard (Windows) screens, and you're ready to log on using the Adobe Online command at the bottom of the File menu (see Figure 3.19).

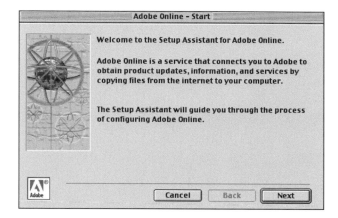

Figure 3.19
Stepping through these screens, along with the Adobe Online command in the File menu, takes you directly to the latest and greatest Adobe has to offer.

The General tab in the Online Preferences screen displays Network Setting and Update Options for determining your download preferences. The Application tab offers Notification Options and Subscription Options that alert you to new downloadable files available, late-breaking Adobe news, and when downloads are complete. You can also be notified of InDesign news via email.

Customizing The Interface

As I mentioned earlier, InDesign ships with a QuarkXPress keystroke set you can activate using File|Edit Shortcuts. You can also add your own keystrokes to unassigned commands and revise the default InDesign key set (see Figure 3.20).

If you have the Edit Shortcuts dialog box open on screen, click the down arrow beside the menu listed in the Product Area box to see and select the category of keystrokes you want to edit. Product Area refers to the InDesign menus and to special tricks that don't appear on any menu, such as Object Editing with shortcuts for Nudging, selecting a specific object in a stack of objects, Swapping Fill and Stroke activation and colors in the Tools palette, and other shortcuts for toggling through multiple open windows, closing documents, and saving all open documents.

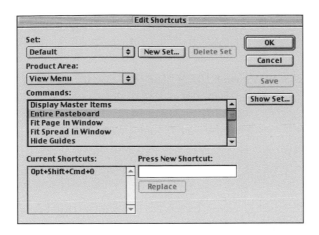

Figure 3.20
Use the New Set button in the Edit Shortcuts dialog box to name your set and base it on an existing set, then enter your shortcut keystrokes for the new set.

With the category selected, highlight the command to which you want to assign a keystroke. If there's already a keystroke assigned to the command, it appears in the Current Shortcuts text box, and the keystroke to press appears under Press New Shortcut. Finally, click the Assign button to store the keystroke, and continue assigning keystrokes to other commands.

Starting A New Publication

You may be the kind of designer who launches into every project with gusto, achieving dazzling results through sheer talent. Count yourself among the fortunate few. Most of us have to do a lot more planning.

Whether you realize it or not, every single thing you do toward final output of a document is prepress, from opening the new file to attending the press run. What you overlook at the start or at any step along the way will surely jump up and bite you in those final moments, so preparing carefully from the beginning is not only helpful—it's good business. Paring down the problem factor also slims the cost factor.

Plan Your Publication

Design your documents for a specific purpose and the intended audience. Yes, I know that you can convert InDesign print documents for the Web. Yes, I've heard clients demand to repurpose a document without realizing what effect that has on document designs. Of course, I know that budgets are forever dwindling and time fleeting, but none of these things render careful preparation impossible. Consider every aspect of the publication. Here's my favorite preproduction checklist:

1. What is the purpose of this publication?

2. Who is the target audience?

3. What is the budget?

4. Is this an ongoing project or a one-off publication?

5. How many pages will it have?

6. If printed, how many copies will there be?

7. What is the final output device?

8. Who will contribute content to the project?

9. Will it include photography?

10. Who is responsible for photo adjustments?

11. What paper stock will be used?

12. How many and what inks are requested?

13. Are there special printing requests, such as die-cuts or lacquers?

14. Can my print resources handle the job?

15. What is the deadline?

16. Who is responsible for signing off on the project?

17. When, how, and how much do I get paid?

You may want to add things to this list, but whatever you do, use a checklist to resolve all possible questions as early in the game as possible.

Document Setup

It helps to be clairvoyant as you set up a document, but it's not required. Just going through a checklist with your client or editor-in-chief or employer resolves much of the need for crystal ball gazing. You can, and no doubt will, revise things on the pages many times, but you don't want to revise the foundational decisions, such as the document size and page margins established in the New Document dialog box. These are based on the size of the page at final output and how margin lines appear on screen.

PROJECT Phase 2 Of Designing A Catalog: Using The New Document Dialog Box

This catalog is to be printed on a standard size 8$\frac{1}{2}$-by-11-inch coated paper stock. Special staples, which allow vendors and salespersons to add the catalog to a ring binder of other catalogs from Turfer, are used to bind the pages. With Preferences set earlier, you're ready to begin creating the Turfer catalog. It may be helpful to have a reference to look at as you work on your catalog. In that case, I suggest you open the file that you looked at earlier.

1. Open Turferct.indd from the CD that accompanies this book.

2. Resize the window to fit in the upper-right corner of your screen. Conveniently, the document magnification automatically adjusts to fit the smaller window.

3. Choose File|New to open the New Document dialog box.

4. Set the following:

   - Number of Pages: 5

   - Click to select: Facing Pages

   - Page Size: Letter

   - Orientation: click the Portrait icon

   - Margins: 0 for Top, Bottom, Inside, and Outside

   - Columns: 1

   - Gutter: 1p0

5. Save your new catalog document right now. Name the document Turfer1.indd.

TOOL PREFERENCES DON'T EXIST

Not to complain, but one thing I like a lot in QuarkXPress is the ability to change default tool behaviors. For instance, you can change the Text Box tool to automatically have the color background you want inside each text box as you draw it rather than the default white background. That's not an option with InDesign. You can set up text boxes on Master pages with a different color background and store one in a Library. That may be your best bet for paralleling the QuarkXPress Tool preference settings.

SOME (POSSIBLY CONFUSING) INDESIGN TERMINOLOGY

I've always been a language addict, and fascinated by the way the same word can mean different things to different folks. The language of DTP applications is no different from any other language. Defining the terminology certainly speeds learning, so, to that end, I've assembled a few terms that might be defined differently by InDesign than the definitions you're accustomed to:

- *Story*—Longstanding PageMaker users know exactly what a Story is, but it's not as clear to those transitioning from other desktop publishing applications. A Story is a continuous body of text contained in one or more text frames. It needn't be a story in the sense that Goldilocks and the Three Bears is a story. It could be statistical data or a list of reference phone numbers, or any combination of text and numbers that are closely related and need to appear in coherent relationships. Maybe a better way to clarify it is to say that a newspaper story continued on page 23 is all considered a single Story by InDesign.

- *Links*—Here is another possibly ambiguous term. Some applications use this word to indicate that text boxes are connected, allowing overflow text to stream to another text box. Not so InDesign. Links, in this application, are connections to source files, and nothing else. Links maintain an internal database that permits InDesign to summon up the application that originally created the items that you import, should you need to edit them in their native environment.

- *Open A Copy*—This is one of the options found in the dialog box when you choose File|Open. The other option is to open the original file, which immediately is a tip-off that you can retain a closed file in its present state of development by opening a copy rather than the original. Again, this is not new to PageMaker users (aren't you glad you chose Adobe again?), but QuarkXPress users haven't had this feature.

TYPOGRAPHY SHORTCUTS

Action	Macintosh Shortcut	Windows Shortcut
All caps apply	Shift+Cmd+K	Shift+Ctrl+K
Baseline grid align to	Opt+Shift+Cmd+G	Alt+Shift+Ctrl+G
Baseline shift decrease	Opt+Shift+Down Arrow	Alt+Shift+Down Arrow
Baseline shift increase	Opt+Shift+Up Arrow	Alt+Shift+Up Arrow
Baseline shift x 5 decrease	Opt+Shift+Cmd+Down Arrow	Alt+Shift+Ctrl+Down Arrow
Baseline shift x 5 increase	Opt+Shift+Cmd+Up Arrow	Alt+Shift+Ctrl+Up Arrow
Bold apply	Shift+Cmd+B	Shift+Ctrl+B
Center align	Shift+Cmd+C	Shift+Ctrl+C
Character style redefine	Opt+Shift+Cmd+C	Alt+Shift+Ctrl+C
Discretionary hyphen insert	Shift+Cmd+- (minus)	Shift+Ctrl+- (minus)
Em space insert	Shift+Cmd+M	Shift+Ctrl+M
Figure space insert	Opt+Shift+Cmd+8	Alt+Shift+Ctrl+8
Force justify align	Opt+Shift+Cmd+J	Alt+Shift+Ctrl+J
Hair space insert	Opt+Shift+Cmd+I	Alt+Shift+Ctrl+I
Horizontal text scale normal	Shift+Cmd+X	Shift+Ctrl+X
Hyphenate auto on/off	Opt+Shift+Cmd+H	Alt+Shift+Ctrl+H
Italic apply	Shift+Cmd+I	Shift+Ctrl+I
Justify align	Shift+Cmd+J	Shift+Ctrl+J
Keep options	Opt+Cmd+K	Alt+Ctrl+K
Kerning and tracking reset	Shift+Cmd+Q	Shift+Ctrl+Q
Kerning/tracking decrease	Opt+Left Arrow	Alt+Left Arrow
Kerning/tracking increase	Opt+Right Arrow	Alt+Right Arrow
Kerning/tracking x 5 decrease	Opt+Cmd+Left Arrow	Alt+Ctrl+Left Arrow
Kerning/tracking x 5 increase	Opt+Cmd+Right Arrow	Alt+Ctrl+Right Arrow
Leading auto	Opt+Shift+Cmd+A	Alt+Shift+Ctrl+A
Leading decrease	Opt+Down Arrow	Alt+Down Arrow
Leading increase	Opt+Up Arrow	Alt+Up Arrow
Leading x 5 decrease	Opt+Cmd+Down Arrow	Alt+Ctrl+Down Arrow
Leading x 5 increase	Opt+Cmd+Up Arrow	Alt+Ctrl+Up Arrow
Left align	Shift+Cmd+L	Shift+Ctrl+L
Nonbreaking hyphen insert	Opt+Cmd+- (minus)	Alt+Ctrl+- (minus)
Nonbreaking space insert	Opt+Cmd+X	Alt+Ctrl+X
Normal apply	Shift+Cmd+Y	Shift+Ctrl+Y
Paragraph rules	Shift+Cmd+J	Shift+Ctrl+J
Paragraph style redefine	Opt+Shift+Cmd+R	Alt+Shift+Ctrl+R
Point size decrease	Shift+Cmd+, (comma)	Shift+Ctrl+, (comma)
Point size increase	Shift+Cmd+. (period)	Shift+Ctrl+. (period)
Point size x 5 decrease	Opt+Shift+Cmd+, (comma)	Alt+Shift+Ctrl+, (comma)
Point size x 5 increase	Opt+Shift+Cmd+. (period)	Alt+Shift+Ctrl+. (period)
Right align	Shift+Cmd+R	Shift+Ctrl+R
Section name insert	Opt+Shift+Cmd+N	Alt+Shift+Ctrl+N
Small caps apply	Shift+Cmd+H	Shift+Ctrl+H
Strikethrough apply	Shift+Cmd+/ (slash)	Shift+Ctrl+/ (slash)
Subscript apply	Opt+Shift+Cmd++ (plus)	Alt+Shift+Ctrl++ (plus)
Superscript apply	Shift+Cmd++ (plus)	Shift+Ctrl++ (plus)
Switch composer	Opt+Shift+Cmd+T	Alt+Shift+Ctrl+T
Thin space insert	Opt+Shift+Cmd+M	Alt+Shift+Ctrl+M
Underline apply	Shift+Cmd+U	Shift+Ctrl+U
Vertical text scale normal	Opt+Shift+Cmd+X	Alt+Shift+Ctrl+X

Take a look at the Pages palette. The lower portion of the palette shows three Master pages: the default single page, None, and facing pages A-Master. The next chapter is all about Master pages, and you'll get to designing those Master pages then.

Saving The Catalog

You all know the perils of not saving your work. A nearby flash of lightning, the unexpected power surge, inadvertent deletions that are saved—any of these and more can obliterate hours of work. Saving immediately after you set up a document and saving often as you work is not just a good habit; it's a survival technique. But what happens if that power surge corrupts your document? InDesign offers two other saving options that can make the difference between missed and met deadlines.

> **Note:** InDesign running under Windows automatically appends the extension .indd to your saved document, but you Macintosh users will have to add that yourself if you expect to open your file on a PC.

The Difference Between Save, Save As, And Save A Copy

Save is so obvious that it needs no further explanation. It can't hurt to mention that the earlier and more often you use that ol' Save, the less likely you are to lose your work.

Save As creates a duplicate of your document and closes your original file as the copy opens on screen. You can rename the duplicate if you want, identifying it as a design phase or some other name that helps you identify the purpose of the development stage of the copy.

Save A Copy is ground already trod by Photoshop users. It's a convenient way to back up your work while keeping the document you're working on open on screen. Save A Copy makes a duplicate of your document in its current configuration, but doesn't close the original, so you can continue working in the original document. Each time you use Save A Copy, the word "copy" is appended to the original file name. If you regularly use Save A Copy without changing the file name in any way, each copy overwrites the earlier backup version of your file. If your original is corrupted, or you've designed yourself into a corner, saving all the while, you can always return to the saved copy and start over from the point where you were when you last saved a copy.

Stationery Option/InDesign Template

Especially for publications that you anticipate producing again and again with only content variations, it behooves you to save a copy of the original publication in a Template (Windows) or Stationery (Macintosh) version. The Windows version of InDesign automatically appends the file-type identifying extension to the name you give a publication. Mac users must add that extension themselves (see Figure 3.21).

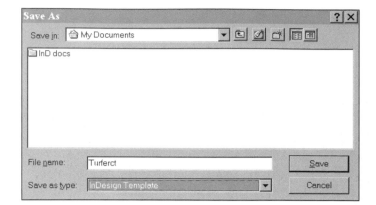

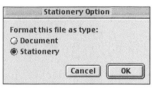

Figure 3.21

As you save a publication as Stationery on a Mac, or as a Template on a PC, the dialog boxes look slightly different, but the result is the same: a reusable copy of your document.

Moving On

In the following chapter you'll continue developing your Turfer catalog by working with Master pages; creating, editing, and adding Master pages and Master spreads; and adding Master Items. You'll create guides on Master pages and Master spreads added to the catalog. Finally, you'll learn about moving, adding, and deleting both document pages and Master pages.

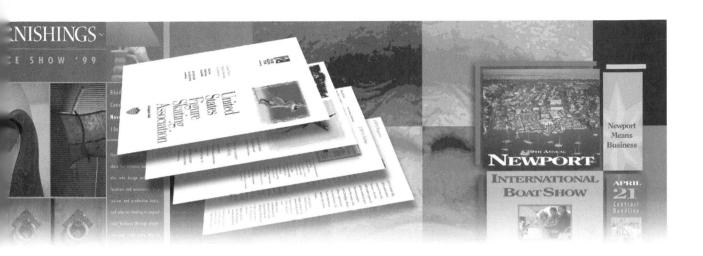

MASTERING
DOCUMENT
PAGES

You're one of the pros. You've designed hundreds and hundreds of pieces. You know all about Master pages. No? Well, you're not alone.

Skills Covered In This Chapter

- Work with guides

- Create a Master page

- Create and work with layers

- Create, fill, and resize picture frames

- Create text frames

- Set default text attributes for a text frame

- Set text specifications in the Transform palette

- Add document pages based on a Master page or Master spread

- Move document pages

- Delete Master pages

It never fails to amaze me how many practicing professional designers overlook the advantages of using Master pages. Unless you're doing a one-page document, or occasionally, a simple folded piece printed on a single sheet of paper, you have nothing to gain by using Master pages...except time. And nothing to lose but aggravation. Master pages act as a cookie cutter for pages in your document. The items you place on a Master page appear on every publication page based on that Master, saving tedious repetition and assuring precision placement of Master items, such as page numbers and graphic elements, throughout your publication pages.

Create Master Pages

In the previous chapter, you opened a new document and set preferences. The next phase of developing the catalog is setting up Master pages for the front cover, spreads, and cross-over spreads.

Use the document created for the previous chapter for projects in this chapter. I definitely suggest you have a go-by open to use as a reference as you work on these projects. The go-by is still Turferct.indd, found on this book's companion CD-ROM.

PROJECT Create Master Pages For The Catalog: Adding The Front Cover Master

The cover of this catalog retains the same page geometry for every issue, but the graphic, the kicker line under the front cover photograph, and the catalog code change with each issue:

1. Using your catalog file, choose Layout|Ruler Guides and set:

- View Threshold: 10%

- Color: Cyan

Close the dialog box. At a magnification less than 10%, these Cyan guides won't show. At any magnification 10% or greater, they do show.

2. Use the pop-up menu on the Pages palette to add a New Master.

3. In the Master Options dialog box, enter:

- Prefix: A

- Name: Front Cover

- Based On Master: None

- Number Of Pages: 1

Close the dialog box (see Figure 4.1).

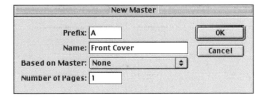

Figure 4.1
Your Master Options for the first Master page should look like this.

4. Add a Master two-page spread now, just as you added the Front Cover Master, and set the two-page spread Master Options:

- Prefix: B

- Name: Spreads

- Based On Master: None

- Number Of Pages: 2

5. Close the dialog box.

Grids And Guides

Grids cover the entire publication or a specific text frame, whereas guides apply to specific pages within the document. You can have objects and text snap to either gridlines or guidelines.

Grids

Two kinds of grids are available in InDesign: Document Grid and Baseline Grid. If you select View|Show Document Grid, you'll see the graph paper–like gridlines spanning the entire pasteboard and catalog pages starting a

Note: If you've spent a career using QuarkXPress and never bothered with Master pages, but built facing page documents by dragging the default A-Master A into the document area of the Layout palette for spreads, you are in for a shock. If, in the Document Setup, your publication is designated as a one page document, you can't place document pages in spreads of InDesign unless you create a Master that is designated in the Master Option dialog box as having two pages!

half inch from the top of the pages, in increments of 0.1667 inches. The Document Grid displays at any magnification. Later, as you work with text frames, you'll discover that at magnifications less than 75%, the Baseline Grid, by default, doesn't show (see Figure 4.2).

The Document Grid is the rank of imaginary lines objects snap to when Snap To Grids is selected for an object, so setting your Preferences for Grids is very important. It determines how many gridlines you have available for snapping, including the subdivisions of each gridline (see Figure 4.3).

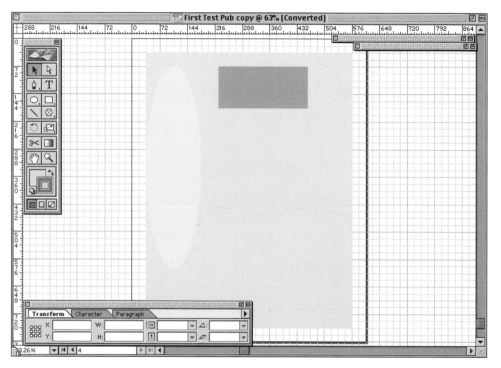

Figure 4.2

The Document Grid covers the entire pasteboard, and every page of a publication.

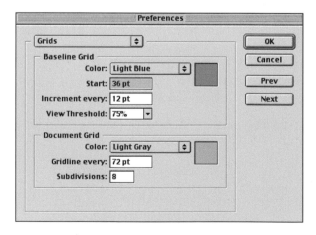

Figure 4.3

Look at the lower portion of the Grids Preferences dialog box to set up your Document Grids.

The difference between Document and Baseline Grids is that you can snap objects to the Document Grid on any page or Master of your document and lock text to the Baseline Grid in any text frame. When you choose View|Snap To Document Grid and drag an object on a page, the object jerks along, snapping to each successive grid, and adhering to the nearest grid when you drop the object. To display or conceal the gridlines, choose View|Show|Hide Document Grid.

For the catalog Master pages, you won't need to use the Document grid, but guides are a must.

Create, Move, And Remove Guides

Before you start setting guides in the catalog, let me remind you: Guides that appear on a Master page also appear on any pages based on the Master, and the magnification set for guides determines when guides are visible on screen as you work with either the Master pages or document pages.

You've already set up guides to show at a magnification of 10% or greater. The first time you zoom in or zoom out and decide to place a guide, it may be a good idea to choose Layout|Ruler Guides and set a different Color and View Threshold before placing any guides at that greater or lesser magnification (see Figure 4.4).

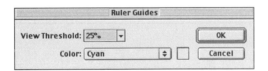

The bonus inherent in having guides that show only at given percentages is that you can use guides for close-in positioning, at say 200% or 400%, that become invisible when you zoom out to get an overview of the page at say 100% or 50%. Away, away with screen clutter without hiding all the guides (see Figure 4.5).

By now, it should be obvious that you can create guides by dragging them from either ruler, but I ought to mention that Create Guides is available to let you create ranks of guides in rows and/or columns, even though you won't use this feature in your catalog. Drop back to Chapter 2 in the section covering the Layout menu for general information about the Create Guides command.

As you draw out a guide from either the horizontal or vertical ruler, keep one eye on the Transform palette. Depending on which ruler the guide is drawn from, the X or Y portion of the palette displays positioning numbers, so you can release the guide at exactly the spot where you want it to be.

Note: *The most recent Ruler Guide settings remain in place* for every guide you drag from a ruler, no matter the percentage at which you are working! If you zoom in and set up positioning guides with a large percentage View Threshold, and then zoom out and drag another guide from the ruler without changing the Threshold, it looks for all the world as if no guide came from the ruler, but it did. You just can't see it at that lower magnification.

Figure 4.4
The color distinguishes Ruler Guides of different thresholds, so you don't do something like removing or moving a guide at one viewing percentage that is essential for aligning objects elsewhere on the page at a different viewing percentage.

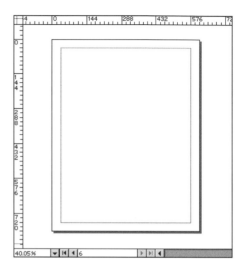

Figure 4.5

These two figures show the same page. The guides are set to a view threshold of 50%. The figure on the left is shown at 60.05% and the figure on the right is at 40.05%.

To move a guide, use the Selection tool to click on the guide you want moved, and drag the guide to a new position. If you want to remove a guide altogether, click on it and press the Delete key.

Guides That Span Pages And The Pasteboard

Just as in QuarkXPress, InDesign guides pulled from the ruler at a position within the vertical boundaries of a page appear only on that one page, even if the page is part of a spread. However, if you pull a ruler guide from a position outside the vertical bounds of a page, the horizontal guide spans the entire pasteboard, including any and all of the pages in a spread.

Hold on now! With InDesign, vertical guides can also stretch beyond the page boundaries, which just isn't possible in QuarkXPress (see Figure 4.6).

Enough of this talk about guides. Better get back to your catalog and use this information to set some guides on the Master pages to learn how they work.

PROJECT Set Guides On Master Pages

1. On the Pages palette, be sure that the Front Cover Master is selected in the Pages palette. If it isn't, double-click on the Front Cover icon.

2. Zoom to view the Master page at 100% and set the Ruler Guides dialog box settings to:

   • View Threshold: 50%

   • Color: Tan

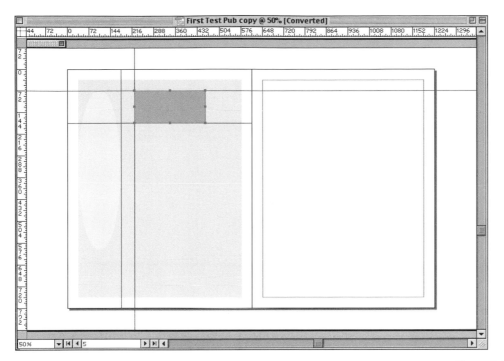

Figure 4.6

If you drag a guide and release the cursor within the page boundaries, the guides remain within the page; otherwise, they span spreads and the pasteboard.

3. Drag out two guides and position them at the following points:

   • Horizontal: 0.333 inches on the Y axis

   • Vertical: 8.197 inches on the X axis

   These will be used as ersatz baselines to position text in frames at right angles to one another. The text frames hold the same reference code that identifies the catalog issue. Yes, you could just as well place this code on the cover page rather than the Master, but this is a learning experience, and you're establishing page geometry for the cover (see Figure 4.7).

4. Continue setting guides on the Front Cover Master at this 100% magnification. Be aware that, unlike in QuarkXPress, the window automatically scrolls as you drag the guides, and the part of the page you want can scoot right away from you:

   • Vertical:

     4.25 inches (Center line of the front cover page contents as measured from the vertical catalog issue code frame)

     3.062 inches (Left edge of the text frame for the year)

     5.418 inches (Right edge of the text frame for the year)

     0.562 inches (Left edge of the front cover picture frame)

     7.937 inches (Right edge of the front cover picture frame)

GUIDES BY THE NUMBERS

You can drag a guide out of a ruler and drop it anywhere, then click on the guide to highlight it, and enter positioning numbers in the Transform palette. The highlighted guide jumps into position, remaining highlighted until you click on the page, or drag out another guide.

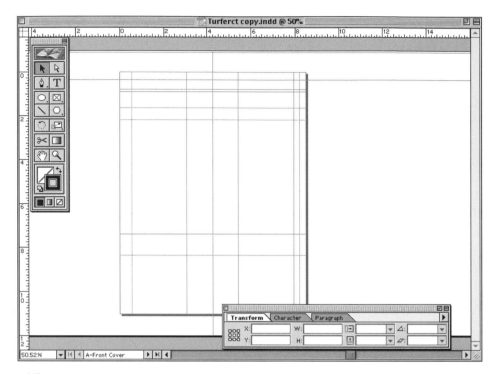

Figure 4.7

Guides on your Front Cover Master page should look like this.

Note: Position numbers in the Transform palette can go up to *four* places after the decimal point, but you need only set these to the three places given. Trailing zeros after the decimal point don't appear in the X and Y positioning numbers.

COLOR-CODED GUIDES

If you're really ambitious, you can color-code your guides to differentiate between text guides and picture guides, for instance, using the same colors for text and graphics at every magnification.

- Horizontal:

  0.791 inches (Ersatz baseline for year in text box)

  0.902 inches (Top edge of the Turfer logo picture frame)

  1.634 inches (Bottom edge of the Turfer logo picture frame)

  2.182 inches (Top edge of the front cover picture frame)

  7.375 inches (Bottom edge of the front cover picture frame)

  8.339 inches (Ersatz baseline for text in the kicker line text frame below the front cover picture)

Now on to the Spreads Master. For a different view, change to a magnification of 50% to see at least some of both pages and a part of the pasteboard.

5. Select both pages of the Spreads Master in the Pages palette.

6. Set guides that span both pages and the pasteboard at these positions:

   - Horizontal:

     1.375 inches (For picture frame banner at the top of each page of the spread)

     10.495 inches (For the top of a page number tile to be added in the next chapter)

     10.75 inches (Another ersatz baseline for the page number text)

- Vertical:

  0.203 inches (Left page margin for the page number text)

  16.816 inches (Right page margin for the page number text)

Masters Based On Masters

The third set of Master pages is similar to the Spreads layout, but has a few changes. C-Cross-over Spread has no photographic banner across the top of each page in the spread, but it does have a photograph that spans both left and right pages of the Master spread. Take a look at the go-by **Turferct.indd** file. There's also a photograph in the lower right section of the right page in the spread.

PROJECT Create The Cross-Over Spread

1. In the Pages palette, highlight both pages of B-Spreads Master pages, then use the Pages palette pop-up menu to select New Master.

2. Select Master Options for the new C-Master and change:

   - Prefix: C

   - Name: Cross-over Spread

   - Based On Master: B-Spreads

   - Number Of Pages: 2

3. Close the dialog box.

For the surprise of your life, double-click on the Cross-over Spread Master page in the Pages palette. Yeowee! All those guides you positioned on the Spreads Master pages are also on the Cross-over Spread Master because, you guessed it, the Cross-over Masters are *based on the Spreads Master*. Now save your work (see Figure 4.8).

You'll need a couple more guides, but you'll add these on a layer made in the next Project.

Layers

Layers aren't new to Adobe. They've been in Photoshop for eons. What makes InDesign layers so wonderful is that InDesign's layers are document-wide, which means that each layer on each page is exactly the same layer that exists on every other page, including the Master pages.

InDesign layers are like a stack of huge acetate sheets covering the entire document. The stacking order remains the same throughout, but, in effect,

PALETTE SHORTCUTS

Use the Tab key (except when in text mode) to move to the next option in the Transform palette. When all options on the palette are set, press the Return or the Enter key to confirm measurements entered in a palette. Be aware that if you press the Tab key after all Transform palette options are set, you'll hide all open palettes.

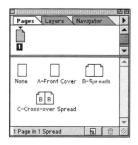

Figure 4.8

The Pages palette should have six Master pages just as this one does (possibly arranged differently): None, A-Front Cover, B-Spreads, and C-Cross-over Spread. The Cross-over Master Spread has the letter B on both pages to remind you it's based on B-Spreads.

you're viewing a different section of the surface of the acetate stack covering each page. Delete Layer 1 on page 6, for instance, and you delete Layer 1 on all pages, taking everything placed on Layer 1 to the ozone layer.

By default, layers show. To hide a layer, click the eye icon to the left of the layer name in the Layers palette (see Figure 4.9).

When you hide the layer, everything on the layer—Master page items and document page items—is hidden. So keep in mind that when you create a layer for Master page items, that layer may also hold items created on document pages. The layer you're about to create will hold guides and frames relating to pictures in the catalog.

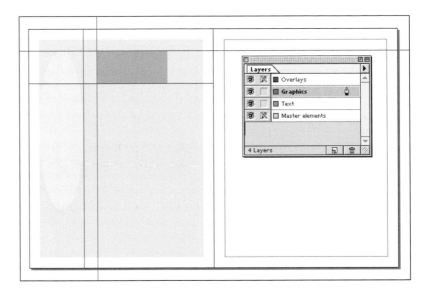

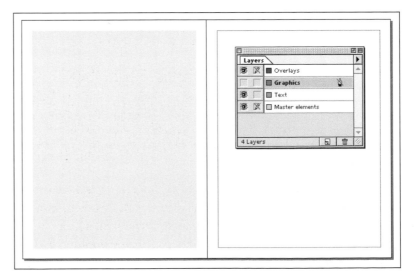

Figure 4.9

On the top you see all the layers displayed, and on the bottom, the Graphics layer is hidden.

Create A New Layer

1. Use the pop-up menu in the Layers palette. By default, the color of the new layer is Red, which means that every object on that layer displays a red frame. It's a good way to tell which layer a item was created on.

2. In Layer Options, set the following:

   - Name: Photos

   - Color: Dark Green

3. Save the document.

At present, the Photos layer has nothing on it, but that's about to change. Take a moment to think about ways you might use layers in things you design.

Guides On Layers

So far, all the guides you've positioned have been on the default Layer 1. To get a sense of how the layers work, choose Window|Layers to show the Layers palette. Click the eye icon to hide the Master Guides Layer 1. Ahhh. Now you see them...now you don't. This should be a tip-off that guides, like items, can be placed on different layers.

Lock Guides On Layers

With guides in place, you can lock them to avoid inadvertently moving any of the guides on a layer. Be sure the layer that holds guides you want locked is active in the Layers palette, and then open the Layer Options dialog box from the pop-up menu of the Layers palette (see Figure 4.10).

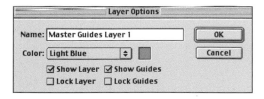

Figure 4.10

Select or deselect the options at the bottom of the Layer Options dialog box at any time as you work on a publication.

In addition to locking and unlocking guides in the Layer Options dialog box, you can temporarily show or hide the layer's guides, or even show or hide the entire layer. These guide options differ slightly from the Hide Guides command in the View menu in that the Layer Options apply to only a single layer, whereas the menu command hides every guide that is not already hidden from the Layer Options dialog box.

It's still a bit early in setting guides on Master pages to lock your catalog guides. You still have additional guides to set for the Cross-over Spread. The guides you'll create in the next Project will be on the Photos layer.

PROJECT Set Layer-Specific Guides

1. Activate the Cross-over Spread Master in the Pages palette, and the Photos layer in the Layers palette. Set guides for the cross-over image at:

    *   Vertical: .
        0875 inches (The left edge of the cross-over image frame)

        11 inches (The right edge of the cross-over image frame)

    *   Horizontal:
        1.5 inches (The top of the cross-over image frame)

        8.125 inches (The bottom of the cross-over image frame)

2. Now you can lock guides on the Master Guides Layer 1 and on the Photos layer using the Layer Options dialog box for each layer (see Figure 4.11).

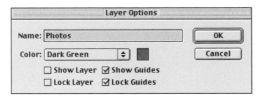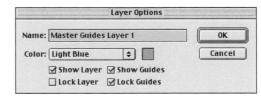

Figure 4.11
Although you can also lock all guides on all layers using the View menu, locking individual layer guides works to your advantage should you decide to unlock and adjust guides related to a single layer. There's no chance of moving or deleting guides on other layers.

Look at each of the Master pages you have. Observe that each Master has a distinct appearance. Some of the guides are Tan, and some are Dark Green. The page geometry is beginning to take shape.

The next thing to do is create some frames for content on the Masters and fill the frames.

Master Items

Master items can be placed on any layer of any Master page. All items on any given layer of a Master page appear on document pages based on that Master unless one or more layers containing Master items is hidden. Later in this chapter you'll learn how to activate and edit Master items on document pages.

Master items on Master pages are intended to give you the biggest bang for the buck. Master items are on Master pages because, in more cases than not, you want these items to appear on pages throughout a publication. As you simply *look* at a document page based on a Master, the Master items that appear on that page can't be changed in any way, so there's no chance of accidentally moving or editing Master items on a document page when you add page content. Later you'll learn how to select Master items on document pages.

Add Master Items To The Front Page Master

Every issue of the catalog needs to have a code number text frame, the Turfer logo, a text frame above the logo for the year, a picture frame, and a text frame for the kicker line below the picture on the Front Cover Master. Guides are already in place for these items, so the next task is to create the frames.

PROJECT Create Frames And Fill Them

1. Use the Rectangle Frame tool to create a frame for the Turfer logo at the top of the Front Cover Master that fits exactly within the guides you set for the logo:

   - W: 2.356

   - H: 0.7312

   Position the frame at:

   - X: 3.06

   - Y: 0.9028

   There's no need to revise the other choices in the Transform palette (see Figure 4.12).

2. To import the logo file, first select the Direct Selection tool and click on the logo picture frame, then choose File|Place and locate the image, TurfLogo.tiff (Mac) or TurfLogo.tif (Win).

   After the logo is placed, if necessary, zoom out far enough to see the frame and handles surrounding the newly placed logo graphic. There are two boxes surrounding the logo graphic. One is the picture frame, and the other is the bounding box of the imported graphic file (see Figure 4.13).

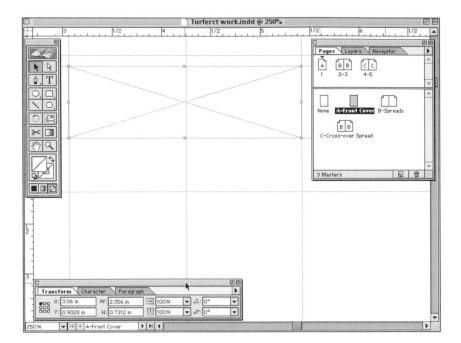

Figure 4.12

You may want to tweak the measurements for width to exactly fit within the guides, and you can nudge the frame in any direction using the arrow keys.

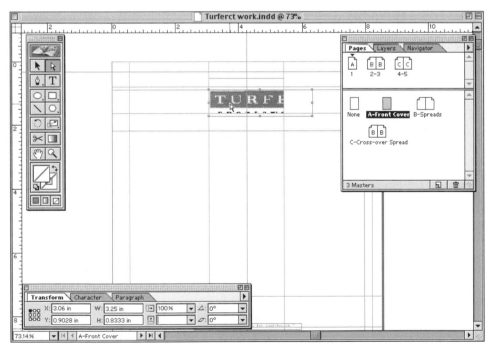

Figure 4.13

The graphic file exceeds the size of the picture frame in which it's placed. It must be reduced.

3. Use the Selection tool to drag a corner handle of the logo file and approximate the size of the picture frame. It's very hard to maintain a proportionate aspect ratio in the file using handles, so use the Transform palette to enter:

- Scale X percentage: 72.55%

- Scale Y percentage: 72.55%

Now the logo file height is smaller than the picture frame, but that doesn't matter in this case because the background of the lower portion of the logo file is white, and the edge of the file bounding frame doesn't show.

If necessary, use the arrow keys to position the file inside the picture frame so the upper-left corner fits properly in the corner of the picture frame.

4. Click outside the picture frame to deselect the placed logo, and save your work.

    The date line, 1999, above the logo, is a text frame. You may need to zoom in to see the guides and have a clear view of the area above the Turfer logo.

5. Use the Type tool to create a frame that is:

    • W: 2.358 inches

    • H: 0.248 inches

    Locate the frame at:

    • X: 3.062 inches

    • Y: 0.5437 inches

    By default, the cursor blinks inside the text frame. You can now assign default text attributes to the text frame.

6. Use the Paragraph palette to choose paragraph alignment and the Character palette to set font attributes:

    • Paragraph—Alignment: Justify with last line centered

    • Character—Font: Bauer Bodoni, 15 pt, Roman

    Leave all other settings in the Character palette as they are.

7. In the date line text frame, type "1999" (see Figure 4.14).

8. For the catalog code in the upper-right corner of the page and a real surprise, use the Rectangle Frame tool to create a frame with these specs (Yes, that's a picture frame you've drawn.):

    • W: 0.731

    • H: 0.199

    • X: 7.582 inches

    • Y: 0.2407 inches

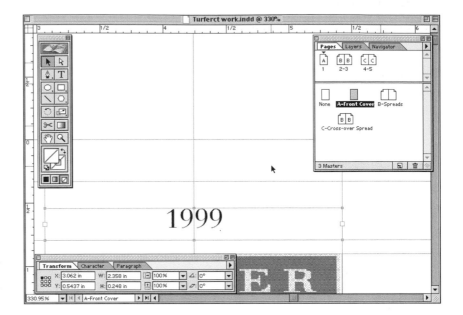

Figure 4.14

As you type in the numbers, they are automatically formatted because you set the attributes before starting to type. You could also set these attributes after the numbers are entered.

9. Now for the surprise. Go back to the Tools palette, select the Type tool, and click in the picture box you just made. Voilà! The frame is converted to a text frame (see Figure 4.15).

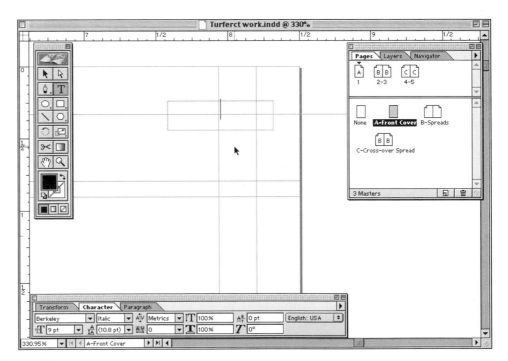

Figure 4.15

If you don't believe me, just move the frame. There's no picture frame buried beneath the text frame.

10. Use the Paragraph palette to choose paragraph alignment and the Character palette to set font attributes:

- Paragraph—Alignment: Justify with last line centered

- Character—Font: Berkley, 9 pt, Italic

11. Type in the catalog code "ASI-92354".

12. Click the Selection tool and press Opt+Cmd+D (Mac) or Ctrl+Alt+D (Win) to duplicate the catalog code text frame.

13. In the Transform palette, set Rotation Angle at minus 90 degrees.

    Position the frame at:

    • X: 8.2928 inches

    • Y: 0.389 inches

14. With the Selection tool, Shift+click to select both catalog code text frames and press Cmd+G (Mac) or Ctrl+G (Win) to group the two code text frames, and save your work (see Figure 4.16).

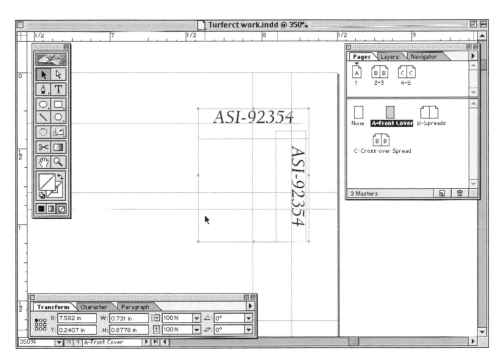

Figure 4.16
Each frame remains independently editable. You can change text or frame attributes, but you can't change the positioning relationship of the frames.

You're on your own for making the trademarked Turfer kicker line text box below the Front Cover photograph frame. This is a test. It's only a test. If it were the real thing, you'd be getting a paycheck! The text you need is: "When you'd rather be outdoors.™"

The text specs are:

• Bauer Bodoni, 11 pt Roman,

• Justify with last line centered

• 7 pt tracking

• Horizontal Scale, 140%

You'll have to create a New Color Swatch (Turfer Logo Green) for coloring the text:

- C: 90
- M: 0
- Y: 45
- K: 22.5

Apply the new Fill color at 100% (set by default in the Color palette)—see Figure 4.17.

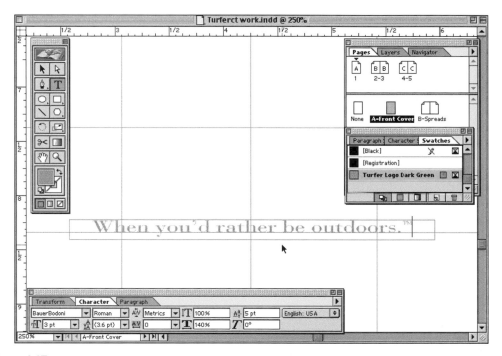

Figure 4.17

The kicker line should look like this.

To create the trademark symbol, type the letters TM, then select the letters and apply:

- Font Size: 3 points
- Baseline Shift: 5 points

You could insert the trademark using the Character palette pop-up to select Superscript, or select Type|Insert Character, but I thought it might be fun to play with shifting the baseline.

Activate Master Items On Document Pages

If, by chance, you need to remove or edit a Master item on a document page, you can select the item by pressing Cmd+Shift (Mac) or Ctrl+Shift (Win) and clicking the Master item to highlight it (see Figure 4.18).

Figure 4.18
The Master item is on the Master page and appears on every document page based on that master, whereas the page item is drawn on a document page and appears only on one page.

Cmd+Shift+click (Mac) or Ctrl+Shift+click (Win) is exactly how you select a Master picture frame on a document page to place a picture inside a Master frame on a document page. You can also, without disrupting the Master page, edit a master item on a document page after you select it on the page.

Work With Frames On Layers

For placing photographic images in the catalog, you need frames. Each frame can hold an image file, a text file, or text you type in the frame. Many catalogs establish a look by positioning images of their wares in the same place on the pages for every issue, so creating picture frames in a Master page or Master spread makes sense for them.

Creating a layer that holds all the pictures in the catalog lets you hide the image layer for fewer distractions as you work with the text. This is not a cast-in-bronze method of working, but it's one way that works for this project.

Remember, layers are document-wide, so the layer you create for a Master page also covers all pages in the document and retains the same layer stacking order for all Masters and all document pages.

PROJECT Create Master Page Picture Frames

If necessary, click the A-Front Cover Master in the Pages palette, and check to be sure the eye icons for both the Master Guides Layer 1 and the Photos layer are showing. The new Photos layer is highlighted in the Layers palette:

1. Use the Rectangle tool to create a picture frame positioned near the middle of the Front Page Master, and enter these measurements in the Transform palette:

   • X: 0.0567 inches

   • Y: 2.181 inches

- W: 7.375 inches

- H: 5.193 inches

2. Use the shortcut keystroke Cmd+Shift+D (Mac) or Ctrl+Shift+D (Win) to place the file, Autumn.tiff (Mac) or Autumn.tif (Win), found on the CD-ROM (see Figure 4.19).

Figure 4.19

The front cover graphic frame for the photograph can be resized or repositioned on the cover page, though its purpose in being on the Master page is to maintain consistency of cover design.

3. Scale the image to fit the box, approximately 94%, plus or minus as your taste dictates. You can use the arrow keys to move the image one pixel at a time or the Direct Selection tool to drag the image inside the picture frame.

For the sake of cementing all these concepts you've had thrown at you, take a moment with the Pages and Layers palettes. Show and hide layers. Activate document pages and Masters. If you inadvertently move a page or a Master, you can always fall back on Undo.

Edit A Master Page

So far in working with the Front Page Master, you've replicated the Turfer 1999 catalog's Cover Page Master, but what happens when Y2K rolls around? Can you edit the date? Yes. What about those grouped catalog code text boxes? Doesn't the code change, too? It sure does, and all you have to do is activate the Front Cover Master, pick up the Type tool, delete the contents, click in the text frame, and type in the new date and code. The defaults for font and paragraph remain the same. Even the rotated and grouped text frame contents can be individually edited. It's a little weird typing sideways, but it's possible.

Of course, you can replace the photographic image with a new one for next year's catalog. Delete an existing photograph by using the Direct Selection tool to activate it, and then press Delete. Place a new photograph on either the Master page or on the document page, but remember that on a document page, you must use Cmd+Shift+click or Ctrl+Shift+click to activate a Master item. What you probably don't want to do is change the page geometry, but even that can be revised. Anything on a Master page can be edited.

Add Document Pages Based On A Master

Like Little Bo Peep's sheep coming home, you can drag a Master into the upper portion of the Pages palette to create a page based on the Master you're dragging. The more times you drag a Master to the upper portion of the palette, the more pages you add to your document. There is no menu equivalent for adding multiple pages based on more than one master, but you can drag more than one Master at a time, thus adding several pages with one drag. Shift+click to select contiguous Master pages and drag them to the document page area of the Pages palette.

Move Document Pages

At the bottom of each page in the document page portion of the Pages palette is a number indicating the sequential order of the pages. Should you take a notion to rearrange the pages, it's rather like playing Solitaire. Drag and drop pages in any sequence you want. Drag any number of pages, as long as they are selected and contiguous. As you drag pages to a new position, a black bar appears on the Pages palette that indicates where the pages will fall if you release the mouse. The Master page applied to the moved document pages remains the same, no matter where in the publication sequence a page is moved.

Delete A Master Page

There's no particular reason to practice deleting a Master page. It's a simple task, but fraught with far-reaching ramifications, depending on how many document pages are based on the Master page you delete. If there are no pages based on the Master, nothing untoward happens. If many pages are based on the Master, the Master items on these pages disappear when the Master is deleted. However, you do have a chance to base these pages on another existing Master.

To delete a Master page, click on the Master you want removed from the Pages palette, and select Delete Master Spread or Delete Master Page with

Note: Chaining Master pages—that is, basing one or more Master pages on another Master page—can be a blessing in time savings, but it can also create big headaches. For example, suppose you create a B Master and use that as the foundation for other Masters, basing C Master on B Master, and then a D Master based on the C Master. The instructions for B Master are included in both C and D Masters.

If you delete B Master, you will affect the appearance of every Master page chained to the B Master, and all document pages based on any Master in the chain. The Master items on B Master are deleted from every Master page and document page based on C or D Master. That may or may not be exactly what you want to accomplish. An Alarm dialog box warns you, but it's better to think ahead at the start of developing Master pages.

the Master name in quotation marks, or drag it to the trash can at the bottom of the Pages palette.

If you delete a Master page that has document pages based on it, items placed on the document page are unaffected, and the pages based on the deleted Master assume None as their Master. You also have fair warning that some pages are based on the Master you're about to delete (see Figure 4.20).

Figure 4.20

If you attempt to delete Master pages that are in use, an alarm box warns you that document pages are based on the Master selected for deletion, and you can choose OK or Cancel.

All Master items are deleted when a Master page is deleted, as I mentioned, so be sure that's what you mean to do.

Apply a new Master, if you like, or leave the pages based on None. You can delete just one page from a Master spread without disturbing its companion Master page. In that case, document pages based on the specific Master page you delete also remain intact.

If you design another Master to replace the deleted one, you'll have to select Apply Master To Pages from the Pages palette pop-up menu, pick the Master from the list of available Masters, and type in the page numbers (separated by commas) that you want the Master applied to (see Figure 4.21).

Figure 4.21

The Apply Master dialog box is for changing the Master applied to pages.

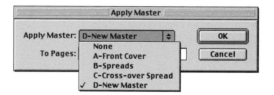

Changing the Master that a document page is based on involves dragging stuff around in the Pages palette, or using the Apply Master dialog box. If you prefer the drag method, drag the Master you want applied on top of a document page and drop it to apply it.

Moving On

In the next chapter, you'll continue working with the Turfer catalog but with a different emphasis. You'll manipulate text and things that InDesign has for working with text, like Multi-line Composer, refining fonts, using styles, and creating special text effects.

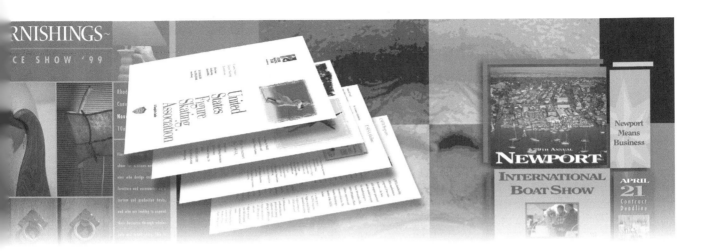

GOOD-LOOKING 5 TEXT

Learn how to place text, wrap text around other objects, apply styles, and make text handling more efficient and better-looking.

Skills Covered In This Chapter

- Create text frames

- Show and hide frame edges

- Use guides for positioning

- Wrap text around an object

- Create specialized text frame corners

- Place text files in frames

- Create threads

- Use tabs to emulate a table

- Define styles

- Import styles

- Use Multi-line Composer

A picture may be worth a thousand words, but not all the pictures in the world can say it alone. Even pictures hanging in museums and art galleries have captions. Typography profoundly affects the impact of all words. The size and proportions of type, the structure of paragraphs, line color within paragraphs—these and other text enhancements convey a powerful visual message that captures attention and subliminally draws people to read the text. There would be no desktop publishing were it not for words.

Text, Type, And Triumphs

A short review of InDesign terminology is in order, especially if you're new to Adobe desktop publishing applications. If you're already familiar with these terms and what they mean to your publication production, skim through to the first project. An interesting technique is employed for making a white drop shadow on certain words.

In that first project, you'll be working with a Library Poster. The Library Poster file is on the CD-ROM accompanying this book. You may want to copy LibrPstr.indd to your hard drive now, and Mac users may want to install the screen fonts it uses. That way you won't have to interrupt your reading when the project comes along. The fonts are on the CD. These need to be installed before you open InDesign. You'll also need to copy the Illustrator file, Books.eps, along with the Library Poster file.

PC users will need to use their system fonts. This will have no adverse effects on completing the projects, though your results may display differently than what's shown in this book.

What's A Story?

In the strictest sense, a story is any unified body of text. That means a headline could be considered a story, and so could a tabbed table of statistics. In InDesign, a story may reside in its entirety in one text frame of any size, or it may flow to other text frames in the publication. Within a story, you can format individual letters, words, and paragraphs independently from other formatting in the story, and define styles for retaining a consistent appearance of both paragraphs and characters of the story.

The visual appearance of a story is based on two factors: typographic settings and settings for the object holding the text, the text frame. InDesign allows you to stack text or picture frames on top of or below text frames, and have text wrap around the stacked frame, or to embed a frame within the text itself so that the frame flows along with the text in which it's embedded, just as if it were another letter in the text of the story.

Text Frames Hold Stories

Every story is bounded by a text frame that can be formatted. Formatting a text frame is different from formatting text inside the frame. You've already had some experience in the Turfer catalog setting attributes for text inside a frame when you applied a font, size, color, and tracking to text on the Front Cover Master page. In the Library Poster, you'll see that a frame can be formatted, in this case, with a colored background.

Text Frame Basics

The good news is that any frame you create can be a text frame. You're not restricted to drawing the "correct" kind of frame for the content you want as you design a page. If you draw placeholder frames for position only, any frame can hold text or graphics. It all depends on the tool you use to click inside the frame after it's created. InDesign automatically understands your intent from the tool, and assigns the corresponding content type. You can change the content type of any frame, even one that you've already used and deleted the contents from for one reason or another.

You can format a text frame with text inset from the edges of the frame, columns, background color, corner effects, and the position of the first baseline within the frame, using the dialog box that opens when you select Object|Text Frame Options. These all affect the flow of text within the frame.

Create A Text Frame

Initially, as you create a text frame, it's just another invisible object on the page, no matter what method you use to get it there, and those ways are many:

Note: Sadly, InDesign doesn't yet support text along a path itself, which is quite amazing because that's been a feature in Illustrator for a long time. Maybe that's what Adobe means by "workflow between applications." If you want text to flow along a path, create the text in Illustrator and place it in InDesign.

- Use the Type tool to draw a rectangle on the page.

- Click the Type tool at the place on the page where you want text to begin.

- Create and convert a picture frame to a text frame.

- Create and convert any closed path—a rectangle, an oval, or a polygon shape—to hold text.

- Use the Pen tool to create an open path for text that flows inside the bounding box of the open path.

To convert a frame to a text frame, create the frame, click the frame to select it, and choose Object|Content|Text, or use the Type tool to click inside the frame, and it's done.

PROJECT Look Over The Library Poster

You'll recall that I mentioned the Renaissance method of training artists: study the artwork, and then replicate it. In this project, you have the chance to do exactly that.

1. Open the Library Poster file for a bit of scrutiny (see Figure 5.1).

2. Select File|Links to open the Links palette.

   Highlight the file name, Books.eps, and select Relink from the menu of the Links palette, or click the Update Link at the bottom of the palette.

   Locate the Books.eps file on your hard drive, click OK, and close the Links palette.

Note: If the fonts look funny, you may have forgotten that fonts need to be installed when InDesign isn't open and running. If necessary, quit or exit InDesign and open it again after installing the fonts, and then open your copy of the Library Poster.

In addition, as you look at the copy of the poster opened from your hard drive, chances are good that the graphic has lost track of where the books graphic file is located. It may (or may not) appear that the poster graphic is a big white blot on the poster. You need to relink the graphic file to display it correctly. Most likely the Links palette has already told you that by opening automatically, but if you closed the Links palette, just reopen it from the File menu.

3. Select View|Show Guides and View|Show Frame Edges.

   The arrangement of frames for text and graphics is an integral part of page geometry. Applying formatting to the frame itself determines the appearance of the frame within the page geometry.

   In a very clever maneuver, every frame on the Black Text layer was grouped, then moved to a newly created layer.

4. Choose Window|Layers, or press F7, to open the Layers palette (see Figure 5.2).

   The text-filled frames on the Text layer were duplicated and placed on the Drop Shadows layer. On the Drop Shadows layer, some of the text was given a white fill, and those words that did not need a drop shadow were filled with the same color as the background of the poster. Each drop shadow text frame was then offset a slightly different amount to create, by eye, a pleasingly proportionate white drop shadow.

Figure 5.1
This poster was designed by Apex Communications for the Rampart Library Fund as a service to the community. You can see the poster in its two-color splendor in this book's InDesign Studio.

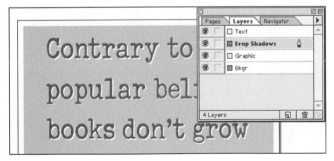

Figure 5.2
You see that there are four layers, Text, Drop Shadows, Graphic, and Bkgr.

5. Use the Type tool to click in the frame that reads "Our Rampart Range..." and zoom in to see the text frame contents more closely. You may want to open the Swatches palette, too (see Figure 5.3).

NUDGE IN TINY INCREMENTS

Sometimes, when you view a page at a very large percentage, 1,000 percent or more, you vividly see that you need to adjust the position of an object in relation to another object. If you use the arrow keys on your keyboard to nudge the object, the distance the object moves may be too great. You could reset the Units & Increments preference to a miniscule increment, but that affects the way the arrow keys work at all times in publication pages, and you may only need a very tiny nudge once in a while.

Try taking advantage of the Transformation palette's capability to accept up to four places after the decimal point to nudge in tiny increments. Add decimal increments to the current X or Y location until you have up to four places after the decimal, or change the existing decimal values.

Selecting a font, size, color, leading, kerning, or tracking, and so on, falls under text formatting.

6. As you can see by selecting the words "way undersized" and "need your help" and looking at the Character palette, these have not only a change of font from the rest of the text in the story, but also a Horizontal Scale reduction to 80 percent.

   In fact, because the spacing pleased Dave's discerning eye, he even made the space between "way" and "undersized" a different font (Courier).

7. Glance at the Character palette as you highlight various words in the text frames on the Drop Shadows layer. All the text set in 18-point Courier is filled to match the background color (Pantone 150 CV in the Swatches palette), leaving only the 32-point SchmutzICG Cleaned text filled with white to emphasize "way undersized" and "need your help."

8. Take a look at the Character palette. The Leading is set to 48 points to accommodate the larger font within the paragraph and give a pleasing readability to the poster (see Figure 5.4).

9. On the Layers palette, click in the right column of the Graphic, White Text, and Background layers, and hide the Graphic and White Text layers. The eye icon is hidden.

10. Use the Selection tool to click on the text frame that reads "Our Rampart Range...," and then choose Object|Text Frame Options.

Figure 5.3

Some words in the Library Poster text are set in a different font and have white drop shadows.

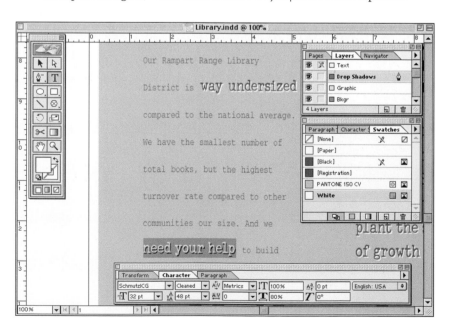

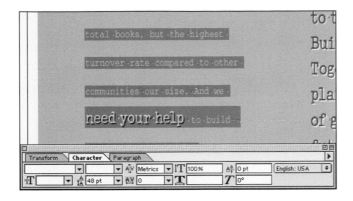

Figure 5.4
Kerning is set to Metrics, the most frequently used automatic kerning, to space letters in a pleasing relationship.

Observe that Fill and Stroke are both set to None, so that the background frame Fill shows through the text frame.

Challenge: Replicate The Library Poster

Now for some fun with the Library Poster. Can you replicate the text frames in the Library Poster layout with only a list of specs (shown in Table 5.1) and the LibrPstr.indd file to go by? Sure you can. You've read about layers and text frames. You've learned about guides. Some of the things, like adding a color to your swatches, haven't been discussed yet, but if you've had experience with other DTP and graphics software, that should be a snap.

Table 5.1   Library poster specs.

Document Setup:	1 page	Tabloid	Portrait		
Background layer:	Rectangle	Upper left corner:		Fill: Pantone	
		X: 0.2669 inches	W: 10.5 inches	150 CV	
		Y: 0.2669 inches	H: 16.5 inches	Stroke: None	
Black Text layer:	Horizontal Guide	Y: 13.4583 inches			
Upper left text frame:					
Contrary to popular belief, (soft return) books don't grow (soft return) on trees.	Rectangle	X: 1.22143 inches Y: 0.4861 inches	W: 8.7249 inches H: 6.8436 inches	Fill: None Stroke: None	Font: SchmutzICG Cleaned Size: 101 pt, Leading: 121.2 pt, Horizontal Scale: 85%
Lower left text frame:					
Our Rampart Range Library District is way undersized compared to the national average. We have the smallest number of total books, but the highest turnover rate compared to other communities our size. And we need your help to build new, larger facilities.	Rectangle	X: 1.33 inches Y: 7.9139 inches	W: 3.9825 inches H: 5.8361 inches	Fill: None Stroke: None Align last line of text to the Horizontal Guide	Font: Courier Regular Size: 18 pt, Leading: 48 pt, Horizontal Scale: 75% and, for the words "way undersized and need your help": Font: SchmutzICG Cleaned, Size: 32 pt, Horizontal Scale: 80%

(continued)

Table 5.1   Library poster specs *(continued)*.

Phone number frame:

Call 687-9281	X: 1.2282 inches Y: 13.797 inches	W: 8.7249 inches H: 1.453 inches		Font: SchmutzICG Cleaned, Size: 101 pt, Leading: 130 pt, Horizon- tal Scale: 85%

Fund address frame:

Or send your donation to: The Rampart Range Library Fund (Return or Enter) P.O. Box 309, Woodland Park, CO 80866-0309	X: 1.2847 inches Y: 15.2722 inches	W: 8.6625 inches H: 1.05 inches		Font: SchmutzICG Cleaned, Size: 130 pt, Leading: Paragraph 1: 42 pt. Leading paragraph 2: 42 pt, Horizontal Scale: 75%

Right text frame:

Please donate (soft return) to the Library Building Fund today. Together, we can (soft return) plant the seeds (soft return) of growth for our future.	X: 6.5613 inches Y: 9.459 inches	W: 3.6887 inches H: 4.3222 inches	Use the guide for the baseline of the word *future*	Font: SchmutzICG Cleaned, Size: 36 pt, Leading: (43.2 pt), Horizontal Scale: 75%

White Text Shadows layer:

	Group every frame on Black Text layer and Paste on White Text Shadows layer	Ungroup frames on White Shadows layer		Fill all text with white except the Library fund address frame, and Fill text, all except "way undersized" and "need your help," with Pantone 150 CV	Rearrange layers, and offset White Text Shadow frames as suits your taste

Figure 5.5

With an object selected, click on
one of the text wrap icons to
determine the way text wraps
around the object.

Text Wrap

The relationship between graphics and text is intimate, especially when text wraps around a picture or another text object. InDesign's text wrap depends on designating the object to be run around, and setting the manner in which text runs around the object.

The simplest way to do that is with the Text Wrap palette. With the object selected, choose Object|Text Wrap, and click one of the wrap icons on the Text Wrap palette (see Figure 5.5).

In Chapter 2, where you looked through the menus and palettes, there is more general information about the Text Wrap palette.

Text Frame Options

Each frame holding text has default options in place for determining the number of columns, their width, and the width of the gutter separating columns. The Text Frame Options dialog box, accessed from the Object menu, also has inset spacing and the first baseline position set. These instructions affect only the characteristics of the frame and how it holds text (see Figure 5.6).

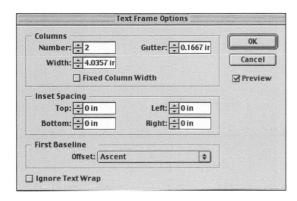

Figure 5.6

In the lower left of the Text Frame Options dialog box, you can select to Ignore Text Wrap for a specific frame, rather than opening the Text Wrap palette and using the None icon to remove text wrap instructions you may have created as a default.

The settings you choose for a frame can be made into defaults for all future text frames you create in a document. Please see the sidebar, Setting Document-Specific Tool Defaults.

By now, it should be evident that the choices for text frames extend beyond the Text Frame Options dialog box. You can use palettes to apply color or a

SETTING DOCUMENT-SPECIFIC TOOL DEFAULTS

Having default settings for objects you create over and over again in InDesign saves untold time, especially during the early phase of designing a layout. Set any specification that applies to any tool on a document-by-document basis.

You may recall that there isn't a Tools Preference for setting the behavior of InDesign tools, but there definitely is a way to set defaults that allow you to preset specifications for every tool. These defaults behave exactly as the Tools Preferences in QuarkXPress do. For instance, you might set frames for a document that automatically have specialized Corner Effects every time you draw a frame, or a specific text inset automatically applied to every frame you draw. Any of the Text Frame Options you consistently apply to frames in your document make appropriate defaults. Analyze your design, and then set specifications for objects created with any tool or dialog box to increase your efficiency factor.

Setting defaults is direct and simple. When you have decided that a particular set of specifications will be used repeatedly throughout your document, and *with the document open*, use the Edit menu to choose Deselect All. This preliminary precaution assures that you aren't applying any changes to items that may be selected in your document.

When nothing in the document is selected, you can set specifications for any menu command and/or dialog box settings to those defaults you want. The new defaults apply henceforth, but only to items created after the defaults are set, and only in the currently open document. Items created before the defaults are set remain unaffected.

gradient to the fill and/or the stroke of text frames, rotate, skew, or scale the frames. These all affect the visual presentation of the content of text frames, the text.

OBJECT PROJECT Experiment With Text Frame Corners

Text frame corner effects are more graphics than text oriented, as the flow of text within a frame that has special corner effects is less readable than straightforward blocks of text. Use the specially designed text frame alone or in conjunction with a graphic (which you'll have a chance to do later, so save the frame you're about to make).

1. Purely for fun, use the pasteboard of the Library file you created to make a text frame:

   • W: 35p3

   • H: 14p9

2. Choose Object|Text Frame Options and set: Inset Spacing, Inset, 0p8 (nothing else needs changing).

3. Apply one of the five special Corner Effects from the Object menu: Fancy, Bevel, Inset, Inverse Rounded, or Rounded, and a 1 point stroke of black.

4. Enter some placeholder text with paragraphs, and see how the various Corner Effects adjust text flow. When you've had enough fun, save your work. You'll do some other things with this frame before deleting it (see Figure 5.7).

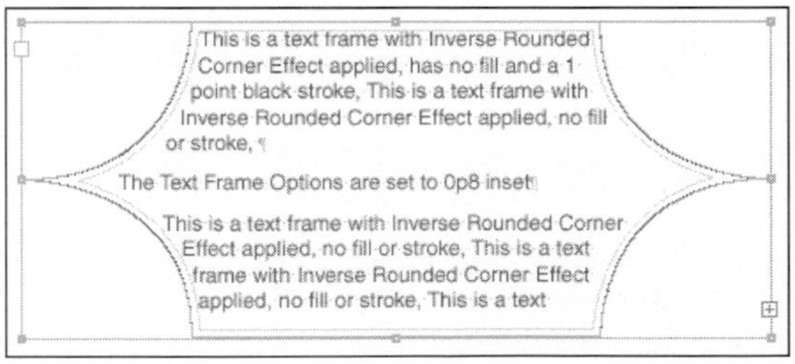

Figure 5.7
This text frame has no background color, a 1-point black stroke applied, and the Inverse Rounded Corner Effect in addition to an 8-point inset applied to the frame. The paragraph attributes are: justify with the last line aligned left, and 8 points of space after each paragraph.

If you look closely at Figure 5.7, you'll see the Overset Text icon in the lower-right corner of the text frame. This indicates that there may be an errant carriage return creating a blank paragraph, or that the text frame is too small in one dimension or the other to accommodate all of the text.

5. Zoom in close and look at the frame at the bottom of the Library Poster that reads "Poster Design..." There it is, the Overset Text icon.

You can resize the text frame to correct the problem, change the text point size, or edit out verbiage, and save your work again.

Text Wrap, Stacking Order, And Layers

Because the stacking order of objects determines the effect of text wrap (an oval behind a text frame still wraps the text, but the stroke on the oval doesn't show, and an oval in front of a text frame is wrapped and does show the stroke of the oval), it's evident that you can place an object on top of a text frame in the same layer and have the text in the frame wrap around the object. But you may not realize that wrapping can happen between layers. Even with a text frame on one layer and the object to be wrapped around on another layer, the text wrap still works—provided the text frame layer is below the object layer in the Layers palette and both layers are visible.

If you experiment with placing an object for text wrapping in your Library Poster, you'll see that, because there are two layers of text, there's a problem. Only one layer of text wraps around the object. The solution to that situation is to move the object to the pasteboard, use multiple Undos, or use Revert in the File menu to return the poster to its former state. Then select both text layers, Black Text and White Text Shadows, and use the menu on the Layers palette to select Merge Layers and make those two layers into one. The text wrap will work correctly now.

So what sorts of objects can you wrap text around? Any of these will work:

- Graphic frames created in the document

- Graphics with a clipping path applied after being created or imported

- Graphics imported with a clipping path

- Other text frames

- A group of objects, which can include graphics and text frames

PROJECT Wrap Text Around A Graphic Frame

The way that text wraps around an image determines the overall graphic effect. You'll want to play around with the options for wrapping, because there are so many.

1. Using the Ellipse Frame tool, create an oval picture frame on top of the text frame with Corner Effects that you created earlier on the pasteboard of your Library poster.

   If you're really ambitious, create a new layer for the document and create the oval on the new layer. (This is a test. If you've been

> **Note:** It's important to understand the distinction between the Ignore Text Wrap checkbox in the Text Frame Options dialog box and choosing None in the Text Wrap palette. The Text Wrap palette establishes the shape and offset specifications for wrapping text around the outside of a selected object, be that a frame, graphic, or group of objects. Ignore Text Wrap in the Text Frame Options dialog box causes the frame holding text to override any instructions applied to the object stacked on top of it.

skipping about in the book, reading only what caught your eye and missed the information about layers, refer to Chapter 4 and the section about layers.)

Enter these dimensions for the oval:

- W: 1.45

- H: 0.95 inches

2. With the new oval still selected, open the Text Wrap palette (Object|Text Wrap) and click each of the wrap icons to see the effect.

3. Keep the oval selected, and experiment with the Inset options on the Text Wrap palette. These can produce some startling results (see Figure 5.8).

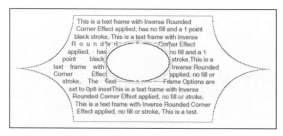

Figure 5.8

You'll discover that you can only enter one measurement because the shape is oval.

4. Finally, in this text-wrapping phase, be sure that you have Wrap Around Object Shape applied to the oval, then click the text frame surrounding the oval, and choose Text Frame Options. Click the Ignore Text Wrap checkbox a couple of times to see the result (see Figure 5.9).

5. Apply to the following to the oval:

- Stroke: 1-point

- Color the stroke: any color but white

Check to be sure the text-wrapping attribute, Wrap Around Object Shape, is still selected.

6. Experiment with sending the oval to the back and bringing it to the front of the stack.

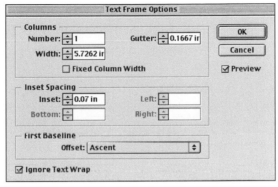

Figure 5.9

Ignore Text Wrap overrides the text wrapping attributes applied to the oval.

7. With the oval selected, choose File|Place to import one of the following files: AngelMAC.tif or AngelPC.tif.

   They're on this book's companion CD-ROM and are located inside the Projects folder.

8. When the angel is in the oval, choose Object|Fitting|Center Content to center the angel within the oval (see Figure 5.10).

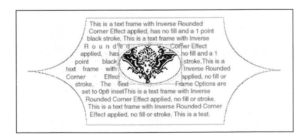

Figure 5.10

If you zoom in, you see that her wings and part of her head are hidden, and the image is not perfectly centered because the angel image was not centered in the original file.

9. Use the Direct Selection tool to click on the angel, and set:

   • Vertical scale: 90%

   • Horizontal scale: 80%

10. Center the image in the oval using the Direct Selection tool and your keen eye. The final result should look like Figure 5.11.

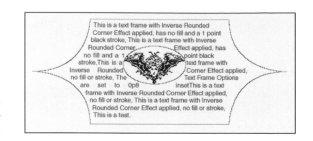

Figure 5.11
The angel is nicely centered in the oval, and text wraps neatly around the oval.

TYPE TEXT IN A MASTER PAGE ON A DOCUMENT PAGE

To add text in a Master frame on a document page, hold down Cmd+Shift or Ctrl+Shift and click in the Master frame appearing on the document page.

Get Text Into Frames

This frames business should be pretty well cemented in your mind by now, and typing text in a frame is easy to grasp. How about filling a frame with text that someone else produces? Use the same methods you always used in desktop publishing applications. Import text by using the Place command on the File menu, using Cut or Copy and Paste, or dragging and dropping text from another document.

Place Text

In QuarkXPress, you use the command Get Text. Adobe products, including InDesign, use Place for the import command, a word choice certain to gladden the heart of English teachers.

In the Place dialog box (shown in Figure 5.12), hold down the Shift key as you select a file name, or click Show Import Options at the bottom of the dialog box to open the Import Options dialog box before flowing text into a text frame.

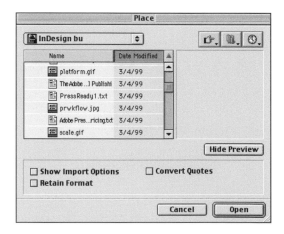

Figure 5.12
The Place dialog box showing the options for importing files.

Imported Text And Teamwork

You have no doubt discovered from sad experience, as have I, that lots and lots of word processing mavens love to preformat documents for you, thinking they're saving you time. The problem is that these WPMs often don't have any page layout experience and not a clue what you do with their files after you get them. It looks good to them, so it must be easy to just plop it into that program, InDesign. Oh, that it were so simple.

If you're hoping to retain formatting applied to documents created in other applications, you'll need to communicate with the person who creates the documents. The documents must be saved in specific formats, and you get to decide which format works best for you.

Text Formats Supported

The most important factor in importing text created in another application is having the proper filter. For instance, if you receive a document saved with an old version of WordPerfect and have only the filter that ships with InDesign (version 6.1 through version 8), you're out of luck.

Four formats that travel well are:

- *Tagged Text*—The guaranteed format for importing text to InDesign that retains all its original formatting is tagged text. The tags indicate the character and paragraph attributes applied to the text. InDesign has filters for reading tags applied in tagged text files from PageMaker 6.5 and QuarkXPress 3, but they can't read InDesign's tags. Adobe InDesign Tagged Text is one of the export options available, and is particularly useful for sending files via electronic media that might otherwise lose formatting in the transmission.

- *Rich Text Format*—RTF is a good Save As option for retaining formatting applied in a document. Many word processors support this option. RTF is application-independent and thus travels well in collaborative work environments using an assortment of word processing applications.

- *Native Format*—Native means the internal format that your word processor (or other program) saves its files in. Some documents saved in their native format import some of their formatting, but it's a chancy situation. Generally, these native format documents retain character and paragraph formatting, but you're almost certain to lose page breaks, margins, and column formatting.

- *Text Only*—A text-only file, because it has no formatting, causes no difficulty in getting text into your InDesign documents. It's the words that count, after all, and you're spared having to clean up someone else's idea of how the words should look.

Speaking of cleaning up text before it works in your layouts, how about those double returns folks use to create open space between paragraphs! Don't you just want to scream? The only thing worse is a document in which someone hits spacebar/spacebar/spacebar to emulate tabs, or consistently

Note: There are 24 different filters for importing text shipped with InDesign, including filters for various versions of MS Word, WordPerfect, Excel spreadsheets, RTF (Rich Text Format), and plain text documents. To see the complete set of filters, look inside the Filters folder nested inside the Plug-ins folder of your InDesign application folder.

Note: Local formatting applied in word processors using keyboard shortcuts, such as Cmd or Ctrl+B for bold, is lost in text imported to InDesign. Your best bet is to have character styles applied in the text before importing it.

SMOOTH THE WAY TO
IMPORTING NATIVE
WORD PROCESSING
FILES

Give your text contributors a
helping hand. Set up a document template for contributors.
Include a set of style sheets
with only features available in
InDesign. Make a cheat sheet
table of instructions for them to
refer to as they create text for
you. Include the character and
paragraph styles you want in
your publication, and when to
apply them. If necessary, give
them a bit of training in using
the template and applying style
sheets. When you get their
documents, you'll be able to
import them, styles and all, to
your layout with as little tweaking as possible after they're in
your layout.

puts two spaces after punctuation marks. Old typing habits die hard. The
only cures are to use a word processor, such as MS Word, with the capacity
to search and replace to remove those extraneous things, or to use the Import Options dialog to squash double returns and change strings of spaces
to tabs. You might also rely on ID's Find/Change to fix the offending characters

Place A PDF

The PDF bandwagon is rolling fast and furiously toward being a standard in
the publishing industry, and for good reason. "Create once, use everywhere,"
that Adobe goal, is exemplified by PDF documents. Placing a PDF in your
InDesign document eliminates all necessity for text import, type, and page
layout design. Placed PDFs can be as simple as a one-page graphic file, or a
multipage document that includes graphics, text, and page geometry.

Presume for a moment that you've already created a publication—the Turfer
catalog, for instance. You want to reuse one of the pages from the catalog
as a mailer or a postcard. An ideal way to accomplish that without re-
creating the entire page is to save the page as a PDF, and import that PDF to
another InDesign publication document. There's more information about
repurposing documents in Chapter 10.

Import pages from any PDF file using File|Place. When loaded with a PDF,
the Place icon bears the Acrobat logo. If you select a PDF with multiple
pages, you have several options:

- *Crop*—Allows for only a portion of each of the pages to be placed.

- *Content*—Places only the area within the PDF pages that contains objects, not the entire page.

- *Art*—Places only things predefined in the PDF as placeable artwork.

- *Trim*—Places only the page area defined as the final trim size of the PDF.

- *Bleed*—Places only the portion of the bleed pages that are actually
  printable, not the bleed that extends beyond the page marks.

- *Media*—Places the actual paper stock size area and page marks.

You can Preserve Halftone Screens and/or select Transparent Background to
have text or graphics in your layout that are stacked under the placed PDF
show through it. When you've made all the decisions about placing a PDF,
click the loaded icon where you want the file placed, just as you would
place any other text or graphic file.

Import Styles

As you import a document to a layout that has your own styles established,
there are a couple of InDesign things you should be aware of. If an im-

Note: If you hope to print
separations of a publication
that includes placed PDF files
that use color, be certain the
original PDF was created
in CMYK.

ported InDesign document has styles with the same name as styles in your layout, the receiving layout's styles override those in the imported document. This is particularly useful when you've created a template for others to use, but have changed your style specs after passing out the template.

You can tell which styles you defined, which InDesign overrides, and which are imported with the text. After you import text, styles with no icon beside their names in the Styles palette are styles you created or that were overridden. Imported styles with names different from those in your layout have a disk icon to the right of the style name (see Figure 5.13).

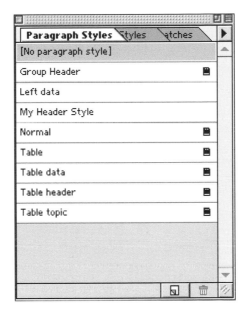

Figure 5.13
Imported paragraph and character styles display the disk icon to the right in the palette.

If you rename or revise the definition of an imported style, the disk icon disappears, and the style becomes native to the InDesign document you are working with. In addition, styles used in other InDesign publications can be loaded into any other publication using the menu on the Paragraph palette or Character Styles palette.

Link Text Frames

Not all stories are short enough to fit in one text frame. Magazines and newspapers, for instance, often have stories that start on one page and continue on later pages in the publication. To make the additional text flow to another frame requires connecting the frames.

A glance at the Tools palette reminds you that InDesign and QuarkXPress handle overflow text differently. There is no linking tool for connecting text frames in advance of filling them, and if you're new to Adobe page layout applications, this can stop you for a moment. The Adobe way is to use the Selection tool to click on the Overset Text icon. Immediately the Selection tool turns into the Loaded Text icon. Click the Loaded Text icon anywhere inside the next frame you want to have text flow to. If the next frame is adequate to hold all of the overflow text, the icon at the lower right of the final text frame is simply a box, not an overflow arrow (see Table 5.2).

I remember all too vividly the first time I tried linking text boxes in QuarkXPress. My page looked more like a plate of spaghetti than a layout design. That was quite the learning process. Well, here comes another one. Adobe uses specific terminology and works completely differently. Linked text frames (called chains in QuarkXPress) are Text Threads in InDesign. Each frame in a thread has an In Port and Out Port, the points of entry and exit for text flow in a frame.

There are no indications of the connection between text frames unless you click in one of the frames in a thread and choose View|Show Thread. My advice to you, if you've never worked with Adobe's method of connecting frames, is to activate Show Text Thread from the View menu before you start flowing text.

Table 5.2   Text thread icons and what they mean.

Icon Or Cursor Indicator	Name	What It Means
	Overset Text	The Overset Text icon indicates that a story exceeds the space available in a single text frame with no thread connecting to another text frame. Use the Selection tool to click on this icon in preparation for continuing the thread in another text frame.
	Loaded Text	The Loaded Text cursor indicates that the Selection tool is loaded with overset text, and ready to be clicked in an empty frame to create a thread of connecting frames to flow more of the story into another text frame. To cancel a Loaded Text cursor, click any tool in the Tools palette.
(image not available)	Thread icon	The Thread icon appears as you move a Loaded Text cursor over a text frame prior to clicking in the frame to flow in more of the story.
	In Port	This In Port icon in the upper-left portion of a threaded text frame indicates the entry point for text flow.
	Out Port	To see the Out Port icon, look at the lower-right portion of a text frame within a thread.

(continued)

Table 5.2 Text thread icons and what they mean *(continued)*.

Icon Or Cursor Indicator	Name	What It Means
	Show Thread	Choose View|Show Thread to see the connection between frames. The in port and out ports of text frames indicate the direction text flows.
	End of text thread out port	If there is sufficient space in a text frame to hold the final line of a story, this icon appears at the lower right of the frame. (This also can indicate that a frame is the first in a thread.)
	Semi-Automatic Text Flow	To activate the Semi-Automatic Text Flow cursor, hold down the Option or Alt key as you click the Loaded Text cursor in a frame or in a page and flow one column of text. When that column is filled, the cursor returns to the Loaded Text cursor in preparation for flowing the next time you click.
	Automatic Text Flow	To activate the Automatic Text Flow cursor, hold down the Shift key and click the Loaded Text cursor in a frame. Columns and pages with text frames are added until the end of the story is flowed into your document.

Yes, you can cut a frame from a thread with no loss of text. You can flow and retract the flow of a story by adjusting the size of a text frame, connecting and disconnecting text frames. Naturally, the more you work with this plethora of text icons and thread options, the easier it becomes, but don't expect perfection the first time out.

> **Note:** Double-click on an In Port or Out Port icon to break the connection between frames.

If you find you've connected the wrong frame to a thread, you can disconnect the frame. To break an unwanted connection between text frames, use the Selection tool to click on either the in port of the frame you want removed from the thread, or the out port of the frame flowing text to that frame. All text in the original frame is maintained, as indicated by an Overflow icon in the text frame you disconnect from. Double-clicking on the in port or out port of a frame breaks the link of all subsequent frames. And, you can select a frame with the Selection tool and choose Cut from the Edit menu to remove the frame from the series of frames in a thread, but all of the remaining frames, previous and subsequent, remain linked. The text simply reflows.

The project file is on this book's companion CD-ROM. Locate and copy the file BkPgct1.indd to your hard drive.

With the project file open, you may want a reference as you work. Open the completed back page of the Turfer catalog. The file name on the CD is BkPgct.indd. Copy that file to your hard drive, open it, and resize it to fit in the upper-right corner of your screen, where you can look at it for clarification should you get lost in trying to read and do the project.

PROJECT Place Text In The Turfer Catalog Back Page

Flowing text from frame to frame on the back page of the Turfer catalog assures that the block of text remains connected, but can be positioned in a pleasing manner on the page based upon the positioning of the linked frames.

1. Locate the text frame immediately below the largest graphic frame, and click the frame with the Selection tool or the Type tool.

2. Select File|Place to open the Place dialog box, and locate the source file named OurDedication.txt on this book's companion CD-ROM.

   Because this is a text-only file, there's no need to select any of the checkboxes in the lower portion of the Place dialog box. Deselect any that may be selected, and click the Choose button.

3. Click the Type tool in the text frame, and select all the text in the frame. Then apply the following formatting to the imported text:

   - Paragraph palette: Align Left

   - Character palette:

     - Font: BauerBodoni Roman

     - Size: 10 pt

     - Leading: 13 pt

     - Kerning: Metrics

     - Tracking: -7

     - Vertical Scale: 100%

     - Horizontal Scale: 140%

     - Baseline Shift: 0 pt

     - Skew: 0 degrees

4. Open the Swatches palette, and Fill the text with Pantone 410 CVC.

5. Now, create a thread by using the Selection tool to click the Overflow icon of the text frame. The cursor you should see replacing the Selection tool is the Loaded Text cursor.

6. Click the Loaded Text cursor in the text frame below and to the left. Refer to Table 5.2 if you aren't sure what the Loaded Text cursor looks like. If you need a tip to locate the correct frame, look for the text frame with a small graphic frame on top of it.

    Some of the text flows into the second frame. To see the connection between the two frames, select View|Show Text Thread.

7. To return the overflow text to the original frame, disconnect the second frame from the thread, position the Selection tool over the out port of the text frame the thread is flowing from, and double-click on the out port.

8. To fit all the text into one frame, you may need to resize the frame. Drag the middle handle of the upper side of the frame toward the larger graphic frame.

This same file is used in the next project. Keep it open if you plan to continue reading, or open it again for the next project.

Long And Short Document Import Options

As you initiate placing text files in your layout, pay particular attention to the checkboxes in the lower portion of the Place dialog box. You can choose Retain Format, Convert Quotes, or Show Import Options. You should select Show Import Options, especially if you're importing a long document. You'll have more choices for the file you're about to place (see Figure 5.14).

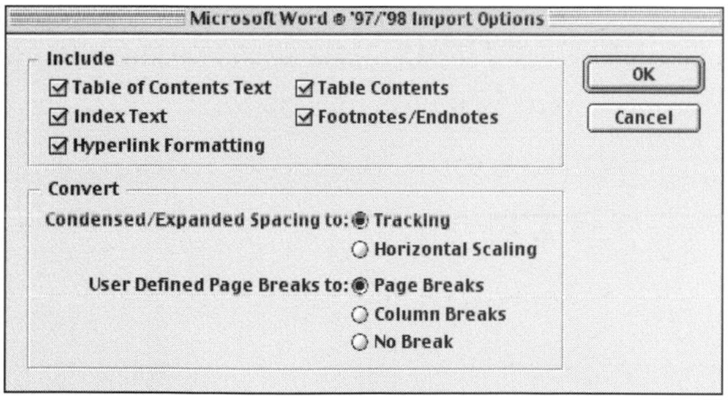

Figure 5.14
The upper portion of the Import Options dialog box applies to long documents or documents with hyperlinks, and the lower portion of the dialog box relates to the appearance of type and text flow. These import options are for the MS Word filter; other filters will show other options.

The good news is that InDesign handles long document elements compiled in other applications. You won't lose a Table of Contents, Index, Footnote, or Endnote as you import a long document. And you can make a single, very long publication with many sections. The bad news is that InDesign has none of the multiple document compiling found in other DTP applications, such as FrameMaker and QuarkXPress 4, to build a book.

REPLACE CHARACTERS

InDesign calls a trademark, copyright, or other symbol a Character. Folks who provide you with text may have used their word processor to insert these symbols, but they don't always travel well. When you import formatted text, the symbols may not be what was intended, and, in text-only documents, sometimes the symbols don't appear at all. These can be bothersome because you must stop the flow of designing the look of your text to insert these characters.

Instead of trundling up to the Type menu and selecting Insert Character, use a contextual menu. Position the text cursor where the special character is needed, then use Ctrl+click (Macintosh) or Ctrl+right-click (Windows) to access the dialog box full of choices from every font you have activated in your system. The dialog box looks remarkably like the MS Word dialog box used to insert a symbol.

Tabs

First, let me tell you that InDesign doesn't make tables. The closest thing you can accomplish without a third-party plug-in is tabbed text that emulates a table, but that's not all bad. Next, let me remind you that tabs apply to paragraphs. If you're importing lots of tabbed text, consider creating a paragraph style with the tab settings you use frequently. There's more about paragraph styles later in this chapter.

The Tabs palette, accessed from the Type menu, consumes much less space on-screen than the QuarkXPress Tabs dialog box, and has the typical variety of left, right, center, and decimal tab stops, and a leader box to enter the character you want between text and tab stops. It also has an X box for positioning tabs more precisely than is possible with the ruler, and an option to enter an alternative to the decimal point (period) for aligning decimal tabs (see Figure 5.15). For instance, you can align a tabbed list of email addresses on the @ symbol by replacing the decimal point with the @ symbol in the Align On box.

Use the menu at the top right of the Tabs palette to Clear All tabs, but don't overlook the other really cool choice there. If you work with tabbed text at all, you'll love this. Set the first tab's parameters, and highlight that tab on the ruler. Then select Repeat Tab to replicate the highlighted tab for the full width of the text line.

Highlighting tabs is remarkably convenient for changing the alignment of a tab. Highlight the tab, and then click a different icon in the Tabs palette. That's it. Do you want to reposition an existing tab? Highlight the tab, and enter a new value in the X box, or drag the tab along the ruler to the position you prefer. To remove tabs, drag them off the ruler, or use Clear All in the menu.

Take the Repeat Tab feature for a test drive on the back page of the Turfer catalog. The data imported to this frame was typed with tabs, but the positioning is unsuitable for the page design.

Figure 5.15

Enter a value in the X box of the Tabs palette to position tabs with deadeye accuracy up to 0.01 points.

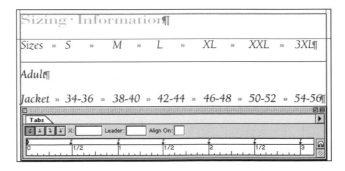

The project file is the same one you used earlier to import text and make and break a text thread, BkPg1.indd. Again, you may want to have the reference file open, as well: BkPgct.indd.

PROJECT Quickly Set Tabs To Emulate A Table

If you don't want to pop for a third-party plug-in that makes tables, you'll need some practice making tables using tabs.

1. Locate the Sizing Information text frame on the Turfer back page.

2. If the Hidden Characters aren't showing, use the Type menu to select Show Hidden Characters.

3. Select Tabs from the Type menu to open the Tabs palette.

4. If you prefer to have the Tabs palette attached to the top of the text frame, click the magnet-shaped icon at the right end of the Tabs palette's ruler.

5. Highlight only the paragraphs of Sizes. Don't include the Sizing Information paragraph or the final credits paragraphs in the frame.

6. Use either the X box, or click on the ruler to position the first tab at Left-Justified: 0.05 inches.

7. Highlight the tab marker on the ruler, and select Repeat Tab from the Tab palette menu.

I grant you, I'm easily amused, but the first time I used this feature, I whooped with delight, knowing how much time it will save me. Now that you're here, experiment with the tabs for a bit, but keep the file open. You'll use it again in the next project.

Text Trapping And Font Issues

I certainly don't need to tell you about formatting text, practiced user that you are. You've worked with fonts all of your career. Instead, let's talk about what InDesign does that may be new to you and some of the things it doesn't do.

General Font Issues

Keep in mind that all printed material is comprised of dots. Though it seems ironic, using outline fonts produces better dots at final output than anything else. InDesign supports three outline font standards:

- *PostScript Type 1* fonts print on PostScript and non-PostScript printers when ATM is installed. They're a standard in the printing industry for output from all PostScript devices.

- *OpenType* fonts are a new industry standard supported by Adobe and should print accurately from all PostScript devices.

- *TrueType* fonts print nicely from most PostScript devices and from non-PostScript devices. Both Macintosh and Windows systems automatically install these kinds of fonts when the system is installed. The major drawback to TrueType fonts is the amount of time it takes to print them on PostScript devices because the fonts must be converted to PostScript outlines by the printing device. Accurate conversion equals accurate printing, but not all printing devices do a perfect job of conversion.

Choosing the best font to convey your message is only part of the issue. It matters not how grand the design on-screen if you have problems getting fonts to print. InDesign has several methods of smoothing out that bumpy road. One is a dialog box that alerts you to fonts not available on your system. If you select a font that has only the screen version installed on your computer, you'll see this alert before InDesign proceeds to use the font (see Figure 5.16).

Figure 5.16

If you select a font listed in the Character palette that has no printer version available, this alert opens before InDesign applies the font you've chosen.

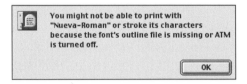

As you can see in Figure 5.16, you may actually have the font installed, but deactivated in ATM. InDesign has a font-matching option, CoolType, to substitute fonts used in documents but not currently available on the system being used to view the publication. Be aware, however, that doesn't mean they print well. This is a reliable look-see feature, but guaranteed to take more time and be less reliable when printed. There's more information about CoolType later in this chapter.

InDesign has no automatic trapping, as in QuarkXPress. Instead, Adobe incorporated In-RIP, a trapping facility, for accurately trapping text to background objects created in InDesign, even filled text frames. (There's more information about trapping in Chapter 11.) That's wonderful, but here are some of the things it doesn't do:

- Bitmap fonts do not trap.

- In-RIP doesn't trap foreground elements to text in the background.

- In-RIP doesn't trap text to other text.

POSTSCRIPT FONTS AND SAVINGS

To ensure that your files image correctly at press time, even if the provider doesn't have the fonts you chose, you can use downloadable PostScript fonts. Naturally, you provide the fonts, but another sure way to save press time is by asking your service provider what PostScript fonts are already resident and available to the particular output device you're using. Using resident PostScript fonts spares download time and saves you money.

Missing Fonts

Have no fear, you'll never have to wonder if all the fonts you see in formatted text you place or in publications you open are correct. InDesign alerts you to missing fonts, and uses CoolType to produce an imitation of the missing font (see Figure 5.17).

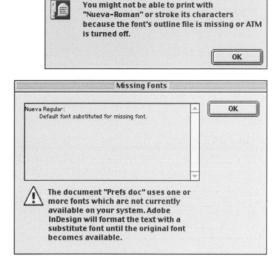

Figure 5.17
InDesign warns you of missing fonts, and CoolType makes every effort to replicate the metrics of the original font—but there's no promise that it replicates everything correctly.

If there is no substitute font available via CoolType, the text with the missing font is set in one of the more common fonts, such as Times or Helvetica, making it fairly easy to spot the substitutes. You can improve the visibility of substitute fonts by setting your Preferences (File|Preferences|Composition) to display Substituted Fonts...highlighted in pink, of all things.

Cross-Platform Font Problems

Especially in workgroup environments with a mixture of Macintosh and Windows computers, fonts can create major hassles. The font names are the same. They're both from Adobe. Everyone uses ATM. So what's the problem?

Simply put, it's the way the two computer platforms handle fonts. Two guys named John aren't exactly the same, and so it is with fonts. Prior to InDesign, the best alternative to ensure the integrity of your layout was to save your publications as EPS files, but that can cause embedded font problems, too, as you probably know. Your best option now is to export your InDesign files as PDFs. That produces a document that is consistent, uneditable, and prints exactly what you design. What's more, PDF files can be separated. Select Export from the File menu, and Adobe PDF for the Format in the Export dialog box. Safe and simple.

Refining Fonts

The Character palette is the place to find most of what you need to choose a font and refine it. Together, the Character and Paragraph palette options determine the appearance of text in your publication pages. But that's not all there is. After all, Adobe started out as a font-based company.

Old Style And Expert Fonts

In most fonts, numerals align to the same baseline as the rest of the text, but Old Style numerals drop descenders of numbers, such as 7 and 9, well below the baseline, creating a rather elegant effect. You can accomplish this lovely design fillip in InDesign, but only if you use OpenType or Expert fonts, highlight the numerals or position the cursor in the text frame, and select Old Style from the Character palette menu.

Leading

InDesign situates leading measurements slightly differently from PageMaker, where it's a Type menu item, and more like QuarkXPress, where it's on a palette. InDesign puts leading on the Character palette. What you may know as relative leading from other desktop publishing applications is called auto leading in InDesign. InDesign sets auto leading for a line of text based on the largest font size used in each line. Individual characters may have auto leading that differs from leading for other text in a line, but overall, auto leading accommodates the largest font size. Parentheses around auto leading measurements in the Character palette make it easy to distinguish auto leading from leading that is absolute.

As with all desktop publishing applications, leading can be absolute rather than dependent on font size. Set the point value for absolute leading in the Characters palette. Then, no matter what size font you set, the leading remains fixed. Sometimes interesting, and sometimes not so interesting, especially when the font size exceeds the vertical space available in the leading setting.

InDesign's baseline-to-baseline leading is, by default, the standard 120 percent of the font size. Using the Justification screen of the New Paragraph Style dialog box (accessed from the Paragraph Styles palette menu), you can revise that standard on a paragraph-by-paragraph basis as you define a style. The adjusted leading ratio applies only to paragraphs to which you assign a style that includes a revised leading ratio.

Kerning And Tracking

PageMaker users are in for a dramatic change. Rather than the nebulous No Track, Very Loose, Loose, and so on, or the daunting Edit Tracks dialog box, InDesign handles precision kerning and tracking from the Character palette. You can use automatic kerning or set manual kerning between

KERNING KEYBOARD SHORTCUTS

Increase or decrease kerning of two letters by holding down the Option or the Alt key and using the right or left arrow key.

pairs of letters, and then manually set overall tracking, if you like, to tighten or loosen an entire range of text. The manually kerned pairs maintain their proportionate relationship even with manual tracking applied.

InDesign offers two modes of automatic kerning, metrics and optical. Whether metric or optical kerning is applied, you can see the kerning value in the Character palette. Values in parentheses are metrics kerning.

Metrics is the default, and uses kern pairs designed into fonts. Optical kerning comes to the aid of those fonts having little or no kern pairs designed into them. InDesign's optical kerning allows you to make the kerning decisions based on the appearance of adjoining letters. Position the cursor between two letters, and enter a value for kerning in the Character palette.

No matter which kerning you choose, keep in mind that kerning and tracking are integrally related. Changing the font size or tracking of a range of text automatically adjusts the kerning to suit the change. You can include tracking instructions in a paragraph style because tracking covers a range of text. Kerning instructions can't be part of a paragraph style.

Ligatures

In addition to kerning, tracking, scaling of text, and shifting text above or below the baseline, InDesign allows you to create ligatures automatically or manually. Pull those pesky letter combinations, such as ff, into a closer relationship automatically as you type by selecting Ligatures from the Character palette, or adjust ligatures individually to suit your taste. Position the cursor between two letters, and use the Character palette to enter a negative value in the Kerning text box, or select one from its pop-up menu.

Automatic ligatures can also be assigned in the Paragraph Styles palette's New Style dialog box. All ligatures print accurately, no matter how they're entered, and the Spell Checker doesn't hiccup on ligatures, as it does in PageMaker.

> **INSERT A LIGATURE**
>
> There are two commonly used ligatures in the English language, fi and fl. To automatically enter the letters fi in ligature format as you type, use the keyboard shortcut Option+Shift+5 or Alt+Shift+5. For fl, use Option+Shift+6 or Alt+Shift+6.

Step Out In Styles

Certainly, by now, you've formatted enough paragraphs in other applications to need no guidance. Suffice it to say that the vast majority of paragraph attributes are set in the Paragraph palette. The range of options there includes icons for alignment, indenting, and aligning to the baseline grid, and a pop-up menu to set Justification, Keep Options for eliminating widows and orphans and controlling how a paragraph moves between frames, Hyphenation and Paragraph Rules, and Single-line or Multi-line Composer.

Some paragraph attributes can only be set up as part of a style, and you regularly use styles, don't you? Drop Caps, for instance. Rather than opening an assortment of palettes to design a paragraph—Paragraph, Character, Tabs—save time and screen clutter by using the Paragraph Styles palette.

Select New Style from its menu and set up everything directly related to the appearance of paragraphs in one place, including character attributes, and you'll only have to do it once because you can apply the style at will. This same timesaver also works well for specialized characters within paragraphs. Use the Character Styles palette to define the look of characters you need repeatedly, and apply the character style at will.

Reuse InDesign Styles

Transfer styles from one InDesign document to another. It's more of the InDesign philosophy, "Create once, use everywhere." Character styles and paragraph styles are easily copied from one InDesign document to another. Select Load Styles from either the Character or Paragraph palette, locate the file that has styles you want to use in the currently open document, and click Open. The set of styles is immediately loaded into the appropriate palette. Delete those you don't need in the current document, and keep those you do need.

If you want, you can import both the character styles and the paragraph styles at one sweep by selecting Load All Styles from the palette menu. In that case, both paragraph styles and character styles from a document are imported.

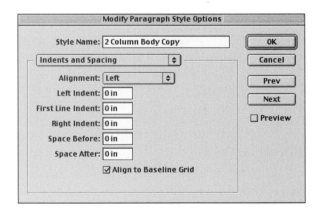

Figure 5.18

There is *no other place* than in the Paragraph Options dialog box, either as you set up a style or after the style exists (as in this figure), to align text to the baseline grid.

Deleting a style that is already applied to text has no effect on the text that has the style applied. It simply removes your option to reuse the style in the current document. If you change any attributes of a style on certain text, the style name shows a plus sign to the right of its name in the palette. If the change you applied to text with a style applied is something you want to keep in place of the original style, you can select Redefine Style while the cursor is in the styled text, and instantly the style's instructions are changed to match the text. Pretty cool.

For this next project, use the same file you worked with earlier to import text and set tabs, BkPgct1.indd.

PROJECT Work With Styles In The Turfer Catalog

In looking over the finished Turfer back page, you quickly see that many instances of text formatting are the same, and styles would be more efficient than replicating text formatting in several places on the page. The Sizing Information is already formatted, and the same formatting is used.

1. Highlight the words "Sizing Information," and select New Style from the Paragraph Styles palette.

2. In the General screen of the New Paragraph Style dialog box, enter:

   - Style Name: Turfer Guar-green

   - Based On: [No paragraph style]

   - Next Style: [No paragraph style]

   - Shortcut: Enter any shortcut that suits you

3. Select each of the other screens in the New Paragraph Style dialog box to see that all the attributes applied to the text on the page are automatically entered in the New Paragraph Style screens, and then change:

   - Hyphenation Limit: 0

   - Hyphenate Capitalized Words: Deselected

4. With your back page file active, use the Paragraph Styles pop-up menu choice, and select Load Paragraph Styles to locate and load the styles from your reference file, BkPgct.indd.

If you're the investigative sort, you've already discovered that there is a hidden layer in the BkPgct1.indd file. If not, open the Layers palette and click to the left of the Text File Names layer to display that layer. This layer has the names of each file to be imported in the position of the text box that needs that file. If you want more practice with styles, use the file names as your guide to place the remaining text. You can apply the loaded styles by referring to the original file, BkPgct.indd. Click in text of the BkPg.indd file to determine which styles are applied where. In some cases, when you click in text in the reference file, styles display a plus (+) beside the name of the style, indicating that something has been added or revised in the style. Your challenge is to discover what the changes are and replicate them.

This challenge is demanding, and takes time, so if you prefer to keep reading, feel free to do so. I can assure you, though, that if you meet the challenge, you'll increase your speed and competency with text so dramatically that your own workflow will improve.

Composer Gives You A Break

Adobe is justifiably proud of its new entrant in the field of desktop publishing, and I suspect they're most proud of its Single-line and Multi-line Composer features. These Composers assess line color and make adjustments to text for optimum line breaks. The principle of the Composers isn't new. Typographers have been doing this sort of copyfitting since Gutenberg, but doing it electronically in a page layout program is new. The goal is even line color with the fewest number of hyphens. Composers take into consideration the parameters set for word spacing, letter spacing, glyph scaling, and hyphenation, assess all the options for line breaks, and select the breaks that best meet all of these specifications.

Both Composers evaluate text, but each in its own way. The Single-line Composer assesses text, one line at a time. That's the more traditional method and lets you retain some control over line breaks. Multi-line Composer works on a broader range of text, assessing multiple lines for a more global effect. In your Composition Preferences, you specify the number of lines Multi-line Composer analyzes, and the maximum number of potential line breaks to be considered.

Composition Preferences

At this point, it becomes crystal clear that your Composition Preferences work in tandem with the Hyphenation and Justification parameters set for a paragraph. That's two different places to set up how the Composers work: File|Preferences|Composition and in the Paragraph or Paragraph Styles palette.

In addition to determining the number of lines to look ahead and the number of alternatives to consider, your Composition Preferences also have options for deciding whether Keep Violations and H&J Violations decisions made by Multi-line Composer are highlighted or not (see Figure 5.19).

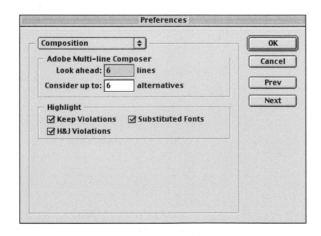

Figure 5.19
Be certain that you have Composition Preferences options selected that work effectively with the Composers.

Because Preferences are specific to a document, if you set a Composition Preference with the document open, it sets the specs for that document only. If you discover that your Composition Preferences don't work well with Multi-line Composer in a given document, change them at any time the document is open.

Hyphenation

Another point that needs consideration, if Multi-line Composer is to work effectively, is the Hyphenation parameters you establish for a paragraph or style. Unlike QuarkXPress, InDesign has no option for saving sets of hyphenation and justification instructions. InDesign treats Hyphenation and Justification exclusively as paragraph attributes. You can, however, change hyphenation settings for each paragraph, so wisdom dictates that you create a Paragraph style with these instructions if you want to save various hyphenation settings (see Figure 5.20).

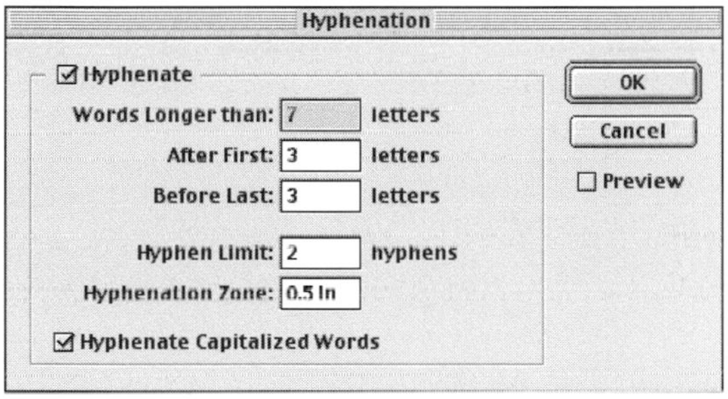

Figure 5.20
This Hyphenation dialog box is accessed from the menu of the Paragraph palette or by selecting New Style from the Paragraph Styles palette.

The font size, leading, tracking, and kerning also play into decisions you make about hyphenation. For instance, you may want to set the Hyphenation zone (that's how close to the frame words must flow before being hyphenated) to a smaller increment for smaller fonts, or tightly tracked text. This is only available when using Single-line Composer, however. Another biggie is the choice to hyphenate capitalized words. It's probably not a good idea to hyphenate company names, or product names with copyrights. Deselecting Hyphenate Capitalized Words prevents that. If you opt to highlight hyphenation violations, you will see a yellow highlight should the composer make an unfortunate choice of line break that results in a hyphen in a capitalized word in a paragraph.

Justification

Settings in the Justification dialog box determine how InDesign handles text when you select a justified alignment. All the characters in a line of text must fit from the left inset margin to the right inset margin of a text frame. You no doubt have experienced in other applications instances of justified text that gangled wildly from edge to edge of a text container looking like a six-year-old missing a few front teeth. In the Justification dialog

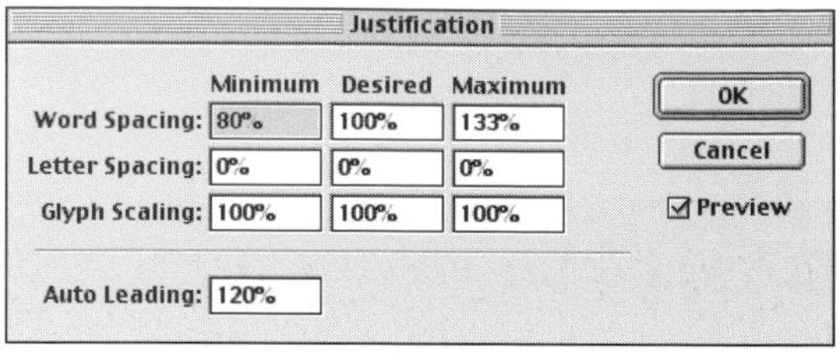

Figure 5.21

Not only does the Justification dialog box give you the option of adjusting word and letter spacing, you also can set the percentage applied when you choose Auto Leading, and Glyph Scaling, a vertical adjustment of text.

box, you set maximum and minimum spacing allowable, and the exact amount of spacing you desire between words and letters (see Figure 5.21).

In the next project, sink your teeth into Multi-line Composer. By default, Multi-line Composer is selected for every paragraph, but it is only evident when you select one of the Justify alignments. The file you'll use is an instruction sheet for patients of the Park Hill Clinic. It was created in QuarkXPress and translated perfectly when opened in InDesign.

Copy the file RxGuides.indd to your hard drive from this book's companion CD-ROM. No special fonts are required because the instruction sheet only uses Helvetica.

PROJECT Use Multi-Line Composer In An Instruction Sheet

With all this talk about the Composers, you probably would like to see how they work.

1. Open your copy of the RxGuides.indd file. All text in the instruction sheet is aligned left.

2. Position your Type tool cursor in the two-column text frame, and select all the text.

3. Check the pop-up menu of the Paragraph palette to assure that Multi-line Composer is selected, and then click the Justify With Last Line Aligned left icon in the Paragraph palette.

Immediately, you see that some of the text is highlighted (yellow highlights indicate composer violations of the settings established in your Preferences), indicating that Multi-line Composer has done its job, and spaced the text to make it easier to read and most pleasing to the eye.

Moving On

In the following chapter you'll find information about InDesign's graphics capabilities. Some are familiar drawing and object manipulation techniques, but may be handled in a slightly different way from other programs. Some involve combinations of text and graphics.

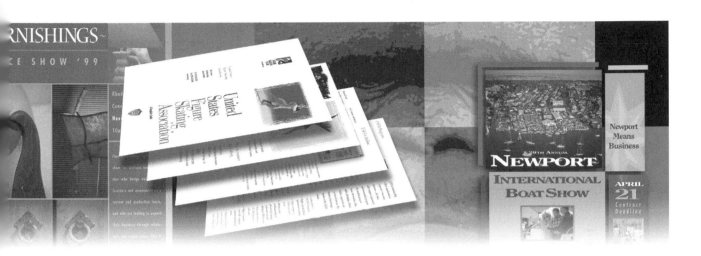

InDesign's
Art Tools
6

Short and sweet, this chapter lets you in on the drawing capabilities of InDesign and has many short projects to help familiarize you with InDesign's way with art.

Skills Covered In This Chapter

- Draw straight and curved lines

- Edit a line segment or anchor point

- Add or remove anchor points

- Close a path

- Convert text to outline paths

- Place and position a graphic in text outlines

- Insert an inline frame in text

In this chapter, you'll have a quick overview of the drawing tools and some ways that InDesign handles drawing differently from other desktop publishing applications. Working with computer-generated artwork both challenges and boggles the mind. As an artist using the computer as your tool, you're distanced from the tactile qualities of traditional media, but the immediacy of the medium and your ability to edit the art go a long way to make up for that. On the one hand, you're returned to the absorbing kindergarten world of cutting and pasting pieces together to create art, and, on the other hand, you're thrown into the endlessly imaginative world of collage artists like Henri Matisse and Antoni Tapies, and the whimsy of Alexander Calder transported to the new millennium. The foundational principles remain the same. Only the medium and the tools differ.

Computer-Generated Drawing

Illustrator, PageMaker, and QuarkXPress users (and those experienced in other art programs) will find little startling about InDesign's art tools. Artwork created in InDesign is based on the principles of object-oriented artwork. The primary difference is the terminology. Each thing you create or import is a discrete object, a frame, contained in an invisible bounding box that defines, in rectangular form, the outer reaches of any frame.

Artwork can be stacked on a single layer, or arranged on numerous layers. Combine artwork and text, if you like. Artwork can be grouped or stand alone, and, in some cases, even blended together to create a completely new frame. (There's more about compound paths in Chapter 7.)

Any frame or closed path you draw can hold an imported graphic file. Any frame can be filled or stroked with color.

Fill And Stroke

Frames can be artwork in and of themselves if designated as unassigned. In Chapter 5, you created special Corner Effects for a rectangular frame. That very same frame can hold a graphic file instead of text. What determines the content type assigned to a frame is a matter of your choice of tool for filling the frame or the assignment you make for Content in the Object menu: Graphic, Text, or Unassigned.

To spice up the design of a frame, apply a Fill color, a Stroke, or both, the same as you would in other desktop publishing applications. There are many choices of color in InDesign, and those are discussed further in Chapter 8.

Far from cast in stone, this is but one of the ways to Fill or Stroke an object:

1. Predefine a color or several colors for the Swatches palette, unless you're using the default [Black] or [Paper] (transparent).

2. Use the Selection tool to click the frame or object.

3. On the Tools palette, activate either the Fill or the Stroke icon, and click a color in the Swatches palette.

4. Using the Color palette, click the Fill or Stroke icon (matching your choice of icon in the Tools palette), and set the color ramp to a percentage for the color you applied. (Be sure to read about creating and saving colors in Chapter 9.)

As the need arises, you can change colors by repeating these steps and selecting a different color or percentage.

Lines

What page layouts exist without lines, alone or in combination? Darn few. There's plenty that's unusual about InDesign's lines, though. Two tools for creating lines start you off. Use the Line tool to create straight lines, and the Pen tool to create either curved or straight lines. These tools produce very different kinds of lines, though the lines may look the same.

No matter which tool you use, make lines any color using the Swatches and Color palette. It's the other attributes of lines, set in the Stroke palette, that make ordinary straight lines into something with graphic impact. The variety of options in the Stroke palette includes a line Weight, set in points, to enter or select from a pop-up menu. No surprises here. Choose Dashed or Solid options, and apply any of the predefined choices for end caps at the Start and End of the line. That's where the fun begins.

To demonstrate one example of the Stroke palette options, I made the line on the left in Figure 6.1, 14 points, dashed, and set only the first dash to 12 points followed by no gap length, no end cap for the Start, and a Circle selected for the End. I then applied a Stroke color, Pantone 5855—a light golden color—and no Fill. By comparison, the line on the right is the same line adjusted by adding a 13.35-point gap to create a more regularly dashed end cap, and then applied a black Fill color that, surprisingly, connected the dashes along the straight portion of the line (see Figure 6.1).

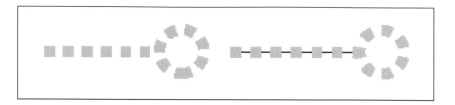

Figure 6.1

Look closely at the line on the left, and you'll see that the lowest juncture of the dashes in the end cap overlap and are unattractive. Adding a gap length cured the problem.

CONSTRAINED STRAIGHT LINES

If you need a perfectly straight line, constrain the Line tool by holding the Shift key as you click and drag to create a line. Draw vertical or horizontal lines at a perfect 90 degrees or at 45 degrees with this trick. Without the Shift key, the line you draw can be at any angle.

Admittedly, it took some tweaking to get the dashes and end cap to work together agreeably in the line at the right, but experimentation paid off. My advice is to take a moment, now or later, to try your hand at that simplest of art tools, the Line tool, and see what results you can come up with.

Curves

If you're familiar with Illustrator, FreeHand, and the most recent version of QuarkXPress, InDesign's curves are better known as Bézier curves. These programs all have tools for creating Bézier curves, so you may already know and use them. However, if you're a convert from QuarkXPress 3.3 or earlier, or have only PageMaker experience, the Pen tool is likely to cause you some consternation. It's unlike any other artist's tool you've ever used.

Creating lines with the Pen tool is a more complex matter than making lines with the Line tool. First, the Pen tool, in addition to being able to create a closed path, creates lines that are actually open paths. That makes for a far wider range of editing possibilities.

Knowing the terminology of paths helps open the way to using the Pen tool effectively. InDesign calls any path created with the Pen tool a frame, even a simple line. Later, as you create and edit paths, you'll see why that term applies. The following terms apply to the components of curves created with the Pen tool:

- *Anchor point*—The square at one end of or along the path of a line. Create the first anchor point by clicking the Pen tool on the page or the pasteboard.

- *Line segment*—The straight or curved portion of a Pen tool line connecting anchor points. To create the second anchor point, and a line segment, click the Pen tool at any distance from the first anchor point. Straight lines are a simple clicking maneuver. Curved line segments result from clicking and dragging an anchor point as you create it.

A straight or curved Bézier path consists of at least two anchor points joined by a line segment. Whether it's straight or curved depends on how you manage the anchor points.

Drawing Curves With The Pen Tool

Bézier principles take practice and regular use to develop proficiency, but in time, you'll discover that there's no more powerful tool in InDesign's lineup of tools. So, make yourself comfortable at the computer, and start practicing.

Open a new InDesign document, and throw caution to the wind. If you miss the perfection mark the first time you try to draw something, don't delete it and start over. All paths are fully editable, so you can repair or revise after you have the general line or shape you want.

Draw A Straight Line

The pasteboard of any open document will do for this practice, but you may want to open a new document and name it Practice.indd.

1. Select the Pen tool from the Tools palette.

2. Click the Pen tool at the starting position for a line. No clicking and dragging allowed, or you'll spoil your chances of creating a straight line. The only thing you see on-screen is the first square anchor point.

3. Click again where you want the end position for the line to create the ending anchor point. Immediately the first and last anchor points are joined by a straight line segment.

4. To stop drawing after you've created a line with only two anchor points, and prevent the Pen tool from creating additional anchor points and line segments, click another tool in the Tools palette, or click *exactly* on the first anchor point of the line with the tip of the Pen tool.

If you want additional connected straight line segments, rather than ending the line after two clicks, continue to click and connect additional line segments. Finish drawing the line using one of the techniques for turning off the Pen tool (see Step 4 above) when you have all the segments you want.

A curved line is also two anchor points joined by a line segment. The curve results from clicking and dragging as you create an anchor point.

One major difference in drawing open paths and closed paths is the way you finish drawing the curve. Open paths require that you click another tool in the Tools palette, or click *exactly* on the first anchor point of the line with the tip of the Pen tool to stop drawing more line segments. Closed paths require you to click exactly on top of the first point you drew to close the path.

With practice, you'll find curves more comprehensible, and the terminology will lose some of it's importance, but for ease of talking you through learning to use the Pen tool, it's a good idea to use the official Adobe terminology for these parts of a curve:

- *Direction point*—As you drag away from an anchor point, two direction lines, each ending in a direction point, appear on either side of the anchor point. If you drag up after clicking, it's not immediately apparent, but the curved line segment connecting to the next anchor point will arc upward. Conversely, dragging down as you create an anchor point sets things up for a line segment that curves below the connected anchor points.

- *Direction line*—The lines connecting direction points to an anchor point determine the length of the arc created by clicking and dragging a second anchor point. (Other applications call these direction handles.)

You can change the direction of an anchor point using the Convert Direction Point tool. Now that could really be confusing. But think of it this way: Changing the direction of an anchor point from smooth to corner affects the subsequent line segment. The Convert Direction Point tool is used after a curve is drawn, because its only function is converting existing anchor points.

PROJECT Draw A Curved Line Segment

As you practice in this project, keep in mind that you don't have to be perfect with every click and drag. You can edit the curve after it's drawn if the shape doesn't please you.

1. Click and drag the Pen tool downward from the anchor point.

   Two direction points with direction lines appear on either side of the anchor point. The direction lines connecting the direction points to the anchor points grow in length as you drag the direction point.

2. Move the Pen tool to the right, click, and drag upward.

   If you drag downward, you create an S-curve rather than a simple arc.

Try drawing several curved line segments, taking note of the direction you drag, and the resulting shape of the line segment. If you feel comfortable with the straight and curved lines, venture into more complex lines.

Try combining straight and curved line segments. Replicate the straight and curved line segments shown in Figure 6.2 to help you grasp the technique of clicking and dragging from anchor points in combination with

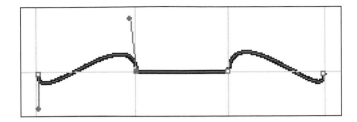

Figure 6.2
One continuous line created with the Pen tool can have both curved and straight segments.

simply clicking to create anchor points. If you can't do it without some guidance, follow the steps in the next project.

PROJECT Replicate The Line In Figure 6.2

On this book's companion CD-ROM, locate the file, Curves.indd, to use for replicating the line. The file has the line already drawn, plus guides and instruction text to help you make the same line.

1. Click and drag down.

2. Move the Pen tool to the right (use the second guide at the 2-inch mark), click and drag down again for the second anchor point. Without releasing the mouse, move the direction point right or left to create a pleasing S-curve. Still without releasing the mouse, move the direction point closer or farther from the anchor point to increase or decrease the magnitude of the arc.

3. When you're satisfied with the curved line, release the mouse.

4. Click *again* on the second anchor point to eliminate the lower direction point and direction line, thus converting the anchor point from a Smooth to a Corner anchor point.

5. Move the Pen tool to the right and click, but don't drag. Release the mouse. This creates the straight line segment.

6. Click again on the third anchor point and drag up to create one direction point and direction line above the line. Release the mouse.

7. Move to the right, click and drag up to make the final S-curve line segment, holding the mouse down and moving the direction point right or left to adjust the position of the arc, and up or down to determine the magnitude of the arc.

8. Release the mouse button, and click another tool in the Tools palette. Your line of mixed curved and straight segments is done.

PROJECT Edit A Line Segment

If you aren't satisfied with the shapes of your curves after the line is drawn, edit them.

1. On the Tools palette, choose the Direct Selection tool.

2. Click on the line segment you want to revise to reveal the direction points and direction lines at both ends of the segment.

3. Use the Direct Selection tool to adjust the length or rotation of the direction points until you're pleased with the curve. There's no need to click another tool when you've gotten just what you want, because you're not drawing—you're editing an existing line using direction points and direction lines.

To adjust the position of the anchor points in the straight line segment, use the Direct Selection tool to drag the straight segment up or down, right or left, but be advised that moving the straight line segment affects the S-curves on both sides of the straight line.

PROJECT Smooth Points And Corner Points

There are two kinds of points, smooth and corner. Smooth points have two direction points and direction lines extending on either side of an anchor point. Corner points have two direction points and direction lines extending on the same side of the anchor point. As you'll soon see, the major difference between a smooth and a corner point is the way the next line segment behaves.

Corner anchor points can set up either a straight line segment or a curved line segment that curves in the same direction as the previous segment, making it possible to create a series of arcing curves that all go upward or all go downward. Try it.

Start your line with an upward curve (drag up). Create the second anchor point (drag down) and convert the second anchor point to a Corner point (click on it), and then draw the next line upward curving segment (drag down). Make as many upward curves as you like. The practice is invaluable.

Continue practicing with the Pen tool until you feel you have a good understanding of all the lines a Pen tool can make. When you're comfortable with lines, closed paths are a breeze.

PROJECT Close A Path

A closed path is nothing more dramatic than an open path that wraps back on itself to make a path with no beginning and no end. For instance, a circle is a closed path.

1. Create line segments, either straight or curved, to draw a geometric or freeform shape.

2. To close the path, create the final anchor point *directly on top of* the beginning anchor point.

Pay particular attention to the shape of the Pen tool on-screen. When you're in the correct position to close the path, a small circle appears at the lower right of the Pen tool icon on-screen. That's when you click to close the path.

PROJECT Add Or Remove Anchor Points

I mentioned earlier, in a tip, that the goal of Bézier paths is the fewest anchor points. With that concept in mind, you'll find times when something you've drawn would benefit from removing some extraneous anchor points. You'll also come across occasions when it would help to have more anchor points to define the exact shape you want. That's the very reason InDesign has additional tools in the Pen tool pop-up menu (see Figure 6.3).

To select a different tool for adding or removing anchor points, or to change the direction of a direction point, click on the small black arrow beside the Pen tool to display the pop-up. Then drag to highlight the tool you need.

To add an anchor point, the path must be selected using the Direct Selection tool. Both the Pen tool and the Add Anchor Point tool can add points to a path. Click, or click and drag, anywhere along the path to create additional points. If your enthusiasm runs away with you, you can always remove points.

To remove anchor points, again, be sure the path is selected, and choose the Remove Anchor Point tool, then click on the anchor points you want to delete. Keep in mind that removing points may dramatically alter the shape of the path. This can be good or bad. If you overdo it, use Edit|Undo to return the anchor point you deleted.

Every anchor point is moveable. That is to say, you can move an anchor point along joined line segments by dragging the anchor point, not the direction points, along the path to reshape the segment. In fact, what you're doing is lengthening one segment and shortening another.

I promised earlier that you'd understand why InDesign calls even a line a frame. Well, draw a straight line with the Pen tool, one that isn't perfectly horizontal or vertical, and then select the line with the Selection tool. Also recall that any frame can contain color, text, or a graphic file. Now it should become clearer. The frame is the line itself, and the bounding box is the rectangle surrounding the frame. You can adjust the bounding box, and thus affect the frame. Try dragging a corner of the bounding box, or a side.

If it hasn't dawned on you already, Bézier principles make clipping paths possible. *Clipping paths* let you to hide some or all of the background of graphic files, displaying only the portion enclosed by the clipping path. All frames you create are closed paths, too, just in case that escaped you,

Figure 6.3
The Pen tool you're currently using determines which icon appears in the Tools palette.

so you can move the existing points, add and delete points in any frame. (Clipping paths are covered more fully in Chapter 7.)

What you've done so far is but a small taste of the power at your fingertips in the Pen tool. A person could spend a lifetime delving into its power and variety. The InDesign documentation has a vast number of other insights to the ways and delights of the Pen tool. I recommend spending some time with that, too. Your investment will be repaid a thousand times over.

Ellipse, Rectangle, And Polygon

There's no magic here. Select the tool, and then click and drag to create the frame. Each of these geometric forms has two tools for creating frames. One is predefined as a graphic frame, and used primarily as a placeholder. Because any frame can be designated as text or graphic or be unassigned in the Object menu, the graphic frame is most useful for blocking out a page before you know the exact content. It works nicely for preparing and saving the document as a template.

Rotate, Shear, And Scale Objects

Rotating, shearing, and scaling are independent attributes applied to objects, but, if the mood strikes you, apply more than one of these to a single selected object, multiple selected objects, or a grouped collection of objects.

The right half of the Transform palette is your command central for rotating, shearing, and scaling objects. The two measurement text boxes at the far right of the Transform palette show the degrees of rotation or shear. The amount of horizontal and vertical scale are displayed in the two measurements text boxes to the left of rotate and shear (see Figure 6.4).

Figure 6.4

All three of the attributes covered in this section, rotate, shear and scale, were applied to a single object. The Transform palette then displays the percentage of scaling, and the degree of rotation and shear for the object.

A delightfully whimsical and informative thing happens in the Transform palette. Before rotating an object, the proxy at the right of the Transform palette appears in a tidy, square arrangement. After rotating an object 25 degrees or more (clockwise or counterclockwise), the proxy rotates to a tidy, diamond configuration, even if the object is not rectangular. That's because InDesign uses the bounding box of objects as the reference for rotation, and bounding boxes are always rectangular, and the visual cue of rotating the proxy lets you see at a glance if an object has been manipulated.

Rotate Objects

It may seem elementary, but if you've never worked with an Adobe application, rotating objects offers a slightly new perspective. Other desktop publishing applications I've used rotate things in either haphazard fashion, relying on you to click where you want the pivot point, and drag out a tiller for controlling the degree of rotation, or a highly left-brain methodology of dialog boxes and measurements. InDesign makes rotating objects more stable and tactile. It gives the left-brain crowd the Transform palette, and the right-brain folks can use the Rotate tool to twist and shout.

Select the object, and, in the proxy at the left side of the Transform palette, click on one of the reference points to establish the object's pivot point. Then select the Rotate tool. Immediately a crosshair icon appears at the pivot point of the frame. Alternatively, you can select the Rotate tool, and then click and drag the pivot point to reposition it.

As you see in Figure 6.5, the first square is neither rotated nor sheared, the second is rotated, and the third sheared. I selected all of the objects to rotate as a unit. I could have grouped the objects, but chose not to.

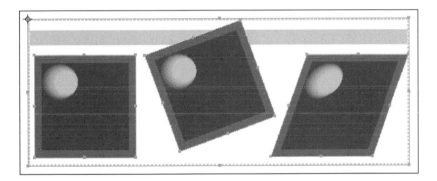

Figure 6.5
The first square on the left is unchanged from the way I drew it, but the second square is rotated, and the third is sheared. Then, I added a frame with a dashed stroke surrounding these objects to emphasize the fact that all three frames are selected for rotation around the Pivot Point icon in the upper-left corner.

Shear Objects

Put a new slant on things with the Transform palette, or use the Shear tool. It's in the pop-up attached to the Scale tool. Shearing can be a by-eye operation using the Shear tool to drag a corner of the bounding box, or you can go by the numbers in the Transform palette. With InDesign shearing has the added advantage of the reference point for shearing that isn't available in some other applications with graphic tools. This reference point gives you greater flexibility in the resulting shear. If you've sheared objects in QuarkXPress (where it's called skewing), you know that the reference point is automatically the upper-left corner, and that limits the results of shearing (see Figure 6.5).

InDesign allows you to shear any object, be it a drawn object, text frame, or a graphic frame. You can even shear lines, which, of course, only shows if the line weight is sufficiently large to allow the shearing to be seen by the human eye.

Note: Resizing grouped objects by dragging the corner or side of the bounding box for the group automatically scales all objects included in the group. This is highly disconcerting if you're unaware of the behavior, particularly when you're working with grouped text frames, say, a headline grouped with a duplicate of the headline that is used as a drop shadow.

Select the object, and set the reference point in the Transform palette proxy, just as for rotating, and enter the number of degrees to shear the frame, or use the Shear tool to drag a corner of the bounding box. It's done. Take a moment to practice with thick lines, rectangles, ellipses, and freeform shapes.

Scale Objects

Again, scaling uses the Transform palette in exactly the same way as shearing, and there's a tool for scaling. If you remember using a vector art program that had the annoying characteristic of redefining 100 percent as the current scaled value, you'll be delighted to find that InDesign doesn't do that. Instead, InDesign remembers the original size of the object, and any adjustment in scale percentage refers only to that 100 percent. Thus, if you scale an object to 58 percent, and decide that isn't quite right, change the percentage to, say, 65 percent. The result is 65 percent of the original size of the object.

Design Artful Text

InDesign offers many ways to manipulate text creatively. One trick I find especially interesting is converting text to outlines. InDesign allows you to embed converted text as inline graphics, as independent frames, or as a nested frame within a nest of multiple frames. (There's more about nested frames in Chapter 7.)

The outlines can be filled with a solid color, a gradient, or an imported file of any sort, text, or graphic. Because the converted text becomes Bézier paths, you can also adjust the shape of letters, moving, adding, and removing anchor points.

In the next project, the APEX Communications baseball team T-shirt, you'll see that, as in all good designs, it went through several manifestations. It began in QuarkXPress as a single layer with multiple stacked picture boxes holding different portions of the same photograph, and text boxes with heavily manipulated text. In converting this version of the T-shirt design to InDesign, it remained one layer, but immediately seemed more suited to four layers: two graphics layers, a text layer, and a background layer.

Mac users should take a moment to install the required screen fonts (Gill Sans) if necessary. That way you'll be able to see the T-shirt file properly. You need to quit or exit InDesign, install the fonts, and then reopen it to make the fonts available to InDesign. The fonts are on the CD-ROM accompanying this book.

PC users will need to use their system fonts. This will have no adverse effects on completing the project, though your files may display differently that what's shown in this book.

Now, open the file from the CD, 1T-Shirt.indd, and save it to your hard drive.

PROJECT ## Analyze T-Shirt 1

You'll need the Tools, Transform, Character, Paragraph, Color, and Layers palettes open, all found in the Window menu, and the Text Wrap palette, found in the Object menu.

All the objects on each layer are locked into position, so there's no danger of mistakenly editing placement as you investigate the way the T-shirt is designed. At first glance, it's deceptively simple.

1. Begin by using the Selection tool to click on the eye icons of the Layers palette to hide or show various layers in the design.

2. As you view a layer, click on the frames, and check out the color and ink value assigned to items in the Colors palette. Also note that Text Wrap is set to None in the Text wrap palette.

    If Text Wrap weren't deactivated, the words in each of the text frames would be affected by the other text and graphics frames. Zoom in close and select all the frames (Cmd/Ctrl+A). You'll see that the text frames overlap one another, and that the Text layer is stacked below the Bkgr Gorilla layer, a perfect situation for text wrapping.

3. Switch to the Direct Selection tool, and, once again, click on the content of various frames to see what color and value is assigned.

    Each graphic frame displays only a portion of the complete gorilla image. The graphic frames and the contents of each are carefully placed to create symmetry   all but the contents of one, that is.

    When you're looking at text, you'll need to have the Type tool active, and highlight letters in the frame.

4. With the letters APEX highlighted, use the Character palette to see some of the ways the font, Gill Sans, is set.

5. Now, click the Type tool between each of the APEX letters to see how the Tracking (in the Character palette) is adjusted to make the letters fit *exactly* across the top of the graphics.

Continue examining the T-shirt design until you have a clear idea of how it was put together. In the next project, you'll convert letters to outlines and place a graphic in some of the outline text.

Convert Text To Outlines

During one phase of experimenting with the T-shirt design, the graphics in the Bkgr Gorilla layer were removed, and the frames left empty, but filled with color. To do that, in preparation for the subsequent project, you'll need to delete the graphics in the Bkgr Gorilla layer, and change the fill and the color of each frame.

PROJECT Revise Frames And Content

Before proceeding with the development of the Gorilla T-shirt design, you'll make settings for the layers that will prevent you from inadvertently editing them. Then, you'll add a fill color to frames on the unlocked layer.

1. Click the Bkgr Gorilla layer in the Layers palette, and select Lock Others and Hide Others from the pop-up of the Layers palette so that only the layer you want to work with is showing and editable.

2. Select all (Cmd/Ctrl+A) on the Bkgr Gorilla layer, and choose Object|Unlock Position.

   These steps are necessary to allow removing the graphics inside the frames without disturbing the remaining layers.

3. Before deleting the graphic in each frame, click outside the selected frames, or choose Edit|Deselect All to assure nothing is selected.

4. Use the Direct Selection tool to click one of the frames, and press the Delete key to remove the imported file.

   Repeat this step for each of the remaining three frames.

5. Select the upper-left and lower-right frames filled with Apex Gold, and change the percentage of ink to 100% on the Colors palette.

6. Select the upper-right and lower-left frames, and fill them with 100% black.

7. Lock and hide the Bkgr Gorilla layer. Show and unlock the Text layer in preparation for the next project. It's a good time to save, as well.

PROJECT Convert Text To Outline

This project gives you a chance to turn text into an art object. The text is no longer editable, but the effect is well worth the trade-off.

1. Use the Type tool to highlight the letters, APEX.

2. In the Type menu, select Create Outlines. The letters become filled with black (see Figure 6.6).

3. Switch to the Direct Selection tool, and click on the converted letters. Each letter is surrounded with a close path, but the entire word acts as one frame (see Figure 6.7).

4. Choose File|Place and import the Gorilla.tif.

Figure 6.6
(Left) Your T-shirt design should now have only black fill in the word, APEX.

Figure 6.7
(Right) Each of the letters, APEX, is outlined, but the image you'll import will appear in all of the letters.

5. Use the Direct Selection tool to move the graphic file around so that the final letter, X, shows none of the imported file, and the gorilla file appears inside the letters, A, P, E (see Figure 6.8).

Feel free to move the graphic around until the portion of the gorilla visible in the letters suits you. To move the graphic file, not the frame you imported to, drag the green line indicating the graphic frame. When you're satisfied, switch to the Selection tool, click on the APEX frame, and use the Object menu to select Lock Position (Cmd/Ctrl+L). The final X remains a solid 100% black, and the graphic fills all the other letters. It should look approximately like Figure 6.9.

Note: You can't place different graphics in a range of text converted to outlines. To do that you need to convert each letter or a range of letters independently.

Figure 6.8
(Left) Here the image you import appears in all of the letters.

Figure 6.9
(Right) Your positioning of the graphic file inside the outline letters APE may differ from this figure.

Note: It's not possible to return converted text to its previous editable text state unless you Undo immediately after converting, or choose File|Revert after performing several actions, but before saving the file.

6. To assess the overall appearance of the design, show all the layers, and save the file.

It's different, but is it better? The answer to that is purely subjective. To see how the final design turned out, look in this book's color InDesign Studio. You'll see that the graphic in APE didn't quite suit Dave Kottler's clean sense of design, and that he spent considerable time revising the text placement, so that the Bkgr Gorilla layer blocks and text aligned more precisely. That involved adjusting the size and horizontal scale of the font, and tweaking the tracking even more.

If you're feeling brave, and have some time, it's well worth it to go through the process of duplicating the final output file. I trust you have enough information to figure out what changes are required. Use the InDesign Studio figure as your go-by.

Embed Inline Graphics In Text

Often, it's necessary to keep a photograph or illustration in immediate proximity to text referring to the graphic. Rather than positioning a graphic frame on top of the text, you want to embed the graphic so that it never loses contact with the text referring to it, even if the text is edited. Any frame of any sort can be embedded in text. That includes lines, drawings, and frames that hold text or graphic frames.

Embedding involves hoodwinking InDesign into thinking of the embedded object as just another letter in a text string. Unlike QuarkXPress, which relies only on the clipboard, there are two ways to embed a graphic file in InDesign publications:

- Create the object within InDesign, select it, and copy it to the clipboard. Next, position the Type tool cursor at the place in the text you want to embed the object, and paste it into place.

- Click the Type tool cursor in the text where you want a graphic file inserted, and select File|Place, locate the file, and click Open.

Both methods result in a graphic that flows along in exactly the same place within the text, even if you edit the text (see Figure 6.10).

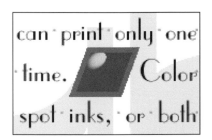

Figure 6.10
InDesign documents that are headed for the Web rely heavily on inline frames.

You can also embed inline graphics in print pieces. For an example of this, check out the Newport Boat Show file, Boat cover.indd, located on the CD-ROM that comes with this book. The inline graphics are symbols found on the page 2–3 spread.

To align the pasted graphic vertically within the text, use the Selection tool to drag the inline frame downward or upward. To align horizontally, use Tracking in the Character palette. Remember, you're fooling InDesign into thinking the frame is more text.

To delete an inline graphic, highlight it as you would any other letter or word, and press the Delete key.

Moving On

The following chapter begins a new part of this book that covers more advanced techniques. Learn how to work with frames after they're created and filled with text or graphics—linking, nesting, stacking, and fitting frames. You'll also discover that imported files are editable in their native application.

InDesign Text Wrap and Inline Graphics

Although it's easier to position an inline frame in InDesign, there is a drawback. If the frame is sufficiently large that it drops below or above the baseline of text it's in line with, the line of text below or above the inline frame doesn't wrap around it, but runs under the frame. Chalk one up for QuarkXPress.

To fix this problem, your only option is to resize the frame using the Selection tool and adjust the handles at each corner of the bounding box of the frame.

INDESIGN
STUDIO

*On the following pages you'll see publications used
in projects throughout this book. These full color
examples show you how your efforts fit into
(or deviate from) the original publications' design.*

ASI 92354

ASI 92354

1999

TURFER
sportswear

When you'd rather be outdoors.™

Catalog: Turfer Performance Sportswear
Garment Photography: Bob Cary Photography
Garment Stylist: Elaine Betts

On this page and the following page are samples from the Turfer catalog, which you will examine in Chapter 3 and in other projects throughout the book.

820 The Striker **Adult**

120 The Striker **Youth**

High-performance, soft, Du Pont Crinkled Nylon® warm-up jacket with jersey lining and nylon lining in sleeves. Striking white athletic design on front, solid back. Set in sleeves. Full front zipper with zip thru collar. Slash pockets. Wind and water resistant.

Sizes:
Adult: S, M, L, XL, XXL, 3XL
Youth: M, L, XL

Black/White   Dark Green/White   Maroon/White

Navy/White   Red/White   Royal/White

821 The Striker Pant **Adult**

121 The Striker Pant **Youth**

Supple Du Pont Crinkled Nylon® warm-up pant with jersey lining and nylon lining from mid-calf for easy on and off. Full athletic cut with elastic drawstring waist. Side pockets. Convenient ankle zippers (12" adult, 8" youth) and elastic cuffs. Wind and water resistant.

Sizes:
Adult: S, M, L, XL, XXL, 3XL
Youth: M, L, XL

Black   Dark Green   Maroon

Navy   Red

For serious play.

Fort Adams State Park, Newport, RI

As the choice of the Olympic Development

Committee and the New York Marathon, you'll find

Turfer on any playing field.

16   17

Turfer Sportswear.

The comfortable choice.

Rugged individuals rely on the superb performance of Turfer Sportswear, as do regular folks who are simply going out for morning coffee. That's because Turfer jackets and sportswear are designed for comfort. We combine the latest brand name fabrics with timeless style for outstanding longevity and value. Perhaps that's why we're the brand that everyone is so comfortable with. Even prestigious groups such as:

- Staff of the New York Marathon
- The cast of "ER"
- Staff of the U.S. Open
- PGA Professionals

- Employees of Microsoft
- Clients of Compaq/ Digital
- Corporate trainees at Arthur Andersen

We think you'll agree, the warmth and comfort of Turfer helps build quality relationships. That's why we invite you to call your Turfer representative today. You'll discover Turfer customer service offers you, too, the ultimate in comfort.

TURFER
sportswear

Narragansett Bay, Newpor

Contrary to popular belief, books don't grow on trees.

Our Rampart Range Library District is **way undersized** compared to the national average. We have the smallest number of total books, but the highest turnover rate compared to other communities our size. And we **need your help** to build new, larger facilities.

Please donate to the Library Building Fund today. Together, we can plant the seeds of growth for our future.

Call 687-9281

Or send your donation to: The Rampart Range Library Fund, P.O. Box 309, Woodland Park, CO 80866-0309

Taking full advantage of InDesign's layers, this library poster relies on only two colors of ink and white paper in its design (see Chapter 5).

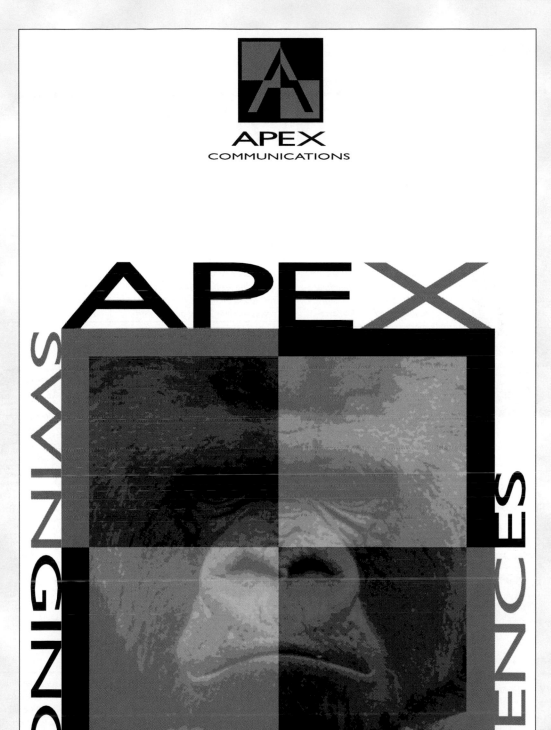

APEX
COMMUNICATIONS

APEX
SWINGING
FENCES
FOR THE

This logo for the APEX Communications baseball team is used in several projects throughout the book, including Chapter 6, where you mix text and graphics.

THEGREENFLAG

THE LATEST NEWS FROM PIKES PEAK INTERNATIONAL RACEWAY

Another major race for 1997: Legendary IMSA cars will roar into PPIR this September.

A sixth major race will cap Pikes Peak International Raceway's inaugural season—a race steeped in history and decades of legend. The awesome sports cars of the International Motor Sports Association (IMSA) will blister the 1.25 mile PPIR road course during the weekend of September 26-28, 1997, when the track hosts four series of IMSA events.

The feature event, scheduled for Sunday, September 28, is a two-hour Exxon World SportsCar Championship race. Sunday will also include a three-hour IMSA Endurance Championship and a 30-minute Black Magic Pro

IMSA's thrilling sportscar series will challenge the 1.25-mile PPIR road course September 26-28.

Series race. In addition to practice and qualifying sessions for each series, Saturday will feature the three-hour Exxon Supreme GT Series race.

This dynamic weekend becomes the sixth major race scheduled for the summer of 1997 at PPIR. For now, the IMSA events are a special bonus for season ticket and suite holders, added at no extra cost.

IMSA was founded in 1969, and is the leading sanctioning body for sports car racing. It organizes championships in five distinctly dif-

stronger than between factory racing teams.

IMSA racing is also attracting major corporate sponsors and "heavy hitters." The group recently announced a sponsorship agreement with Virgin Interactive Entertainment (VIE), a division of Spelling Entertainment and a subsidiary of Viacom.

VIE's sister companies include MTV and VH1 networks, Paramount Pictures, Paramount Television, Simon & Schuster, Showtime, Nickelodeon,

through a corner of shunning the Interstate for a twisting country road? Call (800) 955-RACE (national) or (719) 382-RACE (local) for tickets. And see how your technique compares!

By working with the Pikes Peak International Raceway newsletter (shown on these two pages), you'll discover how importing a graphic effortlessly transfers colors into your InDesign publication's swatches (see Chapter 9).

Paving the way: Surfacing a racetrack leaves no room for error.

"It was a challenge."

Obviously Leonard Miller, Project Manager for Schmidt Construction, is a man prone to understatement. Paving the new PPIR track was his baby, and it quickly became apparent that the silky-smooth surface favored by professional drivers pushing 200 mph requires a bit more effort than creating a road for the family sedan.

"We did our homework," Miller explained. "We went to the new track in Las Vegas and did a lot of research. There are many challenges involved with a racetrack, starting with a very steep grade."

Even the material used in the paving is unusual. "We imported the aggregate from Indiana," Miller said. "It is actually a special by-product of steel mills that doesn't 'polish' when it wears. It has to be good quality."

While no stranger to large projects, Schmidt Construction had to solve several unique problems in laying down the track's surface. Only one joint per pass around the track—a full mile—was acceptable in the asphalt surface to avoid bumps. That meant that once the paving machine started, it couldn't stop. Special equipment was required to continuously feed the paver on its long trip around the oval. Considering that it took seven complete circuits per layer, and three total layers, that's 21 miles of surface that had to be absolutely perfect the first time through.

"We only had one chance to do it right," Miller said, "but that's why we're in business."

The high point for Miller and his crew was watching IRL co-champion Buzz Calkins christen the new surface. "He tested every layer and he gave us rave reviews. It was a thrill watching Buzz hit 160 mph around that track without even trying hard," Miller said.

"We'll all be there when the track opens."

How to build a better racetrack:

First, assemble the most knowledge-able, experienced construction team you can find. Give them a deadline that would chill the faint-hearted. Then get out of the way!

That's exactly what PPIR did with the contractors chosen to build the facility, and it has paid big dividends both in quality and time savings. The June 1997 opening was etched in stone, so the common challenge faced by every member of the team was the clock.

"We had to complete our site work in 60 days," recalled Harlan Jones, Vice President of Engineering and Marketing for Tarco of Arvada, Colorado. "We moved 1.5 million yards of dirt. We had 10 scrapers on site day and night, and had both a day and night shift going almost the entire time doing all the earth work."

As massive as the earthmoving project was, it still required absolute precision when it came to the track itself. "We sub-excavated the track a full four feet," Jones explained, "then replaced it with a homogenous fill to avoid any possibility of swells or dips. The tolerances were extremely precise, down to fractions of an inch."

Tarco also installed the underground utilities and the concrete crash wall, both major projects in themselves. "There are 30 concrete

(Continued on back page)

The view from the blimp.

This birds-eye view of the PPIR track will become familiar to millions of television viewers when the inaugural season kicks off.

The vehicle tunnel between turns 1 and 2 will allow convenient motorized access to the infield.

The view of the permanent garage structures with majestic Pikes Peak as a backdrop will be spectacular.

(Above) A recent aerial photo of the facility shows the newly finished paving for the oval and road course. Garage building construction is well under way and the crash wall is in place.

Blocks of background color used in the Newport Boat Show brochure provide an opportunity to experiment with color and gradients (see Chapter 9).

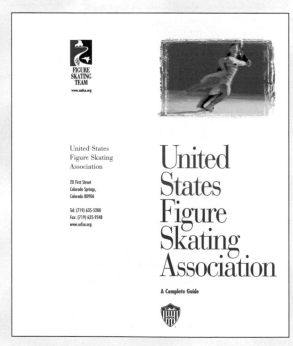

In Chapters 9 and 10, you will use the United States Figure Skating Association brochure to experiment with colors and tints as well as create a postcard.

All of the publications shown in the InDesign Studio were designed by Dave Kottler, art director and founder of APEX Communications, Inc., PO Box 530, Woodland Park, CO 80866-5309

PART II

DELVE
DEEPER
INTO
INDESIGN

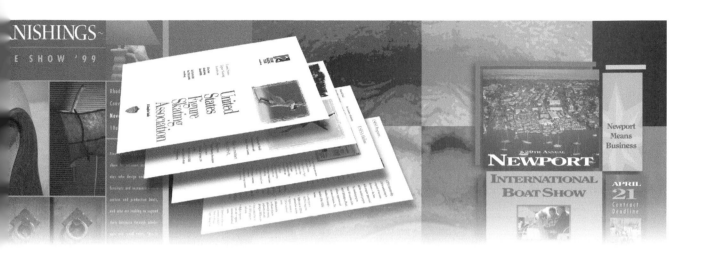

FEATURES TO SPICE UP AND SPEED UP PRODUCTION

This chapter deals with a variety of features that will make your work easier, from long documents and graphics handling to application-specific features you'll love.

Skills Covered In This Chapter

- Add pages automatically to accommodate overflow text

- Define sections of a document

- Apply automatic page numbering for sections to a master page or document page

- Fit a frame and a graphic in all of the four available methods for Fitting

- Create clipping paths using Threshold and Tolerance

- Create clipping paths manually using the Pen tool

- Create compound paths

- Create nested frames

- Use layers to develop alternative designs in a document

- Drag and drop a file created in another application to an InDesign publication

- Edit an Illustrator file using InDesign graphic tools

This chapter offers a handpicked bouquet of features that I like or need, and I presume you will like and need them, too. A few sections cover in greater detail topics that were mentioned only in passing earlier in the book. Others are topics that many experienced layout designers demand. You'll learn about long document features, interesting tips and tricks, graphic formats that can be imported, and unusual drawing and graphic features.

Long Documents

Starting with the bad news, InDesign has no book compiling feature such as you find in QuarkXPress. You have to scratch your head about this when you realize that FrameMaker and PageMaker assemble books, but maybe this oversight will be fixed in the next release of InDesign.

There are some long document aids, however. In Chapter 5, you read about placing text and other things you can do with text. What wasn't mentioned is a special feature that is rather interesting. In long documents created using other applications—documents that include things like tables, a table of contents, an index, footnotes or endnotes, and hyperlinks—InDesign lets you decide which components to import along with the body of text. It's not possible to import one or more of these elements without the text, but it certainly is possible to import the text without any of these long document elements. Simply make your selection or deselect all of the options in the Import Options dialog box as you place a long document.

Add Pages Automatically To Accommodate Overflow Text

As you prepare a long document, you needn't guesstimate the number of pages required to accommodate all the text and document components you're importing. InDesign adds pages automatically...if you know the secret.

1. Set up a New Document with the following settings:

    - Number Of Pages: 1

    - Facing Pages: selected

    - Master Text Frame: selected

    - Paper Size: Letter

    - Orientation: Portrait

    Specify the Margins as:

    - Top: 1.5 inch

    - Bottom: 0.5 inch

    - Inside: 1 inch (for a binding gutter)

    - Outside: 0.5

    Under Columns, set:

    - Number: 2

    - Gutter: 0.1667 inch

2. Save the document and name it Long Document.indd.

3. Be sure you are viewing Page 1 of the document, not a Master page, and have the Pages palette open.

    Do not click the Type tool on the page.

4. Choose File|Place, to locate and select the Word document, Employee Guidelines.rtf, on the CD-ROM that comes with this book.

    Be sure that Import Options is selected in the Place dialog box.

5. In the Import Options dialog box, deselect all the options under Include.

    Under Convert, set:

    - Condensed/Expanded Spacing To: Tracking

    - User Defined Page Breaks To: No Break

Note: You can perform an Autoflow anywhere in a document. Add to existing text in a thread by positioning the cursor where you want the text to start flowing when you choose File|Place, or begin flowing text into new frames.

This will import only the text of the document, not the accompanying table of contents.

6. When the cursor is loaded with the text of this 15-page document, hold down the Shift key. The cursor icon becomes the Autoflow icon, shaped like an S-curve on its side. Refer to Table 5.2 in Chapter 5 for a picture of this icon, if you need a reference.

7. Still holding down the Shift key, click the Autoflow icon at the top of the left column in the text frame on page 1 of your document (1.5 inches from the top edge of the document page).

   When the text has flowed into your InDesign document, glance at the Pages palette. You should see approximately 10 pages in your layout.

8. Save your document and leave it open. You'll use it in the next project.

   If you were to open the source document for this project in MS Word, you'd see that it has 15 pages, but, after being placed, it has fewer pages in the layout. That's because the user-defined page breaks in Word weren't translated to page breaks in your layout. This has a significant impact on the page numbers if you import a table of contents. The original Word TOC page numbers differ from the InDesign page numbers.

   The Word document has a table of contents, but, magically, InDesign recognizes the style identifying its entries, and bypasses paragraphs styled in a table of contents format when that option is deselected. When the TOC arrives in your layout, you'll have to edit the page numbers, but the sections are already defined.

9. To test the long document import feature further, delete the imported text, and place the document again. This time, select Table Of Contents in the Import Options dialog box.

   The table of contents will be helpful in the next project.

Once the text and TOC are in place, proceed with formatting and copy fitting, adding any inline graphics you may need, and go on with the usual business of creating a dynamite document out of what was just an ordinary blizzard of information that nobody wanted to wade through.

Document Sections

Not all long documents fall into the category of books divided into chapters. Newspapers and magazines qualify as long documents with sections. Whatever the thrust of a long publication may be, it surely needs some means of identifying one section from another, and discrete page numbering for sections is an integral part of the design.

Sections in InDesign documents are exclusively for page numbering changes. A section can have any master pages applied, but there's no such thing as section-specific master pages that the application understands as applicable only to pages within a specific section. You could, of course, design a section master page and limit the places it's applied to pages in a section.

In this project, you'll use the Employee Guidelines text you imported earlier—with a TOC—and create sections with page numbering.

PROJECT Define Sections And Apply Page Numbering

Section definition and page numbering are handled in the Pages palette. You'll need to go through the imported text to identify the page on which each section begins before starting the actual numbering.

1. In the document, locate the section header, Policy (approximately page 7), and make a note of what page it's on. (Click the Type tool in front of the word "Policy" and look at the lower-left corner of the publication window.)

2. In the Pages palette, click on the page icon for the beginning of the Policy section.

   InDesign understands only the beginning of sections, so a section runs on until it encounters the beginning of another section or the end of the document.

3. Use the pop-up menu to select Section Options (see Figure 7.1).

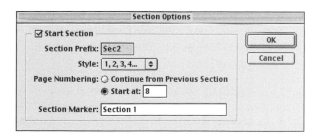

Figure 7.1

Each of the choices in the Section Options dialog box affects the display in the document pages or in the Pages palette.

4. Enter the following settings for the section you are creating:

   • Start Section: selected

   • Section Prefix: Plcy

   You can enter a maximum of five characters in the Section Prefix field, because this shows only in a Tool Tip on the Pages palette.

Do not enter dashes, slashes, or any other weird character in this portion of the dialog box, or InDesign will scold you.

- Style: Arabic numerals

  The predefined numbering styles include Roman numerals in capitalized and lowercase form in addition to upper- and lowercase letters for page numbering.

Set page numbering as follows:

- Start At: 1

  Defining a section, though done in the Pages palette, is not always reliant on fixed page numbers. Sections can begin and end while the sequence of numbers continues from the previous section.

- Section Marker: Policy

  This Section Marker text can appear on all pages included in a section if you insert the Section Marker on a Master page, or it can appear on only certain document pages if the marker is inserted within the section publication pages.

In addition to the visual cues for sections in the Pages palette, there is yet another helper, a Tool Tip. Place your cursor over one of the black triangles indicating the start of a section, and a Tool Tip pops forth to identify the section by the characters you entered in the Section Prefix text box of the Section Options dialog box.

Remove A Section Start

To remove a section start, in the Pages palette, highlight the page icon that starts a section. The start of a section is identified by a black triangle above the page icon (see Figure 7.2).

Open the Section Options dialog box from the Pages palette pop-up in order to deselect Start Section. Honestly, it takes more brain power to think up how to describe this than to actually do it.

Automatic Page And Section Numbering

If you want page numbers on only a few pages of your publication, click in the frame where you want to display a page number and use the Layout menu to select Insert Page Number. You need to repeat this for every page you want numbered, but, thank goodness, the numbering sequence is always accurate, whether you skip numbering some pages or not.

By using a frame on Master pages, you can have each page number in the same position on every page based on the master that has the numbering code (A) inside a master text frame. But where the heck is the automatic

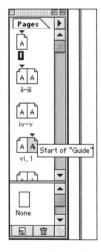

Figure 7.2

Sections are indicated with a Section Start triangle above the page icon in the Pages palette. Another indicator can be a change in numbering conventions and sequences that you've chosen and that show in the Pages palette.

page numbering and section numbering command? What's the keyboard shortcut? Go ahead. Cruise every menu. It's not there. Where oh where can it be?

The answer: There isn't a keyboard shortcut for Auto Page Numbering, and the way to do it is through a pop-up menu attached to a contextual menu that appears *only* when:

1. You have the Type tool active in a text frame on a Master page.

2. Then, you Ctrl+click (Mac) or right-click (Windows) in the text frame on the Master page to open the contextual menu where you highlight Insert Special Character to open its pop-up menu. There, at the top of the list, is Auto Page Numbering. When you select this, a capital letter A appears in the Master text frame, and you can select the A and apply any font or paragraph attributes that suit you.

Circle these two points with a bright yellow highlighter, because it isn't easy to find this feature (see Figure 7.3).

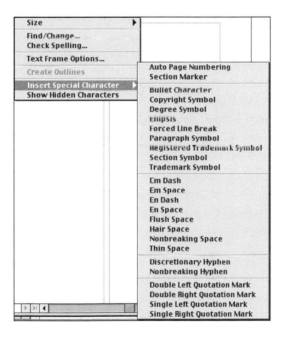

Figure 7.3
You see Auto Page Numbering or Section Marker on a contextual menu when you have the Type tool active in a text frame on a Master page and Ctrl+click or right-click in a text frame on a document page or master page.

This contextual menu's submenu is worth scouting for. As you see in Figure 7.3, there are more choices than just Auto Page Numbering. Look down the list, and you'll discover an option to insert a Section Symbol. Aha! Use this menu choice first (to insert the section symbol), and then Ctrl+click or right-click following the symbol (you still have the Type tool active, don't you?), and select Insert Special Character|Section Marker. What you get is a lovely section symbol followed by the Section Marker text you entered in the Section Options dialog box (see Figure 7.4).

Figure 7.4

The word "page" is text entered in the frame, followed by the contextual menu command, Insert Special Character|Auto Page Numbering. Below the page number you see the inserted section symbol followed by the result of selecting Insert Special Character|Section Marker.

InDesign sections are truly powerful, if not exactly straightforward. Once you've latched on to the secrets of sections and numbering, you'll use them, and see how they apply to other, shorter layouts.

Move A Section

After struggling with automatic page numbers, you deserve something easy. Here's a really good, straightforward, easy thing to do. You can move an entire section as easily as if you were moving a single page.

1. Click the first page icon of the section in the Pages palette.

2. Shift+click the last page icon in the section, to highlight and identify every page in the section.

3. Drag and drop the entire section to a new position on the Pages palette.

Oh, that it all were so easy. You don't even need a picture to figure it out. Speaking of pictures, it's time to freshen that herbal tea, feed the fish, and move on to some essential information about images.

Image Insights

InDesign has many ways of getting graphics into a document. Sometimes importing an image is the way to go. Other times creating an image on the page is right, and often graphic images use both techniques. But you know that. What you need to know is the "hows."

Imported Graphics

The nature of frames is to hold things, often things that are already created. When you import a photograph or drawing, it can automatically be placed in its own frame, or inside an existing frame. The difference lies in the method you employ during the importing process.

If an existing empty frame is selected when you choose File|Place, the artwork is imported to the selected frame. If no frame is selected when you locate and place a file, the cursor is loaded with the incoming artwork, and when you click on a page or the pasteboard, InDesign automatically creates a frame big enough to hold the artwork.

Content/Frame Fitting

Developers (Extensis, for one) have made a name for themselves by listening to the grousing of the graphic design crowd, and have sold lots of packages of XTensions to do things like fit the picture to the box or the box to the picture. You save that small chunk of change with InDesign, because Adobe programmed in the graphic fitting.

RESIZING BITMAP HAZARD

It's important to avoid increasing the physical size of a bitmap image file because any imported file has a specific amount of information about color and content. Increasing the file beyond its original dimensions simply spreads that finite information a little thinner, leaving you with a less sharp focus, less smooth edges, less subtlety of color, less of everything. EPS graphics can be resized, but most print providers suggest you rescale the graphic before importing it.

If you must resize, always opt for sizing down or for cropping. Unlike other desktop publishing applications, InDesign actually ignores the data from the portion of the file that you crop before printing, so there's less information sent to the printer and fewer printing problems. The image remains intact. It's just the extraneous data that's ignored.

When you design a frame that's exactly the right size to fit the space available, and import a graphic that is not exactly that size, you have several Fitting choices:

- *Fit Content To Frame*—This seems clear enough. The imported image will be sized to fit within the confines and the inset parameters of the frame, whether or not that suits the proportions of the image.

- *Fit Frame To Content*—This is a much more genteel way of handling an imported image. It retains the original size and proportions of the imported image, but that may not work in your layout design.

- *Center Content*—This is for situations when you import a file that is symmetrically placed on its original document page, and you want the center of the image placed dead center in the frame you're importing it to.

- *Fit Content Proportionally*—This is the choice you'll find easiest and, probably, the one you'll use most frequently when you have set-in-stone graphic frames in a layout. No matter what the size, Fit Content Proportionally adjusts the imported image kindly, maintaining its original proportions and fitting all of the image file inside the frame as neatly as possible.

To give you an idea of how this Fitting goes, use the Gorilla.tif image (from this book's companion CD-ROM) that is meant for the T-shirt design and the pasteboard of any InDesign document you have open at the moment. If these concepts are clear to you, you may want to skip the following project and continue reading, or return later to practice graphic fitting.

PROJECT Graphic Fitting

Each situation calls for a different solution as you import graphic files. With a good grasp of how InDesign's graphic fitting options function, you'll know immediately which will work best.

1. On the pasteboard of an open document, import the Gorilla.tif file without drawing a frame for it. The size of the file is 5.5 inches by 5.5 inches.

2. Still on the pasteboard, use the Rectangle Frame tool to draw a frame with the following size:

   - W: 4.3 inches

   - H: 6.7 inches

3. Choose File|Place and import the Gorilla.tif file again.

4. When the file is inside the frame, select Object|Fitting|Fit Content To Frame. Somehow the gorilla looks as if he's lost a few pounds.

Continue selecting each of the fitting options to see how each choice changes the relationship of the graphic file to the frame. When you feel confident that you understand these Fitting options, you're welcome to delete the gorilla and any frames you created during experimentation.

Graphic Import Formats

Working with a wide variety of contributors and sources for page layout components can bring joy and problems in about equal measure, especially when it comes to graphics. There are so many different formats, it's sometimes hard to figure out which works well for what. It's also darned hard to figure this out if you haven't any idea what file extensions are telling you, or worse, if there's no extension on a file name.

Macintosh users have never had to worry about adding extensions at the end of file names, but in today's world of cross-platform workflow, extensions are a necessity. Each format has its purpose, and choosing the best format for the job can forestall problems at output or upload time.

InDesign handles all of these graphic file formats:

- *AI (Adobe Illustrator)*—Graphics created or saved in Illustrator typically are line art, vector graphics, and they import or drag and drop seamlessly to InDesign, and then print well on any device.

- *BMP (Bitmap)*—Developed for PCs, the color support is limited and not suited for commercial printing, but this format produces acceptable images on desktop printers.

- *DCS (Desktop Color Separations)*—A version of .EPS, this format produces separated plates for final output. DCS is often used with Scitex and high-end prepress systems.

- *EPS (Encapsulated PostScript)*—EPS is a resolution-independent format, and it's not normally suitable for on-screen display, however. Placing an EPS file in InDesign offers two options:

  - *Read Embedded OPI Image Links (Open Press Interface)*—Automatically replaces a low-res, FPO version of embedded OPI images with links included in a graphic file to the high-res version at output, but only if your prepress service provider supports this. With this option turned off, only the low-res images included in the image file are imported.

  - *Create Frame From Clipping Path*—Imports a Photoshop 4 or 5 clipping path with the image and automatically converts that clipping path to a frame.

- *GIF (Graphics Interchange Format)*—Best suited to flat color and line art Web graphics, GIF images can have a maximum of 256 colors.

- *JPG (Joint Photographic Experts Group)*—The JPG format is best suited to continuous tone images displayed on screen, either via the Web, an intranet, or through a projector. There are instances (when file size is an issue and resolution isn't) that this format is used in print. File size is reduced by an automatic compression, and the compressed image automatically decompresses when it's displayed.

- *PCX*—This format has some limitations because it was originally created for PC Paintbrush rather than for cross-platform compatibility or consistent color. The current version is PCX 5, but it's worth noting that images saved in version 3 of PCX display in a VGA color palette rather than the file's original palette. These images print black and white and offer a fairly good color image from desktop printers, but, in general, PCX should be avoided for on-screen display or commercially printed work.

- *PDF (Portable Document Format)*—This format falls under the category of graphics because, essentially, it's an image of a page or series of pages. PDF is rapidly becoming an industry standard for delivering documents over the Web, for prepress, and for printing PostScript quality to a non-PostScript printer, because it preserves the integrity of layout, typography, and most of the color information in imported images, whether bitmap or vector.

- *PNG (Portable Network Graphics)*—An alternative to GIF format for displaying images on screen, images saved in PNG have proven more

Note: If you've ever had trouble importing an EPS file, it's probably because the file is saved in an earlier version of PostScript. Those earlier version files have only grayscale vector bitmap images.

If you see only an X after importing an EPS file, you can bet it was created in a program that doesn't support a preview image. Never fear. It will print well, nonetheless. You just won't want to show it to your clients on screen.

suitable in printed form than GIF, though neither is ideal for printed output.

- *PSD (Photoshop Document)*—Well established as the continuous tone image format, PSD images import or drag and drop seamlessly to InDesign and print well on any device.

- *SCT (Scitex Continuous Tone)*—High-quality scanned images suitable for commercial printed output to Scitex compatible systems.

- *TIFF (Tagged Image File Format)*—Supported by all desktop publishing applications, this is a bitmap image format that also allows you to determine the kind of compression, JPEG or LZW. Of the two methods of compression, LZW is the more desirable because it loses none of its color information in the compression process.

Drag And Drop Files

InDesign has a neat feature that allows you to drag and drop text or graphic files saved in compatible formats from the desktop, the Finder on a Macintosh or the Explorer on a PC. This completely bypasses the Place command, but it requires that you have both the publication and the document you're dragging in view simultaneously.

Links to the original file are established, but the import options available when you place a file aren't. In other words, if you drag and drop a text file, the usual options to include information about the character set, platform, remove extra carriage returns and spaces, and set a dictionary aren't available. If you drag and drop a graphic file that wasn't created using InDesign tools, any clipping paths, image settings, or color settings applied to the graphic in its native application are left behind.

Graphic File Drag And Drop

As with text files you drag and drop, when you drag and drop a graphic file into a publication, a link is established, and the file name appears in the Links palette. You can edit that graphic from within the publication if the file is saved in a compatible format.

Not everyone has every graphics application ever sold, but Adobe has made it easy to edit graphic files after they're placed or dragged and dropped in an InDesign publication. After the file is in the publication, you can edit the file in Photoshop or Illustrator, presuming the file is saved in a format that one of these programs can read and that you have these applications installed. Mind you, Photoshop and Illustrator are not the only applications to use when you choose to edit a linked graphic file, but you'll need to experiment to see if the different applications you may have installed work successfully for native editing.

> **Note:** You can also import a file using copy and paste. In that case, no link is established to the original file, so it can only be edited within the publication, not in its native application. Copying and pasting between two InDesign publications retains all the attributes applied and the linking information attached to the original file, but in the transition from another application to InDesign, the link is broken, and some attributes may be lost.

> **Note:** EPS graphics can't be edited. That's one reason why you save graphics in EPS format.

To edit a graphic in Photoshop or Illustrator:

1. Select the dragged and dropped graphic file.

2. Open the Links palette.

3. Select the file name you want to edit.

4. Click the Edit Original button at the lower right of the Links palette.

   If you have Photoshop or Illustrator installed on your hard drive and the file can be read by either application, the file you want to edit will open in one of these applications.

5. After you've made the revisions you want, save the file (not Save As, that doesn't work!), close the file or leave it open, and return to your publication.

   The Links palette now shows an Alert triangle beside the name of the revised file.

6. Click the Update button, and the graphic (and its preview) in your publication assumes the changes you applied in Photoshop or Illustrator.

Characteristics Of Illustrator Drag And Drop Files

Illustrator files saved in native (.ai) format arrive in InDesign publications as EPS files, whether placed or dragged and dropped from anywhere other than the native application. The conversion is automatic, and means that you can't edit the graphic using InDesign tools. If, however, you drag and drop directly from the open Illustrator window (sadly, not Photoshop) to an open publication page, you can edit the graphic using InDesign's tools.

To demonstrate my point, the next two projects give you a chance to drag and drop Illustrator files and a Photoshop file into a publication. The first project works whether you have Illustrator installed or not, because you'll drag from this book's companion CD-ROM. After that, if you have Illustrator 7 or 8 installed, you can do the second project. Earlier versions of Illustrator don't allow you to edit dragged and dropped files within InDesign, although they will drag and drop from the Finder or Explorer, arriving as EPS files.

Note: Gradients in Illustrator files don't migrate well in the drag-and-drop-directly-from-Illustrator method of placing files. In fact, Illustrator gradients are lost altogether, and objects filled with a gradient are filled with black in the dropped graphic. Illustrator files placed using File|Place do maintain their gradients, but they can't be edited with InDesign tools.

PROJECT Drag And Drop A Graphic File Into A Publication

This is your chance to experiment with dragging and dropping from external media to an InDesign publication. There are three files for you to experiment with. One is a TIFF, and the other two are identical Illustrator files saved in different versions of Illustrator, just in case you have version 7 rather than 8.

To begin, open the InDesign publication, Drag n Drop.indd. It's located inside the Projects folder on this book's companion CD-ROM. You'll also want to open the Links palette after the Drag n Drop file is open.

1. Resize the publication window so that you can see both the publication file, Drag n Drop.indd, and the window showing the contents of the Drag & Drop folder.

2. Drag and drop the AngelPC.tif or AngelMAC.tif file on to page 1 of the publication. There is no difference in dragging either file; I gave you the option to reassure you that both formats work successfully.

   The Links palette should show the name of the dragged and dropped file (see Figure 7.5).

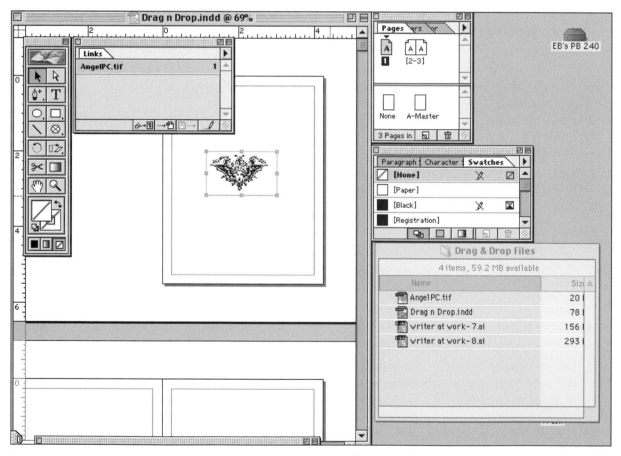

Figure 7.5

The Links palette displays the name of a dragged and dropped file. The Edit Original button at the bottom right of the Links palette allows you to edit the imported file in another application.

3. Use the Pages palette to activate page 2, and drag and drop the writer at work-7.ai. file from this book's companion CD-ROM to the publication. Notice that the Illustrator gradients applied to the eraser band are intact.

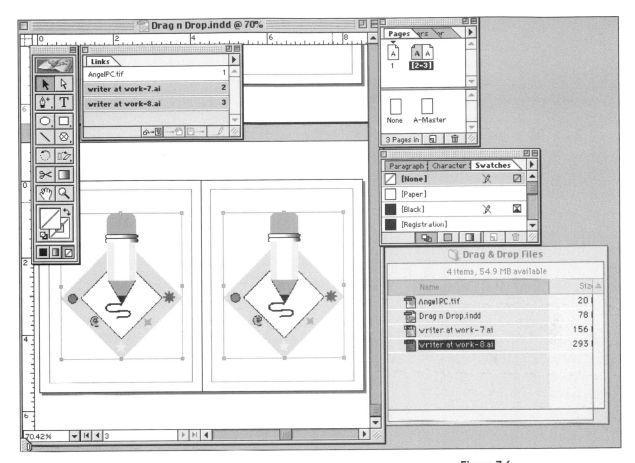

Figure 7.6

Both the dragged and dropped Illustrator files include the gradient applied in Illustrator.

4. Activate page 3 of the publication, and drag and drop the remaining file, writer at work-8.ai, to the InDesign publication (see Figure 7.6).

With these files in place in your publication, you can now edit any or all of these graphics in another application without closing InDesign.

PROJECT Edit A Dragged And Dropped Graphic In Another Application

Experiment with editing any or all of these graphics, but only if you have Photoshop or Illustrator, or another graphic application that will open the files.

1. In the Links palette, select the name of the file you want to edit.

2. Click the Edit Original button at the lower-right corner of the Links palette.

   Based on which file you choose and the graphic applications you have installed, a dialog box may ask you to select the application to use for editing or else Illustrator or Photoshop may open automatically.

3. Make any edits you like, and save the file in the graphics application.

4. Click on the InDesign publication window and glance at the Links palette. You should see an alert next to the name of the file you just edited and saved (see Figure 7.7).

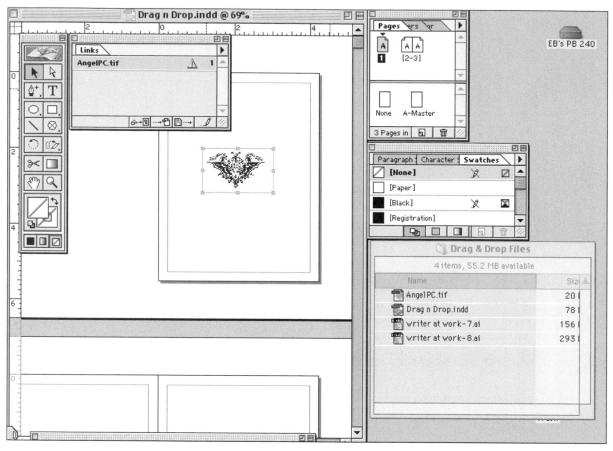

Figure 7.7
The alert advises you that the original file has changed, and you need to update the preview file inserted in your InDesign publication.

5. Click the Update Link button at the bottom of the Links palette. (The button looks like a floppy disk.)

The file is updated, and you can go on to the next task, editing and updating the other graphics you dragged and dropped in the publication.

PROJECT Direct Drag, Drop, And Edit An Illustrator File

If you completed the previous project and still have the Drag n Drop.indd file open, you can add a page to the Drag n Drop.indd publication. If not, any publication will suffice.

1. Open one of the writer at work.ai files in Illustrator. Either file will work in Illustrator 8, but only writer at work-7.ai opens in version 7.

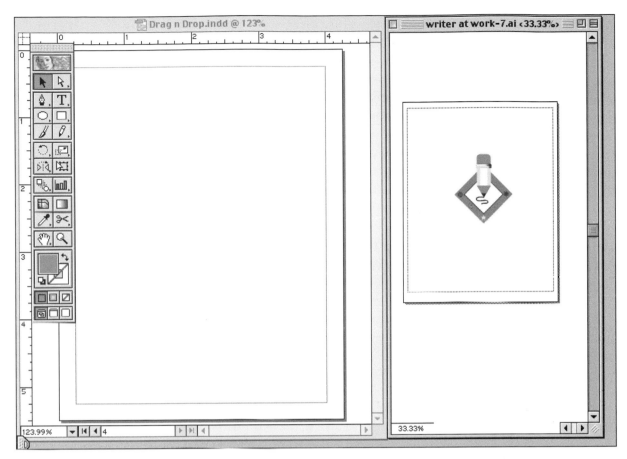

Figure 7.8

The size of your Illustrator file
and InDesign page may differ
from this figure, but you must be
able to see both application
windows at the same time to
drag directly from Illustrator to
InDesign.

2. Resize the Illustrator and InDesign windows so you can see both the
   graphic and the publication page at the same time (see Figure 7.8).

3. Click and drag the Illustrator graphic to the InDesign page. Notice
   that there is no additional link shown in the Links palette and that
   the gradient applied to the eraser band in Illustrator doesn't appear
   in the InDesign version (see Figure 7.9).

4. In your publication, select the eraser (or any other component of the
   Illustrator graphic) and recolor it, reshape it, or edit it in any way
   you like, using InDesign's graphic tools.

5. Save your work, and sit back and marvel.

Because there is no link to the original Illustrator file, none of the changes
you make in InDesign are saved in the original Illustrator file. You can re-
import the original file and be assured of its original integrity or drag and
drop the revised version elsewhere. If this isn't the slickest way of working
efficiently, I don't know what is.

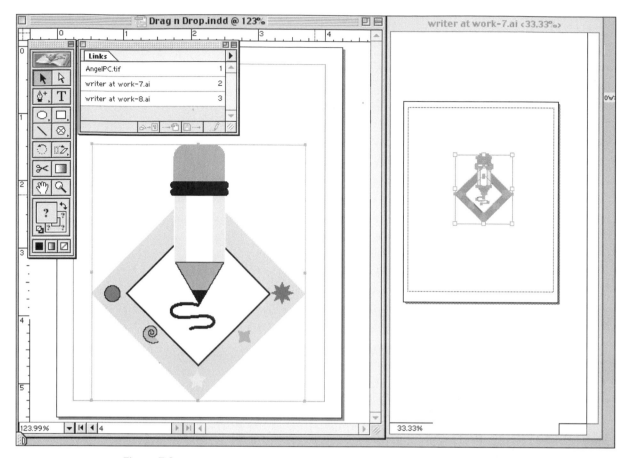

Figure 7.9

The graphic dragged and dropped directly from Illustrator to InDesign can be edited directly in the publication using the InDesign tools.

Clipping Paths

All imported graphic files are rectangular. Clipping paths mask off portions of the rectangle, and they are best suited to bitmap images such as photographs. Every clipping path is made up of Bézier anchor points and line segments called nodes. The shape of the Bézier path clips off portions of the image and allows other portions to show through the hole created by the closed clipping path. Although it sounds as if a clipping path cuts off portions of an image, in fact, it renders portions of the image transparent.

The portion of an image that's clipped is based on a selection of tones in the image and the number of nodes in the path. Because a clipping path is tone-based, it's possible to make a clipping path that makes portions of an image within the perimeter selection become transparent. For example, you can clip the space between the crook of an elbow in the sleeve of a jacket and the body of the jacket as well as the background of the photograph if these all are similar tones.

InDesign can import a clipping path created in another application, such as Photoshop. It's almost always preferable to import a clipping path, but you can also create the clipping path after an image is placed.

Import A Clipping Path

When you import a Photoshop, EPS, or TIFF file that already has a clipping path, nothing more need be done than to place the file. The clipped image is automatically placed in a rectangular bounding box, and the clipping path cannot be edited. If you select Create Frame From Clipping Path in the Import Options dialog box, the result is an editable clipping path surrounding the clipped image (see Figure 7.10).

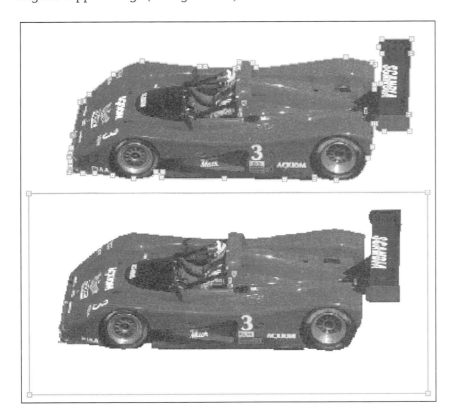

Figure 7.10
The upper racing car image, with a clipping path created in Photoshop, was imported with the Import Option, Create Frame From Clipping Path, selected, while the lower image was simply placed.

InDesign allows you to render the path uneditable by turning off the option Create Frame From Clipping Path. If this Image Import Option is grayed out in the dialog box, it simply means the image has no clipping path.

When you create a frame from an imported clipping path, you can use the Pen tools to adjust the frame, thus hiding or revealing portions of the clipped image, or use the Direct Selection tool to move the image inside the clipping path. Placing a clipped image without creating a frame from the path only lets you move the image within the bounding box.

- To select the bounding box, click the Direct Selection anywhere inside the image.

- To select the clipping path, click along the edge of the image.

Adjust the clipping path with the Pen tools, and the position of the image with the Selection or Direct Selection tool. Move the entire clipping path, image, and bounding box with the Selection tool.

Make A Clipping Path

Although InDesign has fewer options for creating a clipping path than those available in Photoshop, you can make a clipping path for an image after it's placed. InDesign has two ways to create clipping paths. One uses Object|Clipping Path, to open a dialog box where you determine the portion of the image to be clipped (see Figure 7.11). The other is to create the path manually, which comes a bit later in this chapter.

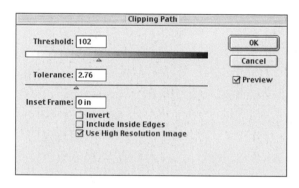

Figure 7.11

Move the sliders or enter numeric values in the upper portion of the Clipping Path dialog box, and use the checkboxes in the lower portion to determine the behaviors of the path.

Each setting in the Clipping Path dialog box has an effect on the way a clipping path is made and what's included or excluded. You should know that clipping paths are second only to fonts for creating problems with high-end PostScript output. That's not to say you should avoid them. It's possible to make clipping paths that work well if you're aware that excess in the Clipping Path dialog box spoils success at output, and you have a good grasp of the Pen tools for editing a clipping path. The Threshold setting is based in light and dark values for pixels. The Tolerance setting determines how the path is drawn:

- *Threshold*—This setting determines how much tonal difference there must be between pixels in order to be included in the selection that will become the clipping path. The lower the Threshold, the more dark value pixels you include (see Figure 7.12).

  Push the Threshold too low, and you'll include more of the image than you want. The higher the Threshold, the lighter in value pixels must be to be included in the selection. As you push the Threshold to a higher and higher number, you eliminate more and more pixels from the selection until, finally, you can't see any of the image.

- *Tolerance*—This setting determines how precisely the clipping path created follows the on-screen selection of pixels. A clipping path can

Figure 7.12
The jacket on the top left has no clipping path. The top right is set to a Threshold of 55, showing none of the drop shadow. The lower left one is set to 25, and the last jacket is set to 3, just one number above disappearing. The drop shadow is rather bulkier than the one set to 25 because more dark pixels are selected.

slice pixels at a diagonal, whereas on screen, each square pixel is selected. Higher Tolerance values usually make for a smoother path.

Be sure to turn on the Preview. This shows you the selection in the image on your document page (see Figure 7.13).

Lower Tolerance values pick up more of the pixels selected based on the Threshold setting. Set the tolerance too low, and there will be too many nodes. That all but guarantees PostScript printing problems. Set the Tolerance too high, and the portion of the image you want to show will be less than you need. It's a balancing act, and experience is your best guide. As with any Bézier shape, you want the lowest possible number of nodes that still retains the outline of the portion of the image you want to show.

- *Inset Frame*—This setting shrinks the frame that automatically is outside the clipping path created by your Threshold and Tolerance settings. If you have difficulty selecting and clipping exactly around the edges of the portion of the image you want to show, adjust the Inset Frame to cover up unwanted pixels around the perimeter.

Figure 7.13
Again, the top left jacket image has no clipping path. The top right is set to a Tolerance of 2, the lower left is set to 7, and the last is set to 10 (maximum). Just right.

- *Inverse*—Sometimes it's easier and faster to select what you *don't* want included, and then use the Invert checkbox to create the clipping path around what you do want to show. This works especially well when an image has a very light (or very dark) background, and the part you want to show is full of varied values.

- *Include Inside Edges*—If, in selecting pixels surrounding the portion of the image you want to display, you also want pixels within the image to become transparent, click this option. The same Threshold and Tolerance settings are applied to the interior pixels.

- *Use High Resolution Image*—Slower, but more precise, this option calculates the transparent portions of an image based not on the low-res proxy image on screen, but on the high-res image it refers to.

The other method of making a clipping path is a do-it-yourself operation. In actual practice, it's more of a cropping action than a clipping path, because your image is pasted into a closed path rather than the path shaping to a selection within the image. This works for images that are so complex, or have tones so similar, that selecting only the portion you want to show is all but impossible (see Figure 7.14).

Figure 7.14

A manual clipping path worked best on this image to display only the interior of the image because the surrounding tones were too close in value to the tones I wanted to display. The top right image shows the drawn path. At the lower left you see the path selected after the image was cut, and the lower-right image is how the image appears after using Paste Into and positioning.

Manually Create A Clipping Path

All that time spent with the Pen tool earlier in this book is about to come home and prove its worth. In this project, you draw the clipping path shown in Figure 7.14.

1. Place the image, Frame.jpg, on your document page. (The file is on this book's companion CD-ROM.)

2. Use the Pen tool to draw a closed path on top of the imported Frame.jpg image surrounding the portion of the image you want to show.

3. Use the Selection tool to select just the imported image (not the path you just created), and cut it to the clipboard.

4. Use the Direct Selection tool to select the path you drew (if you can't see the path to select it, you may need to drag a selection rectangle over the area where the path is located to activate it), and choose Edit|Paste Into.

5. With the Direct Selection tool or the arrow keys, position the portion of the image you want to show inside the path.

6. To conclude duplicating the same paths as shown in Figure 7.14, use the Pen tool to draw around the hand print, and fill that path with 100% black.

PASTE VS. PASTE INTO

There's a distinct difference between Paste and Paste Into. Paste simply glues an object on a document page. Nothing else on the page need be selected, although it can be. Paste Into *requires* that some frame be selected in order for the Paste Into command to understand the destination of the clipboard contents.

I always try the automatically drawn clipping path first. I like automated stuff. But when it's clear that I'll spend too much time messing with numbers, or, if the parts of the image I want to show are scattered all over the image and not easily singled out by tone, I quickly head for the Pen tool. This is a tedious process, granted, but it's often less time-consuming than fiddling with Threshold and Tolerance settings that don't quite do the job.

Fitting Frames And Artwork

As with any frame, you can resize a graphic frame or its contents, but with InDesign graphic frames, you get a special treat. If you've worked with QuarkXPress, you know that there are keystrokes, but no menu command for fitting and positioning a graphic in a frame—but InDesign has no secrets. In the Object menu, look for Fitting. There are four fitting choices in a pop-up menu, and their corresponding keyboard shortcuts: Fit Contents To Frame, Fit Frame To Content, Center Content, and Fit Content Proportionally. The graphic and frame fitting commands are right out where you need them, and quickly and easily cover all your imported graphic fitting requirements. Place the graphic and make your choice.

Edit Graphics From Within InDesign

When graphic files are imported, by default, they are linked to their source document. If you decide to edit that linked file in its original application, use the Links palette button Edit Original to open the application that created the original file. This editing capability isn't limited to graphic files. You can edit any imported file in its native application, provided, of course, you have that application installed.

To perform native application edits from within InDesign:

1. Open the Links palette.

2. Highlight the name of the file you want to edit.

3. Click the Edit Original button along the lower edge of the Links palette.

4. Make any changes or additions you want, and then Save, and close the file and the application, if you want. The imported file is still in place in your layout, but with the most recent edits.

This certainly expedites matters when you have many files imported from the same application and are familiar with its tools.

Nested Frames

Nested frames are another way of creating complex graphics. It's hard to say whether nested frames are a boon or a toy. I, for one, find them fascinating, if initially frustrating. Nested frames are different from stacked frames. The effect of nesting is a little bit like inline graphics, and a lot more like creating a collage. You create the first frame, then paste another frame inside that, and another inside the second frame, and so on.

Any kind of frame can be nested inside another frame, but remember that each frame can only hold one other frame. You can work around the one nested frame limit by nesting a grouped set of frames, because the group is considered one object. Nesting objects converted to Compound Paths also works. (Compound paths are discussed in the next section of this chapter.) Nest frames that are text converted to outlines, if you like. The visual possibilities are vast.

Adobe likes to call a frame holding another frame the parent frame. I call the frame pasted into it a child. To nest frames, you need at least two frames already created, a parent and a child.

1. Select the child frame.

2. Copy it to the clipboard.

3. Select the parent frame.

4. Choose Edit|Paste Into.

There you have it. A nested frame.

Each frame, as it is selected to be pasted into, is the parent. Any of the frames and the contents of frames can be edited. Change the content, the style of the contents, and the frame itself, within the confines of its parent frame. Use the Direct Selection tool to activate a nested frame, and then do whatever you need to do inside the frame.

As you nest frame in frame in frame, there is no limit to the number that can be nested. The first frame determines the outermost boundary of the entire nest, and the size of each subsequent nested frame determines how large the next nested frame can be. If you've ever seen those charming Russian dolls, one inside another, diminishing in size as you open each doll to discover another even smaller one inside, you have a perfect idea of how the size ratio of nested frames works.

> **Note:** Paste Into is grayed out in the Edit menu if the parent frame holds a photograph, but, if you want to paste a photograph into another frame, go right ahead. That works.

The nested frames needn't be concentric. For instance, you could create a text frame that holds a graphic drawn in InDesign with the Pen tool, and nest a text frame inside that, then convert some text to outlines, and fill the text with a photograph, and nest the outline text inside the text frame.

If you change your mind about the content type of a nested frame, select the nested frame, and choose Object|Content to select the type content you want, Graphic, Text, or Unassigned.

> **Note:** Nesting images with clipping paths loses contact with any original link that might have been a part of the file before nesting.

Compound Paths

The truly imaginative artists always seem to come up with ideas that no mere mortals conceive of. Perhaps that's the inspiration for Compound Paths. Create any shape, frame, or combination of these, and then meld them together to make something unique and more than the sum of its parts.

As a trial, use the pasteboard of an open InDesign document to assemble several objects. Some can overlap, and others can be freestanding. Select the entire group of objects, and choose Object|Compound Paths|Make.

The results I got were certainly different than I thought I would get, though what exactly that was, I'm not sure. I did expect to create a single object from many objects, and that some of the resulting single object would be negative space (see Figure 7.15).

Figure 7.15

These three examples show you objects before they are made into a Compound Path (left), after being converted (middle), and after they're released and made independent objects again.

To disassemble multiple objects made into a compound path:

1. Select the compound path.

2. Choose Object|Compound Paths|Release.

In Figure 7.15, the last group of objects on the right are an example of what happens when you make and then release a compound path. As you see in the first group (at the left), each object is filled with a different tint or gradient of black. In the center objects, those made into a Compound Path, the attributes applied to the lowermost object in the stack (the first object created) control the attributes applied to every object in the compound path. Naturally, when the compound path is released, the objects retain their newly assumed attributes after being disassembled, but the negative space created where independent objects overlapped is eliminated.

Layers

Anyone who uses Photoshop or PageMaker very much knows about layers. Sometimes I wonder how we worked before the era of layers. Their uses are as varied as those who use them.

One interesting way to use layers came to me from a Web developer friend who decided to use layers to create different versions of the same Web pages for client approval. "Brilliant," I thought. And, "Why shouldn't graphic designers do that, too?" Well, for a long time, the answer was, "Because you don't have layers in your desktop publishing application, silly." But now you do, thanks to Adobe.

The foundational concept of InDesign layers is the fact that each layer is document-pervasive, that is, it covers every page of a document at exactly the same level throughout. You want to be clear about how layers can be used so that turning off a layer doesn't hide things elsewhere in your publication that you want incorporated in the overall design.

Layers and master pages differ slightly. Master page elements reside on a layer, but a layer can be devoid of master elements, too. Rearranging layers in any view, including a master page view, rearranges every design element throughout the document that was placed or created on the layers.

To use layers effectively for proposals, or for trying out ideas, you need to consider what elements are likely to be relatively consistent throughout the publication, and what things you think will be optional or changeable. For example, if you're working with a variety of logos on a page, you could create a layer with nothing but logos, and another with those same logos rearranged, to give you and your client something visual to make decisions with. Things that are likely to change deserve a layer of their own. Things you're testing should be on yet another layer, and so on. It's not rocket science. It's just thinking ahead, and preparing.

Each time you hide a layer, the effect of the spread is changed. With these versions available to see either on screen or in a proof print, you'll save tons of time and aggravation.

Moving On

In the following chapter, you'll learn about InDesign's Color Management System and Practice applying CMS to a document converted from QuarkXPress.

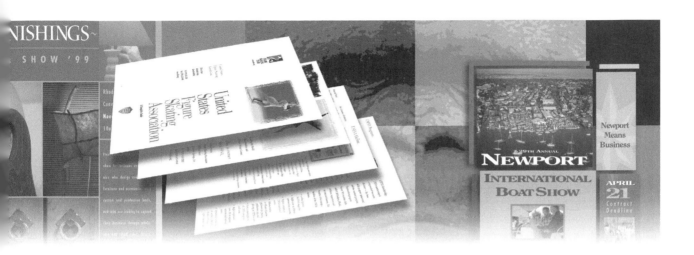

COLOR
MANAGEMENT

Take a deep breath and prepare yourself for what just may be the most important concern in desktop publishing today: color management.

Note: Color management is a big topic. This chapter offers basic information so that you can see the difference CMS can make. However, the use of CMS in high-level color work is beyond the scope of this book.

Skills Covered In This Chapter

- Calibrate your monitor

- Set Application Color Settings

- Set Document Color Settings

- Set up Color Management System (CMS) to more closely parallel monitor view and final output

- Convert a QuarkXPress document and apply CMS

- Correct the text flow in the converted document

- Quickly transfer items from one layer to another layer

I don't need to tell you that color is a loaded topic. The road to final output is up and down, and full of potential axle-breaking pitfalls because there are so many aspects of color, from color spaces to the devices used for printing or viewing color. In fact, the size and kind of monitor you use as you develop a color publication has an impact on color. Even the paper involved in a printed publication affects color.

Despite all these variables, some things do remain in your hands. You can apply a Color Management System (CMS) or not. That can be a good thing, because you have some control over your work, and a bad thing, because you carry much of the responsibility for the end product. Remember, CMS doesn't guarantee truer or better color. It gives you consistent color from monitor to proof printer to output printer by displaying and printing colors within the gamuts of input and output devices.

CMS Terminology

If you were trained as a graphic designer, you certainly have some color theory under your belt, but there's no assurance that you also received training as a pressman or an electronic color technician. You may need a primer just to discuss the subject, let alone achieve a proficiency level that lets you feel comfortable with the mechanics of digital color.

- *CMS (Color Management System)*—This acts similarly to a language interpreter. It recognizes the gamut in which a graphic was created and the gamut of the graphic's target output device, and it makes whatever adjustments are required to ensure that the printed colors look like the colors on screen.

- *Gamut*—This indicates the range of color a device can produce. It is synonymous with "color space." The gamut of the human eye has a far wider range of colors than, say, the gamut of an RGB monitor, which, in turn, has a greater gamut than a web press can produce.

Each device—a scanner, a monitor, a printer—has a different gamut, so clearly, a color management system has a place in your design concepts.

- *Gamma*—Gamma is the measurement of the mid-tone values of a monitor. The new Adobe Gamma, which comes free with InDesign, creates profiles for your monitor—profiles that are used in conjunction with the profiles of output devices to assure consistency of color from the concept to the delivery of a publication.

- *ICC (International Color Consortium)*—This organization established standardized profiles that describe the color gamut of a specific device, be it a printer, scanner, or monitor. You can use the standard ICC profiles or create your own. InDesign automatically embeds profile information in graphics created within the application.

- *Profile* A set of parameters describing the way a monitor displays color, or a description of the range of colors an output device is capable of producing.

- *Color Space*—A synonym for gamut, the color spaces available in InDesign are RGB, CMYK, and LAB.

- *CSA (Color Space Array)*—The PostScript equivalent of the source profiles for colors.

- *CRD (Color Rendering Dictionary)*—The PostScript equivalent of the destination profiles for colors. Together, CSA and CRD provide specific kinds of output devices with the information needed to convert colors to the gamut of the device.

Why Use CMS?

The more sources you tap for graphics in your publications, the more you need a CMS. The best reason for using a CMS is to ensure that every file, whether it's an image or a final publication, has consistent color aimed at its final output destination. A CMS allows you to sleep easier at night, knowing that, if nothing else, *your* files are all headed in the right direction. The very first question that must be settled before launching into a new publication is what CMS your print provider uses. If you and your output supplier are on the same page, the results will be quicker and cheaper as well as more reliable.

One service bureau that I'm familiar with handles thousands of electronic images and page layout documents, and they strongly recommend a three-step approach to color management:

1. Be sure the final version of your color files is saved in the same color space as the intended output. It's perfectly acceptable to use RGB

during your design development of a printed piece, but when it comes time to print the publication, convert colors to CMYK. RGB and LAB are suitable for on-screen viewing or photo-imaging, but they are unsuited to print because their gamut is so broad that colors you see on screen may not be within the gamut of a CMYK printer.

2. Check for out-of-gamut colors before handing off your files. It's easy to do, but it's often overlooked in the rush to deadlines. (There's more information about out-of-gamut colors in Chapter 9.)

3. Always present your service bureau or print provider with the profiles of your monitor that you used as you created a file. That way, they can compare what you saw as the file grew with the way the output device will produce it and make any necessary corrections.

Monitors And Calibration

Conventional wisdom suggests that, if you have even a hope of correlating on-screen color with final output, you'd better have the biggest, highest-resolution monitor you can afford. Some say a 21-inch monitor is a must, but, more important is the resolution. Why? Because you want the electronic image files' resolution and monitor pixels to correlate one-to-one; otherwise, the digital data on screen is merely interpolated to display at a different ratio, and color data on screen is either dropped or added to accommodate the difference in resolution.

With that in mind, and an eye to your budget, remember that all monitors sold these days are multisync monitors. A multisync monitor can be set to emulate different sizes of monitors. It's possible to make even a 13-inch monitor display the equivalent of a 21-inch monitor. The display will be mighty small, but it's possible.

If you're looking for another argument to justify popping for a large monitor, this one states the obvious, but it is often overlooked. You want to see as much of your publication as possible at 100 percent, and on a 21-inch monitor, you can see a two-page spread of 8^1/$_2$–by-11-inch pages. No, I don't hold stock in any monitor companies, but I do take stock of the discomfort levels and of the time and money lost by using a monitor that doesn't do the most helpful job of showing your work.

Stabilize your surroundings so you consistently see colors on your monitor under the same influences:

1. Keep the walls and furnishings of your office or studio in a neutral palette, such as a polychrome medium gray.

2. Maintain a consistent light level in the office or studio so that your monitor calibration needs no adjustment for ambient light changes throughout the day and year. You also need to parallel the light temperature for your work environment and your light table. Typically, both should be 5,000 degrees Kelvin, but that's not a rigid requirement, either. As long as you keep everything consistent, you should be all right.

3. Make the background of your monitor a solid, medium gray. PC users can choose Start|Settings|Control Panel|Display and set up a medium gray Desktop in the Appearance tab. If you're using a Mac, you may need to create the gray background for yourself (see the "Neutralize A Macintosh Desktop" sidebar).

4. Calibrate your monitor.

NEUTRALIZE A MACINTOSH DESKTOP

In the most recent systems releases for the Macintosh, there is no medium tone gray background for the desktop. I've found a way to work around that, however. Create a color tile in your favorite graphic program, and choose the tile as a Picture in the Appearance Control Panel. It takes only a couple of minutes, and it averts the distraction of colors that confuse your eye as you mix and use publication colors on screen.

Begin by opening Photoshop or Illustrator, and then follow these steps:

1. Open a new document that is 0.5 inch by 0.5 inch (36 pixels by 36 pixels) with a resolution of 72 pixels per inch in RGB mode. These measurements needn't be exact. I simply chose them because they create a small file, and there's no need for a large file to make a background for your desktop.

2. Fill the document with a mid-tone gray. I chose a setting of 199 for each R, G, and B.

3. Save the file as gray.pct.

4. Store the file inside the system Photos folder by following this path: System Folder|Appearance|Photos.

5. Close the System Folder, and from the Apple Menu, choose Control Panels|Appearance.

6. On the Desktop tab, select any Pattern you like. It will show only briefly as you boot up.

7. Click the Place Picture button, highlight your new gray.pct file in the list of pictures, and click Choose.

8. In the pop-up menu below Place|Remove Picture, select Fill Screen.

9. Click the Set Desktop button to test your new background, and close the Appearance dialog box. The ersatz picture file completely obscures the pattern you chose as soon as the booting process is finished, and you're at the Finder, ready to open an application.

There's an alternative way, too. Follow Steps 1 and 2, then select the entire gray swatch document, and copy it to the clipboard. Select Control Panels|Appearance|Desktop, and Paste. There's no need to save the swatch document because the name Untitled Pattern appears among other Patterns listed, and it can be used or deactivated at any time. To change the name of the new pattern, with the Appearance|Desktop open and the Untitled Pattern highlighted, choose Edit|Pattern Name, and call it what you will. Be sure the new gray pattern is selected when you close the Appearance dialog box.

No matter what size monitor you work with, calibration is an essential beginning. Whether you require and use CMS or not, you have at least a couple calibration options. You could buy a device to measure a light stream from your monitor and compare that light stream to a measuring constant the device generates. There are a number of inexpensive (under $300) calibrators coming on market. Or, calibrate by adjusting your monitor using software.

Profiles

"In all honesty, you really don't have to spend hard-earned money buying expensive monitor calibration devices or extra software." So sayeth the output experts I rely on. There are drawbacks, even if you do buy calibration hardware. For instance, OptiCal and Lamda calibrators are limited to certain video cards, and if you don't have the right one, you're out of luck. X-Rite 92 sometimes doesn't match your output device properly. Kodak's ColorBlind is purported to be the best, but it, too, relies on video cards, and you can't use Adobe Gamma in conjunction with ColorBlind. So what's a designer to do?

> **Note:** Because this is a book about Adobe InDesign and InDesign comes with Adobe Gamma, I've focused on Adobe Gamma. Other software and hardware profiling packages are beyond the scope of this book.

Start with your system software, ColorSync, on the Mac, and progress to the free utility shipped with InDesign, Adobe Gamma. On a PC, go directly to Adobe Gamma. Though limited to creating profiles for your monitor, Adobe Gamma, an ICC-compliant utility, is perfectly fine for working with DTP documents.

When it's time to print, if your print provider has a complete set of the profiles you used during the design phases of your document, they can see exactly the same colors on screen as you saw while you worked. With that assured, they can reliably adjust the gamut of their output device and avert quirky, unexpected color shifts. Chances are greatly reduced that you'll face a surprise similar to the one a designer I know encountered after creating a sumptuous purple on screen that printed a rich, but unanticipated, brown.

Macintosh Profiles

The Macintosh OS 8.5 or later includes Apple's color management utility, ColorSync. To work effectively, you must have version 2.5 or later installed. Version 2.1.1 doesn't cut it. Using ColorSync is remarkably simple. It has an assistant to guide you through all the steps involved in calibrating your monitor. Your goal is to see on screen the closest possible approximation of the actual colors you choose or mix, and that depends on monitor calibration.

After your monitor has been turned on for at least half an hour:

1. Choose Apple|Control Panels|Monitors & Sound (see Figure 8.1).

2. Select the Color icon at the top of the dialog box.

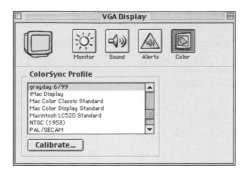

Figure 8.1

Click the icon at the top of the Monitors & Sound dialog box to access the Color settings.

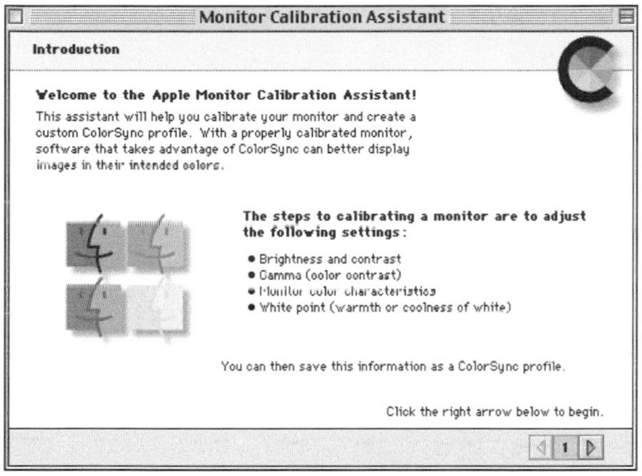

Figure 8.2

Click the arrow at the bottom of the Monitor Calibration Assistant to advance through the screens and calibrate your monitor.

3. Click the Calibrate button to access the assistant (see Figure 8.2).

4. Save your profile with an identifying name, such as Sunny Morning June or Gray Day-Fall, and close the assistant.

If you can't stabilize your work environment light without moving everything into a closet, you'll need profiles for various hours of the day, various kinds of days (sunny or gray), and various times of the year (spring, summer, fall, winter). Create and save profiles of your monitor regularly. You need to calibrate your monitor often, at a minimum, every 30 days, and more often if your monitor remains on for extended time periods. The more hours of use a monitor has, the quicker it slips out of calibration.

When it's time to hand off your publication, include the profiles you've used as you worked on your publication's design. The profiles are located in the ColorSync Profiles folder inside the System Folder.

Note: If you open the Color screen of the Monitors & Sound dialog box and see no Calibrate button, the solution lies in the Extensions Manager. The Default Calibrator is not turned on, and it needs to be. As always, after locating the Default Calibrator under the list of Extensions, and activating it, you need to restart your computer. Then you can proceed to create profiles for your monitor.

Windows Profiles

After your monitor has been turned on for at least half an hour:

1. Choose Start|Settings|Control Panel|Adobe Gamma (see Figure 8.3).

2. In the first screen, select Step-By-Step (Wizard), and proceed through the instructions on subsequent screens.

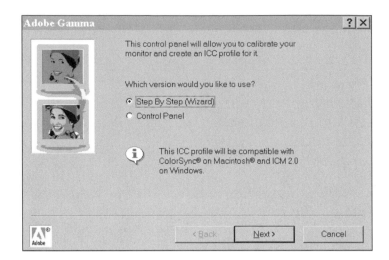

Figure 8.3

The PC version of Adobe Gamma varies from the Mac version only in its appearance, not its steps or its function.

3. Save your profile with an identifying name such as SunAMJun.icm, and close the wizard.

   The path to Windows profiles is Windows|System|Color. All profiles have the extension .icm.

Color Settings

Two different sets of color settings, document and application, determine what's specific to and saved with the document, and what's saved with the application. Establish application settings that you're likely to use frequently, default application settings, the same way other defaults are set, with no document open.

You may need to change color settings if you or someone else working on a publication is using a computer other than the one it was originally created on. Changing color settings is a simple process and doesn't affect any defaults. The application or document color settings that need to be revised from the default color settings set up on a different installation of InDesign will apply exclusively to the open publication; they will not revise the default settings. The changes you make with the publication open are specific to the open publication, and they don't affect default settings made when all publications are closed.

In many respects, color settings perform in the same way as preferences. If you consistently work on the same computer and use the same proofing device, you can establish color settings with no document open to apply your settings to every newly created document. Individual graphics can have settings different from your defaults applied if necessary.

CMS WEB RESOURCES

Expand your CMS information and your stash of profiles by visiting these Web sites. Things constantly change in the print world and on the Web, so you probably should visit frequently to keep current.

- **www.barco-usa.com**—Calibrator Talk software and a Personal Calibrator to mention two of this site's offerings. It has lots of verbiage and interesting information.
- **www.chromix.com**—Profile Central from CHROMiX. Drop by this site for profiles you may need.
- **www.cim.mcgill.ca/~image529/TA529_98/projects97/62_Wen/sensor.html**—An interesting student project with relevant site links. The site, however, loads like molasses.
- **www.color.com**—Perfect Color White Paper, ColorBlind ICC Workflow. An interesting treatise.
- **www.kodak.com.tr/global/en/professional/products/software/colorFlow/iccProfile/features.shtml**—Profile Editor and hints for using ICC Production Tools.
- **www.lacie.com/scripts/color/calibration.cfm**—Free La Cie color profiles.
- **www.lhag.de/lhag/press/i_color_man.html**—Color management links and other pertinent info from Linotype-Hell.
- **www.light-source.com**—Light Source Colortron II measurement device for color and optical density. The company is now owned by X-Rite.
- **www.picto.com**—ColorSynergy is an affordable Macintosh aid to matching color from scanner to output. Granted, this is advertising, but its capabilities are full for fewer bucks.
- **www.pantone.com**—Everything Pantone has to offer, plus interesting information about their Color Institute.
- **www.printbid.com**—A directory of commercial printing related companies—and it's absolutely free. This site has useful resources for anyone who buys or sells commercial printing.
- **www.publish.com/features/9606/prepress/toolbax.html**—An extensive list of links to resources for color management.
- **www.rodsandcones.com**—ICC profiles and Macintosh ColorSync information. This site has plenty to entertain and inform.
- **www.xrite.com**—Hardware calibration solutions especially for the PC, but also for the Mac. In addition to selling its wares, this is possibly the richest site in information about firmware for color management. Check out their Industry Links page.
- **www.colorpartnership.com**—An interesting, if glib, site. You'll find downloadable PDF files that cover color and printing-related topics. It sells various products, including OptiCal calibration software, and have a list of the video boards required to use their wares.
- **www.digitaldog.net/tips.html**—A fine source of informative PDF downloadable files covering all manner of tips about color management, Photoshop, scanners, and digital camera issues.

Application Color Settings

To open the Application Color Settings, choose File|Color Settings|Application. In the Application Color Settings dialog box, specify which color management engine you want to use, and the profiles you prefer for the monitor, composites, and separations (see Figure 8.4).

The color management engine and other settings you choose in the Application Color Settings dialog box are global, and they are the defaults for all newly created documents, or documents you open after the Application

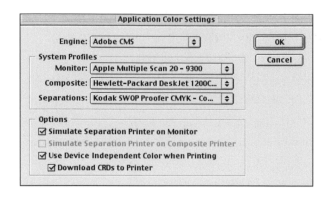

Figure 8.4

These Application Color Settings options don't need to be saved with a specific file because they can differ widely as you move a document from an application installation on one computer to another computer.

Settings are in place. Your choices are saved as a part of InDesign's instruction sets, not with individual documents.

- *Monitor*—This setting is for the profile you created or installed and have activated for this publication. This need only be changed if you change monitors or if a publication is moved from one computer to another and, therefore, you're working with a monitor that differs from the one used for creating the publication.

- *Composite*—Select the color proofing device you plan to use. If you're doing professionally produced overlay or laminate proofs, consult your print provider before selecting the composite setting.

- *Separations*—This setting identifies the final output device you plan to use.

Application Color Settings Options

In most instances, you'll set these Application Color Settings with no publication open to establish defaults. As always, you can revise your defaults with no publication open, or establish settings specific to a publication when it is open.

- *Simulate Separation Printer On Monitor*—For print pieces, be sure to select this option to have the most accurate view of colors on screen. With this active, InDesign calculates and displays colors within the gamut of your final output device. It's a soft proofing method, on screen. If your publication is headed for on-screen viewing over the Web or an intranet, be sure this is deselected, because your publication will be using a monitor gamut.

- *Simulate Separation Printer On Composite Printer*—With this option selected, InDesign compares the composite printer profile to the separations profile and produces the closest possible composite from your proof printing printer. You may print a bit faster when this is deselected, but you may be unpleasantly surprised when you see the final printout.

- *Use Device Independent Color When Printing*—This choice works only when your PostScript printer has built-in device-independent color management. (Consult your provider or the user manual of your desktop printer.) With this option selected, InDesign sends images' source profiles, unadjusted, to the output device.

- *Download CRDs To Printer*—If the printer you plan to use for final separations has CRDs built-in, you needn't activate this option unless your print provider specifically requests that you do so. When activated, it generates a PostScript Color Rendering Dictionary based on the Separations profile selected.

Document Color Settings

Document settings are embedded in the document. Anything you set in the Document Color Settings dialog box is saved with the document and travels along to any other workstation the document is opened on. Your choice of rendering intents is also saved with the document. (There's more in the "Rendering Intent" section later in this chapter.)

Activate CMS

With the groundwork laid, you're ready to activate color management. By default, CMS is turned *off*. The logic behind that is that you have so many things to set up correctly before CMS does any good, that there'd be no purpose in enabling color management before these are attended to. After you've established profiles, gamuts, and devices, then you're ready to turn on CMS.

To activate CMS:

1. Select File|Color Settings| Document Color Settings to open the Document Color Settings dialog box (see Figure 8.5).

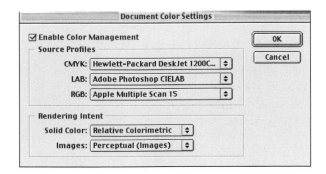

Figure 8.5

Turn color management on or off in the Document Color Settings dialog box using the Enable Color Management checkbox.

2. Specify which Source Profiles to use as defaults for graphics you create in InDesign, and for imported graphics that weren't saved with embedded ICC profiles.

Rendering Intent

The rendering intent applies to both imported and native InDesign graphics. Settings made in the Document Settings dialog box are document defaults. You may have occasion to override these defaults, and that's covered in this chapter, too.

- *Perceptual (Images)*—Good for continuous tone images, such as photographs, this properly represents color by scaling the source gamut to the destination gamut with the emphasis on hue and the way colors relate to one another. If colors shift in this method of transitioning because the destination gamut is smaller than the source gamut, all the colors will shift proportionately.

- *Saturation (Graphics)*—Good for flat color illustrations, such as presentation graphics, this doesn't do continuous tones well. It produces vivid colors by scaling the source gamut to the destination gamut while retaining the relative saturation. Consequently, the hue may shift.

- *Relative Colorimetric*—Best used for flat color illustrations; doesn't do continuous tones well because it doesn't span the entire gamut. Good for maintaining the original color accuracy in graphics, such as logos. Colors outside the destination gamut are clipped, that is, out-of-gamut colors are shifted to the closest match within the destination gamut. Relative Colorimetric compensates for the white point setting.

- *Absolute Colorimetric*—This doesn't scale the gamut, nor does it compensate for the white point setting to maintain color accuracy—*not* the ratio of one color to another. Also best used for flat color illustrations, as it, too, doesn't do continuous tones well (for the same reason Relative Colorimetric doesn't).

Rendering Intent For Imported Images

By default, InDesign Document Color Settings override any profiles embedded in imported graphics unless you specifically request that an imported image retain its color settings. Such a situation might arise if your document color setting option is Perceptual (continuous tone images) and you're importing a bitmap solid color graphic, say, from Illustrator. You'll want to apply Relative Colorimetric rendering to that image only. Yes, you can apply CMS to individual objects. Photoshop 5 and Illustrator 8 can embed color profiles in their documents, if the documents are saved correctly before being imported to InDesign. You probably want to retain those profiles.

Documents produced in earlier versions or in applications that don't support ICC color management will most likely use the Windows or Macintosh monitor gamut. These graphics can use some attention as they're imported.

Select a generic profile in the Rendering Intent options available in the Image Import Options dialog box, which is accessed from the Place dialog box (see Figure 8.6).

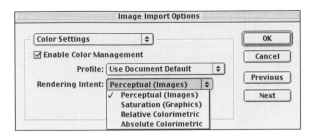

Figure 8.6
The Import Options dialog box offers the same Rendering Intent options as the Document Color Settings.

Checking For Embedded Profiles

All this talk about color management and importing graphics is fine, but you're still at sea if you don't have any idea what, if any, color management was applied to an image. It's okay. InDesign thought of that, too. You can assign color settings as you place an image or after it's in the layout.

If the graphic is already placed in your layout, click on it and select Object|Image Color Settings to open the Image Color Settings dialog box (see Figure 8.7).

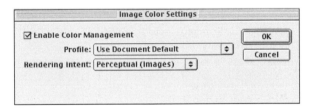

Figure 8.7
The Image Color Settings dialog box applies settings to specific graphics in your layouts.

In the Image Color Settings dialog box, choose the Profile you want applied to the image. These include Use Document Default, and an array of monitors. If the image was created and set with a monitor profile other than the one you are using, rectify that right here. Choose one that parallels the monitor on which you are working, or use the document default if you're at your own workstation. Choose the Rendering Intent appropriate to the image, and you're all set.

As you import a graphic that you're not certain has CMS applied, be sure to check Show Image Options in the Place dialog box to see the Image Import Options dialog box (see Figure 8.8).

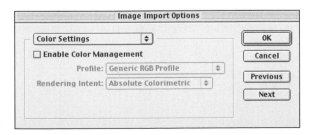

Figure 8.8
The Image Import Options dialog box gives you CMS feedback about an image before you place the image.

In the Image Import Options dialog box, select Color Settings from the drop-down menu. If Enable Color Management is grayed out, no CMS is applied, and if the image has CMS instructions applied, the settings for monitor profile and rendering intent are displayed. Make any changes you may need for the incoming image, and click OK.

PROJECT Convert A QuarkXPress Document And Apply CMS

Converting documents made in other DTP applications to InDesign documents may be something you need to do frequently. In this project, you have a chance to convert a completed QuarkXPress document included on the CD-ROM that comes with this book. In the process, you'll set up and activate CMS for the newly converted document. If you own and have QuarkXPress 3.3 or later installed, you can compare the conversion before and after applying CMS settings. The comparison is a real stunner.

There's no problem if you don't have QuarkXPress. The conversion to InDesign is still the same: You just won't have an opportunity to view the original file as it was created. The CMS tasks remain fruitful and informative, and you'll definitely see the difference that activating CMS can make as you work with converted or native InDesign documents.

Before starting to work on this project, Mac users need to install the screen fonts required: Futura, Futura Condensed, Minion, and Waters Titling. These are included on this book's companion CD-ROM. PC users will need to use their system fonts.

You also need to calibrate your monitor, if you haven't done that already. Refer to the earlier section of this chapter, "Macintosh Profiles" or "Windows Profiles."

1. With InDesign open, select File|Open, locate and open the QuarkXPress document, FFurn.qxd, on this book's companion CD-ROM.

2. As you are converting the document, a dialog box appears asking if you want to replace other instances of a color in the document with the color of the same name used in an EPS graphic in the brochure (see Figure 8.9).

   The answer in this instance is No.

   That color is from Illustrator, and it's embedded in one of the brochure's images. It should make no difference in what you're doing in this project. In other documents you convert, the answer may be Yes, if you have the same color swatches available to InDesign. It's also a matter of determining how many plates might be added if you don't click Yes.

Figure 8.9
As you convert documents to InDesign, if duplicate color names are encountered, you see this dialog box asking if you want to replace the color in the document, or simply import the color in the image.

3. When the Conversion Warnings dialog box appears, you see that the keyboard shortcuts from QuarkXPress can't be converted (see Figure 8.10).

   Click the Close button, and proceed with the conversion.

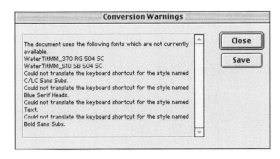

Figure 8.10
Conversion Warnings alert you to incompatibilities between programs before opening the converted document.

4. After the conversion is complete, save your publication, and peruse the spread. There are many things that need correcting.

5. For a view of the way the document should look, open the file, FineFurn.idd., on this book's CD-ROM.

   If you have QuarkXPress 3.x or later, you might want to open the original of the imported file in QuarkXPress for comparison purposes.

   In the finished InDesign file, I've made four layers, and done a lot, a whole lot, of font tweaking. The text flow differs because InDesign applies fonts differently, InDesign uses a different set of tracking values from those used by Quark, and Quark has only a single-line composer.

   Glance again at Figure 8.10 if you didn't save the Conversion Warnings.txt file as you converted the QuarkXPress version of the brochure. There is a font alert. Layers and text are not the concern right now. It's color management first, and then you can play with the other things. The other fixes are listed later.

6. Choose File|Color Settings|Application Color Settings, and set the Engine and System Profiles appropriately for your computer and monitor.

7. Select a Composite printing device, and set Separations to Adobe InDesign Default CMYK.

8. In the Options area, select the following:

- Simulate Printer On Monitor

- Simulate Separation Printer On Composite Printer

So far, there's no dramatic improvement in the monitor color simulation of the final output, but the foundational specs are in place. The next step is to set Document Color Settings.

1. Select File|Color Settings|Document Color Settings.

2. Click Enable Color Management.

3. Set the Source Profiles:

- CMYK: Use Separations Profile

- LAB: Adobe InDesign Default LAB

- RGB: Select the same profile you applied in calibrating your monitor, or override that setting with a custom setting you created, such as grayday, if the sun disappeared in the last half hour.

4. For Rendering Intent, set:

- Solid Color: Relative Colorimetric

- Images: Perceptual (Images)

You should see a dramatic change in the InDesign document's appearance on screen. The PMS color is no longer a glowing neon periwinkle purple, but a dull, grayed purple. The yellows are no longer school bus orange, but a softer golden color. This is much closer to the way the final, printed piece will look.

Save your publication. If you have a desktop color proof printer available, run a test printout to compare with your on-screen view of the document. It's destined to be closer than the original, imported on-screen colors. If the printout and your monitor view vary widely, you'll have to change some of the Document Color Settings until you achieve the balance between the two. That's the whole purpose of CMS.

You may want to complete the transitioning process, because this file will be used in later projects. As you make corrections, be sure you have the go-by InDesign version of the brochure open, and select Window|Tile, to have a quick reference to the corrections you need to make. Other things that can be fixed in the imported InDesign document include the following:

- There's a lot of the dreaded Courier in the InDesign version of the brochure. Courier, you recall, signals the absence of the correct font. In this case, the correct font is available. It simply didn't make the transition well because of differences in the way the two applications handle fonts.

Every place that WaterTitMM_370 RG 504 SC or WaterTitMM_510 SB 504 SC was used in the original file is now Courier. The first thing you need to do is change each instance of Courier to Waters Titling MM. Neither the font size nor the color needs changing right now. After the correct font is assigned, you can proceed with other corrections.

- The tracking of the headline, Fine Furnishings ~ (which flows to a second line) needs to be adjusted to –45, and scaled to 85 percent for every character except the tilde.

  The tilde is tracked –25, and scaled to 95 percent.

- Although you may not realize it, there are two text frames lying on top of one another at the upper-left corner. The top text frame is small (0.75 inches by 1.4355 inches) and has the number 4 in it that doesn't show because QuarkXPress and InDesign handle font attributes differently. Lying beneath that frame is another frame that should read, 4 Easy Steps. There's an extra character, 4, typed in the frame, and that needs to be deleted to reveal the rest of the headline text, Easy Steps.

- In the text frame below the headline, 4 Easy Steps, select all the text and apply the Single-line Composer from the pop-up menu of the Paragraph palette.

- The text frame under the picture of the lamp (Rhode Island…) at the upper-right corner of the spread needs to be repositioned because InDesign doesn't have the capability to justify text from top to bottom within a frame.

- The duotone photographs of the crowd and the lamp cannot be made transparent, as they were in QuarkXPress, so the imported versions have a picture frame that is the correct color, but that color doesn't show through the placed photograph. The duotoning must be done in Photoshop, and the edited photographs reimported to the InDesign layout.

  CMYK Yellow is a Spot Color made up of:

  - Cyan 0%

  - Magenta 40%

  - Yellow 100%

- Black 0%

- Applied at 30%

The PMS Metallic 8163 is applied at 100%.

- Finally, if you want to make multiple layers, as I did, it's much easier than you might think.

  1. Click to select all the objects you want on a different layer.

  2. Look closely at the Layers palette. On the far right is a small box icon indicating that objects on the layer, Default, are selected.

  3. Use the Layers palette pop-up to make a new layer to hold the selected items, and drag the small square icon from the Default layer to the newly created layer. That's it. Every selected object is now residing on the new layer in exactly the same position it was in on the Default layer.

If you discover other things that you feel need your attention, please feel free to make those adjustments.

And now you have a handle on CMS. You'll wonder how you ever got along without it.

Moving On

In the next chapter, you'll be immersed in color and things that InDesign does with color that are new, different, or unusual. You'll have an opportunity to learn about the Swatch libraries, things over which you have control when importing color images and out of gamut colors and working with gradients.

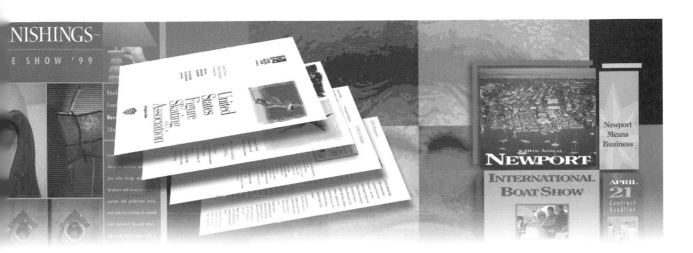

CREATING COLOR

As interesting as black-and-white and grayscale artwork can be, the world of publishing would be pretty dull without color. In this chapter, you'll see how InDesign handles colors.

Skills Covered In This Chapter

- Create and replace colors and tints
- Import colors from other publications and from graphics made in other applications
- Create and apply gradients
- Use color Libraries
- Set default colors

Foundations Of Color

At this point in your design career, you surely know that there are different color spaces, and that each has its place. RGB is great for working on screen, and for on-screen publications. CMYK works for prepress, and LAB color produces device-independent color. So those topics need no further elaboration. What may need some explaining is the way InDesign handles color.

First, if you're an Illustrator user, you'll soon discover that InDesign handles color slightly differently. You're accustomed to having process colors in Illustrator that can be either global or not, meaning that global colors are linked to the color in the Color palette. When you revise a global color swatch, every instance of that color throughout a document is revised. Illustrator's nonglobal colors are independent of the swatches, and they don't automatically update if the swatch is revised.

Well, InDesign has no nonglobal colors, but that doesn't mean there's a problem with printing imported graphics created with nonglobal colors in Illustrator. Global or nonglobal imported colors separate, so the absence of nonglobal InDesign colors is a nonissue. All swatch color revisions in InDesign are reflected in all objects to which the color you revise is applied.

Color-Related Palettes

By far the majority of your color work will be done in one of the color-related palettes. InDesign has two palettes directly related to creating color, Color and Swatches, and two that are best used after colors are created, the Gradient and Stroke palettes, though you can use these palettes before adding colors to your Swatches.

Color Palette

The Color palette pop-up menu allows you to assign a color space (LAB, CMYK, or RGB) for a new color, and the palette itself offers the means of creating the color. The Color palette is used to create "unnamed colors" for separations or on-screen documents that aren't headed for the Web. An

Note: Adobe doesn't plan to support Hexachrome in the first release of InDesign. That's something users will have to let Adobe know is a priority.

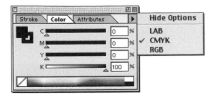

Figure 9.1

Colors can be created directly in the Color palette colors.

unnamed color is one created in the Color palette, but *not* saved in the Swatches palette (see Figure 9.1). Unnamed colors are discussed more fully in the sidebar, "Unnamed Color Pitfalls."

Look closely at the color ramp on the bottom of the palette. You see on the right, a split box for 100% of the color, and a white one above the other, to select either of these colors for the Fill or Stroke, and a None box at the left of the ramp for removing color from either the Fill or the Stroke.

Each color model offers a color ramp at the bottom of the Color palette in addition to the ability to enter numeric values or drag the sliders for colors. The color ramp lets you select a color by clicking anywhere along the length of the ramp. If you prefer the ramp-clicking method, you can also adjust the amount of black or white in the color according to whether you click near the top of the ramp or near the bottom.

A sample swatch of the color you create appears in one of two boxes at the upper-left corner of the palette, one for Fill and one for Stroke. These boxes also indicate whether the color you're creating will be applied to the Fill or the Stroke of currently selected objects. The color you create is shown as well in the Fill or Stroke box at the bottom of the Tools palette where colors remain in place and usable, even if you close the Color palette.

If you create a color in the LAB or RGB color space that is out of gamut for the document color management system you've set up, an alarm icon appears above the color ramp of the Colors Palette. To the right of the alarm is a color swatch that shows the nearest CMYK equivalent. Click on the CMYK swatch to make the required adjustments to the color values if you want the color to print correctly. (There's more about out-of-gamut colors later in this chapter and about color management in Chapter 8.)

UNNAMED COLOR PITFALLS

Because you can apply a color to objects directly from the Color palette or the Tools palette, bypassing the Swatches palette altogether, it's possible to create a problem. Consider the possibility of using the same color during different phases of developing your design, and inadvertently or intentionally changing the color space from RGB to CMYK. There is no way to be sure that every occurrence of that color in your document will change color space. You could wind up with an unwanted separation during final printing.

My suggestion is to always add newly created colors to the Swatches palette. Then you can edit the color in any way and be assured that every place you've applied that color will be edited. If you decide you don't really want the color, use the Swatches pop-up menu to delete the color.

Swatches Palette

After you've created a color in the Color palette, you know the next step. Add that color to the Swatches palette. Yes, it's possible to apply it without adding the color to the Swatches, though frankly, I can't imagine not adding colors to the Swatches palette. You never know when you might want to use it again, or revise it slightly, and that's only easy after colors are in the Swatches palette.

To add a color from the Color palette to the Swatches palette:

1. Create the color in the Color palette.

2. Use the Swatches palette's pop-up menu to select New Color Swatch (see Figure 9.2).

Figure 9.2
Creating colors from the Swatches palette automatically adds the color to the palette, and then you can apply the color, create tints, and edit the color whenever necessary.

3. In the New Color Swatch dialog box, enter a Name for the color, review, and, if necessary, revise the Color Type, Color Mode, and values for the color (see Figure 9.3).

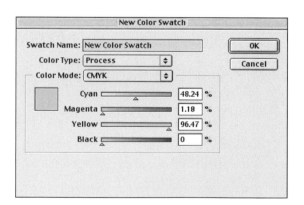

Figure 9.3
The choice of Swatch Name, Color Type, and Color Mode in the New Color Swatch dialog box can be changed at any time after the color is saved in the Swatches palette.

4. Close the New Color Swatch dialog box to add the new color to your Swatches palette (see Figure 9.4).

Figure 9.4
The color values set in the Color palette remain in place, and the new color, Green Bean, is added in the Swatches palette.

Each swatch in the palette has helpful reminder icons on the right. The pencil with a red slash indicates that the color cannot be deleted from the palette. The square made up of four triangles indicates the color is a process color. A square with three vertical stripes is an RGB color. A gray square indicates a process color, and a circle inside a square indicates a spot color. Hover the cursor over these icons to display a tip with the values that make up each color.

To add a custom color swatch to the Swatches palette without using the Color palette, perform the following steps:

1. Choose New Color Swatch from the Swatches palette pop-up menu.

2. Enter a name for your color.

3. Select the Color Type: Process or Spot.

4. Select a Color Mode: LAB, CMYK, or RGB.

5. Use the sliders at the bottom of the dialog box to set values for the color, or type in the values.

6. Check the resulting color in the swatch to the left of the sliders, and click OK if you're satisfied.

If you forget to type in a name for your color or you want to change the color type or color mode, you can double-click on the swatch to open the Swatch options dialog box and rename the color (see Figure 9.5).

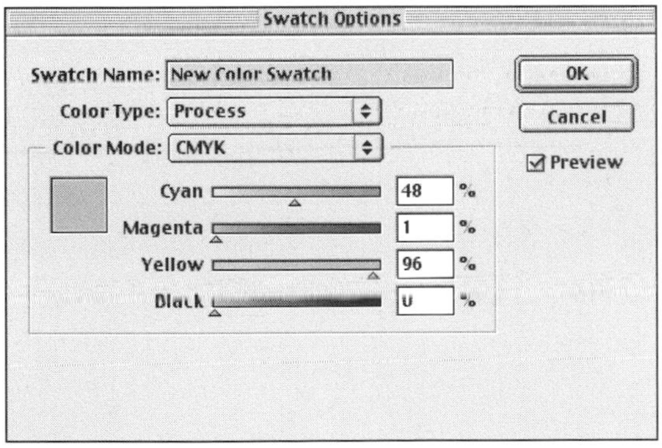

Figure 9.5
The only discernible difference between the Swatch Options dialog box and the New Color dialog box is the name in the title bar of the window.

To add a swatch to the Swatches palette after you've applied it from the Color palette, follow these steps:

1. Fill or stroke an object with a color created in the Color palette.

2. Click either the box in the Tools palette that displays the color you want in your Swatches palette, Fill or Stroke.

3. Use the pop-up menu of the Swatches palette to choose New Color Swatch, or click the New Swatch button at the bottom of the Swatches palette.

The values, color type, and mode are already entered in the New Color Swatch dialog box, and you can change them immediately, or at a later time.

Tints

Tints, in Adobe products, are various percentages of a color. The moment a color is available in the Swatches palette, and selected, the Color palette makes a shift in its appearance to allow you to make tints (see Figure 9.6).

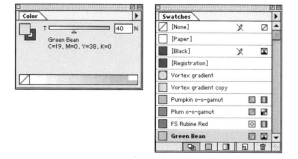

Figure 9.6

The new color, Green Bean, in the Swatches palette can now be made into any percentage tint using the Color palette.

To create a tint do the following:

1. With both the Color and Swatches palettes open, select one of the Swatches colors.

2. In the Color palette, set the percentage of ink for the tint by typing in the percentage, using the sliders, or clicking in the color ramp.

   The swatch in the Color palette shows a sample of the percentage you choose, as does one of the boxes at the bottom of the Tools palette, either Fill or Stroke.

   The same swatches caveat applies. If you use a tint, it's wise to add that tint to your swatches.

3. With the tint still displayed in the Color palette, select New Tint from the Swatches palette (see Figure 9.7).

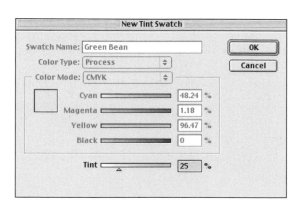

Figure 9.7

The New Tint Swatch dialog box can also be used without having the Color palette open. In that case, click on a color in the Swatches palette, and then open the New Tint Swatch dialog box from the Swatches pop-up.

The name of the new tint is the same as the original color. You might be accustomed to adding the percentage to the name of the swatch, but in InDesign there's really no need to do that, because the new swatch displays the percentage in the Swatches palette (see Figure 9.8).

"Why bother with a New Tint Swatch dialog box?" you might say. "I like doing things my own way! I'll just use the Color palette to set a percentage and apply it, or make a new color of the tint using the New Color dialog box. So there." Well, the result is sort of the same, but not exactly.

Tints created in the New Tint Swatch dialog box are linked to the original color from which the tint is made. Edit the original color, and all tints based on that color are revised throughout the publication. If you use the New Color Swatch dialog box to make the tint, there is no connection to the original color, so when you edit that original color, the tint won't change.

So there's your pivot point for decision making. Do you want the new tint to be a color unto itself? Use the New Color Swatch choice. Do you want the tint to change along with changes made to the color it's based on? Use the New Tint Swatch choice.

Delete Colors From The Swatches Palette

If you follow the recommended workflow, and save every color and tint to the swatches, or after importing a document from another application there are some swatches you know you won't use in the publication, you can reduce swatches clutter by eliminating the unused swatches.

If you know exactly the swatches you want to delete, you can remove individual swatches.

1. Select a swatch in the palette.

2. Choose Delete Swatch from the Swatches palette pop-up menu.

If you're not exactly sure what swatches are no longer in use, InDesign lends a helping hand. To remove all the swatches you haven't applied in one swoop:

1. Use the pop-up menu of the Swatches palette to choose Select All Unused.

2. With the unused colors selected, choose Delete Swatch from the pop-up.

With either method, should you, by chance, attempt to delete a color that is applied somewhere in your publication, an alarm dialog box opens, giving you options to replace the color with any other color in your swatches, or an unnamed color (see Figure 9.9).

Figure 9.8
Look to the right of a new tint name in the Swatches palette to see the exact percentage of ink for the new tint swatch.

ADDING SWATCHES AFTER THE FACT

It happens sometimes. You create and use a color or a tint, but forget to add it to the Swatches. Well, all's not lost. Select an object with the color or tint applied, and then choose New Color Swatch or New Tint Swatch from the Swatches palette menu. You'll have to reapply the color or tint to objects already filled or stroked before you added the swatch to be sure that every object filled or stroked with the color or tint is also revised should you edit the new swatch.

Note: A tint percentage set in the Color palette without being saved in the Swatches is also an unnamed color, but these *retain a link to the color the tint is based upon.*

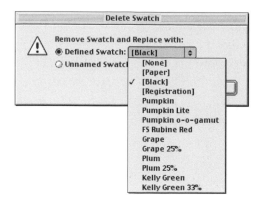

Figure 9.9

The default replacement color in the Delete Swatch alarm dialog box is Black to identify objects that previously had the deleted color applied.

Now here's another unnamed color hazard to skirt. If you replace a deleted color with an unnamed color, the objects filled or stroked with that color don't show any outward sign of change! All you've done is to delete the swatch, and undefine the color. It could add a plate to your printing. For the life of me, I can't think why you'd ever want to do that, but I can't think of everything, and you may have a very logical reason for it.

PROJECT Create And Replace Colors And Tints In Figure Skating Brochure

The file used for this project includes four pages extracted from the original 16-page brochure created for the U.S. Figure Skating Association: the front cover, back cover, and a two-page centerfold. Throughout the brochure, two colors and various tints of those colors are applied to objects and text. Your task is to create colors and tints, store them in the Swatches palette, and apply them to text and graphic elements on page 9 of the brochure. See this book's color InDesign Studio for a sample from this brochure.

Before beginning, you know the drill. Fonts used in the layout must be installed if you don't already have them in your active fonts. The Mac screen fonts are located on the CD-ROM that came with this book. Look for Bauer Bodoni, Berkley, and Futura Condensed. PC users will need to use their system fonts.

Open the project file, Skate1.indd, and, for a completed reference file, I've included Skate.indd.

I venture to say that the first thing you'll notice is that the colors of the completed file and the project file differ dramatically. That's because, for one thing, I used different colors in the project file. For another, I intentionally didn't activate CMS for the project file, but I did activate it for the reference file. This gives you a chance to compare the before and after CMS, and to practice things you read about in Chapter 8.

You'll also see that there are Pantone colors in the Swatches palette that have a pencil icon with a red slash to the right of their names. These are colors embedded in EPS graphics in the original QuarkXPress file I converted to InDesign, and then deleted pages for the project files. The swatches travel with the document, and the only way to delete or edit those colors is to first delete the EPS graphic.

Use the File menu to select Color Settings, and, if necessary, set the appropriate Application Color Settings, and then set the Document Color Settings to match your input and output devices on both the project file and the reference file.

With CMS settings in place, it's time to create colors.

1. Open the Swatches palette, and the Color palette.

    Be sure Show Options is selected in the Color palette.

    For ease of navigation, you may want the Pages, Layers, and Navigator palettes open, too.

2. To ensure that color is not unintentionally applied as you create it, choose Edit|Deselect All. This spares all sorts of aggravation and is one of the most useful work habits in InDesign.

3. Activate the project file, Skate1.indd.

4. In the Swatches palette, select New Color Swatch, and set the color as follows:

    • Swatch Name: FS Rubine Red

    • Color Type: Spot

    • Color Mode: CMYK

        • Cyan: 0

        • Magenta: 100

        • Yellow: 15

        • Black: 0

    Because nothing is selected in the publication, there's no need to Preview the color, but do look at the Colors palette.

5. Click OK to close the dialog box and add the new swatch to the Swatches palette.

At this point in developing a color, you have two options. If you want to globally replace an existing color applied with this new color, you can simply select the existing color, and delete it, instructing InDesign to replace every instance of the deleted color with the new color. Throughout the entire publication, the new color is applied.

Note: Unfortunately, if you feel it's necessary to change or remove the locked colors, there's no way programmed into InDesign to pinpoint which graphics have those colors. (I'll give you a hint: The logo on the back cover page is the culprit.) You can create a script to locate each graphic on each page based on its Fill color, the colors with the pencil/slash icon.

The other option is to locate and select individual objects and text you want to have this color, and then click the new color in the Swatches palette.

To see how global color replacement works:

1. Be sure the project file, Skate1.indd, is active.

2. In the Swatches palette, select the color I named Replace with Rubine Red.

3. Use the Swatches pop-up menu to select Delete Swatch.

4. In the Delete Swatch dialog box, be sure the Define Swatch radio button is clicked, and choose FS Rubine Red.

5. Close the Delete Swatch dialog box, and cruise through the pages of the publication to see that every place the deleted green color was applied is now FS Rubine Red. Pay special attention to the places that a lower percentage of the green was applied (in the ellipses on the right-hand page of the two-page spread). The replacement FS Rubine Red is applied at the same percentage as was the green.

If you need to apply the color to individual objects or text, they must be individually selected and the full 100 percent value of ink applied directly from the Swatches palette, or a tint value set in the Color palette after the color is applied. This works fine for limited changes in ink value, but what about situations where you need to reuse the same tint of the newly created color in a number of places? Again, you can manually apply the color and adjust the tint, but it might be more efficient to create and store a tint swatch.

Note: Do not set the tint value in the Color Palette. If you do set the percentage and then choose New Tint Swatch, InDesign assumes that the value set in the Color palette is your 100 percent color, not a percentage tint of the original color.

PROJECT Create A New Tint Swatch

Be sure nothing is selected in the publication before you create this new tint swatch; otherwise, the new tint is automatically applied to selected objects or text.

1. In the Swatches palette, click on the color, Replace with Steel.

2. Use the Swatches palette pop-up to choose New Tint Swatch.

3. In the New Tint Swatch dialog box, enter the new value in the tint ramp for Replace with Steel: 60%.

   Close the New Tint Swatch dialog box. The new tint appears in your swatches, and can be applied at will.

The new tint is based on the original color. When you delete and replace the original color globally, even defined tints of that color change, too, and you still have the tint swatch to use in additional places with but a click in the Swatches palette.

To test the veracity of my statement about tint swatches, just create some additional tints and then do a global replacement.

Follow the steps for creating a new tint swatch, and make an additional swatch for Replace with Steel at 30%. Apply the swatches to the ellipses on the right-hand page of the two-page spread as follows:

- US Championship: 100%
- Sectionals: 60%
- Regionals: 30%

Now, create the replacement color:

- Swatch name: Steel
- Color Type: Spot
- Color Mode: CMYK
  - Cyan: 100
  - Magenta: 70
  - Yellow: 0
  - Black: 0

Finally, delete the color Replace with Steel, and, what a surprise, replace it with the 100% Steel color.

Every place the deleted color was applied is now Steel, or one of the tints of Steel, and you still have the same value tint swatches of the new Steel color in your swatches to use elsewhere.

With this practice concluded, you can save the project file, and close both the reference and project file. You're all set to create colors and tints in your own publications.

Swatch Libraries

InDesign has a rather small collection of color libraries that may seem, at first blush, an oversight. There is logic to the small number, however. The swatch libraries available are those most commonly used: Pantone coated, uncoated, and process; Trumatch; Focoltone; Toyo; DIC; Web; and System libraries for both Macintosh and Windows (see Figure 9.10).

But that's not the end of your choices. The swatch libraries that come with Illustrator can be imported, and so can the color swatches in an Illustrator EPS file, and other InDesign publications. Third-party color libraries compatible with InDesign are sure to be developed. Pantone is making noises to suggest that it will expand their available libraries. So, you see, there was no need to load up the shipped version of InDesign with color libraries you may never use.

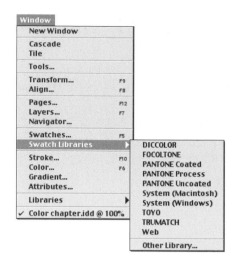

Figure 9.10
Access Swatch Libraries from the Windows menu.

Any Swatch Library you open remains open only during the current work session, but colors copied from a library to the Swatches palette are saved with the publication and are available any time you work with it. If you want to add more colors from a library during subsequent work sessions, you'll have to reopen the library.

Import Other Swatches

Because Swatch Libraries are independent files, they can be stored anywhere on your hard drive or network. You only need to navigate to locate the library you want to use.

Sometimes you need to build and reuse a custom set of colors. For instance, your company has a directive to use only certain colors to maintain its corporate identity, or a client regularly uses a specific set of colors. Making a reusable library of colors is little more than creating the color set in one document, and then importing that collection of swatches to another InDesign document.

Figure 9.11
Colors imported from other documents display the name of the source document in the title tab of a newly created Swatches Library palette.

Color swatches imported from other documents appear in their own palette, and they are accessed exactly as you'd open one of the other color libraries, from the Window menu (see Figure 9.11).

With color libraries, it's all or nothing. Individual colors can't be removed from a library. For example, glance at Figure 9.11 again. There are RGB colors that aren't used in this publication—Cyan, Magenta, and Yellow—but those swatches weren't deleted. This is another reason to remove unused colors from publications. (Deleting swatches was discussed earlier in this chapter.)

To import colors from another InDesign document:

1. Make sure you have the publication that needs colors from another document open when you start this process.

CREATE YOUR OWN DEFAULT LIBRARY OF COLORS

If you work for a company or organization that uses a specific set of colors, and those colors only, for its publications (government entities such as the Air Force Academy do this), why not create your colors in a document named "Company Colors," or some other equally identifiable name. Remember, the name of the document becomes the name of the library.

After the colors are defined, close the document. In the next publication you create, you can create a new library by importing the colors from your dummy publication, and have that library available for all future publications. If you want to, dispose of the dummy publication after the library is created. Your new library is an independent file, so you can reload it at any time.

2. Select Window|Swatch Libraries|Other Library, and locate the publication that uses the colors you want to import.

3. Click Open in the navigation dialog box. All the color swatches from the publication are copied to a new library palette of colors.

Every color, gradient, and pattern in the source document swatches is included in the newly created Swatches Library, and the name of the source publication is listed below Other Library in the list of Swatch Libraries in the Windows menu. After the library is created, it's available to all InDesign documents, whether new or already designed.

Add Illustrator Swatch Libraries

Any Swatch Libraries you've acquired to work with Illustrator 8 can be imported and used by InDesign.

1. Choose Swatch Libraries|Other Library, and locate the Illustrator Swatches Library.

2. Click Open in the navigation dialog box. Imported Illustrator swatches appear as a new palette in InDesign, just as imported document colors do.

Add Colors From Illustrator Documents

I haven't talked about drag and drop or copy and paste as a means of getting graphics from Illustrator into open InDesign layouts, but you can do that, and it's an easy way to add colors to your publication swatches.

Before you make this Illustrator-to-InDesign transfer, no matter which method you use—import, drag and drop, or copy and paste—you need to be sure that process colors used in the Illustrator graphic are global. This ensures that the colors carry the necessary information about color space, values, and name to InDesign. Pretty neat way to get more colors, too, don't you agree?

1. Open the Illustrator document along with your InDesign publication, and make sure you have a clear view of both documents.

Note: Sad but true, PageMaker swatch libraries don't import to InDesign. Could this be another hint as to why Adobe found it not only desirable but necessary to expand its desktop publishing applications with the more sophisticated code of InDesign for its suite of desktop publishing applications? You can, however, import colors used in specific PageMaker documents.

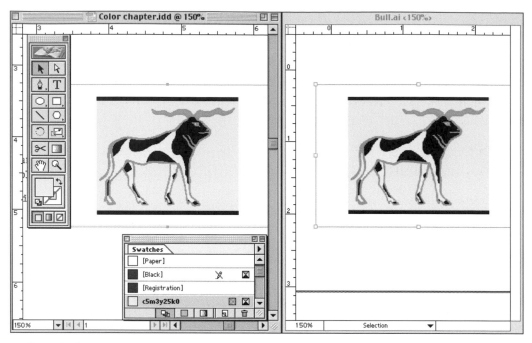

Figure 9.12

The dragged-and-dropped image of a bull, from Illustrator 8 on the right to InDesign, automatically saved the Illustrator background fill color as an InDesign swatch.

2. Drag and drop, or copy and paste what you want from the open Illustrator document to the open layout (see Figure 9.12).

Illustrator colors saved in your InDesign swatches can be used again anywhere throughout the publication. Can there be any doubt that this is a major time saver?

PROJECT Import Illustrator Colors Using Drag And Drop Or Place

If you have Illustrator 8, your Adobe workflow has begun, and here you'll see how smoothly things can go. You'll open an Illustrator document, and then drag and drop that logo document into an existing InDesign newsletter layout.

If you don't have Illustrator 8, you can still play! Simply place the Illustrator file. The resulting colors added to your InDesign Swatches palette are identical, and that's the point of this project.

As ever, fonts are required, and Mac users may need to install these before opening the InDesign Rocky Mountain Raceway newsletter. Locate and install the screen fonts City, Frutiger, and Zapf Dingbats on this book's companion CD-ROM. PC users will need to use their system fonts.

With fonts in place and available to InDesign, you can open the reference file, Raceway.indd, to see where the logo should be inserted. Everything in that file is locked into position, and the only reason for its existence is to show you the final file's appearance. As with other project files, this newsletter was designed by APEX Communications, and originally done in

QuarkXPress 3.3. I converted the file and took advantage of InDesign features that aren't included in QuarkXPress, features such as layers and the drag-and-drop feature used in the following project.

The files you work with, Raceway1.indd and PPIRLogo.ai, are on this book's companion CD-ROM. See examples from the newsletter in this book's InDesign Studio.

To drag and drop the Pikes Peak International Raceway logo into place:

1. Open Illustrator 8, and then locate and open the file, PPIRLogo.ai.

2. In InDesign, open the layout file, Raceway1.indd.

3. Arrange the Illustrator and InDesign windows to conveniently show both files on screen.

   Be sure that the first page of the newsletter is the active page and that the upper-right corner of the page is visible. That's where the logo is dropped first. Later you can drop the logo on page 3 of the newsletter, too.

   To make things easier, I applied a stroke to an empty destination frame that's your guide to positioning and resizing the dropped logo. After the logo is placed, you can remove that positioning frame.

   Although the magnification of either the Illustrator file or the InDesign layout is irrelevant, it's easier to see how dragging and dropping works if both files show the entire page in their application windows.

4. Be sure the Graphics layer is active and the only unlocked layer in the InDesign layout, and then position your cursor on the logo in Illustrator, and drag it to the newsletter.

   The logo is converted to an EPS image, and appears significantly larger in the layout because of the conversion.

5. Resize the dragged-and-dropped Illustrator image proportionately to 25%.

6. Position the logo in the upper-right frame, and take a look at the Swatches palette (see Figure 9.13).

You can now rename the imported swatches, if you like, or leave them as-is for easy identification of the imported colors. If you delete the dragged-and-dropped logo, the Illustrator colors remain in the InDesign swatches. And, as a bonus, if you don't delete the logo, you can select and edit each item in the dragged-and-dropped logo within InDesign!

Note: If you apply the imported colors elsewhere in your layout and then delete the logo, the colors remain in the layout's Swatches palette, and there is no need to replace colors used from the listed Illustrator colors.

Figure 9.13
The colors from the Illustrator file are imported to your layout and displayed in the Swatches palette with their CMYK values as the name of each imported color.

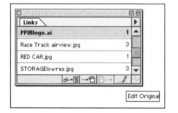

Figure 9.14
Clicking the Edit Original button in the Links palette automatically opens Illustrator and displays the original logo file, ready for editing within Illustrator.

Also take a look at the Links palette. The dragged logo is not listed, and thus is not linked, but embedded in the layout.

If you don't have Illustrator, or prefer not to drag and drop because you lose the link, simply place the Illustrator files in the usual way. (There's information about importing graphics in Chapter 7.) The logo file is located on the CD-ROM that comes with this book. The file name is PPIRlogo.ai. Again, it needs proportionate resizing to 25 percent, and the Illustrator colors *do not* appear in the layout's Swatches palette.

To edit the logo, you must use the Links palette. You can't edit the placed logo within InDesign, but highlight the name of the imported logo file in the Links palette, and click the Edit Original button at the lower-right corner of the palette (see Figure 9.14).

Add Third-Party Swatch Libraries

Surely by the time you're reading this, third-party developers will have Swatch Libraries to add to the list of Swatch Libraries that come with InDesign. Among them, I expect Pantone to be a front-runner.

The Pantone Web site has oceans of information about color and its libraries. At the time of this writing, there is no confirmation as to which among its lavish assortment of Pantone swatch libraries will be made accessible to InDesign, but you can bet there'll be plenty to choose from. Point your browser to **www.pantone.com/catalog/catalog.asp** for a look at the currently available libraries (see Figure 9.15).

Use Swatch Library Colors

Libraries of color swatches are simply holding tanks for colors. You can't apply the colors directly from the library. To use colors from an open swatch library, you must add the color to your publication's Swatches palette.

1. Choose Window|Swatch Libraries, and select the library of colors you want to use.

Figure 9.15
Each choice on this page of the Pantone Web site has a set of color-related products specific to your needs.

2. Click on a library color, and select Add To Swatches from the library's pop-up menu, or double-click the name of the color in the library palette to add it to the Swatches palette. If you want to add multiple colors, use Cmd+click (Mac) or Ctrl+click (Windows) to select those colors.

After copying a swatch from a library to the Swatches palette, you can edit the newly added swatch. Perhaps you copied an RGB color into the Swatches palette of a print document. What you really want is a color in a mode suitable to ink, not light. Simply double-click on the new color to open the Swatch Options dialog box, and change the Color Mode to CMYK (see Figure 9.16).

The LAB color mode is used primarily as an internal InDesign tool for converting colors from one color space to another, the same as in Photoshop.

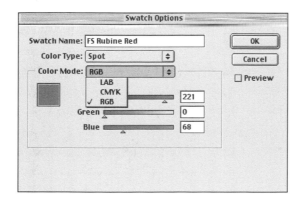

Figure 9.16
Click the Preview checkbox in the Swatch Options dialog box when you change Color Mode to see how the change will affect the color.

Remove A Swatch Library

If you no longer need to use a swatch library you've imported, you can remove it from the Swatch Libraries listings. Doing this means that the swatches will not be available to any InDesign publication, but it has no effect on colors transferred to the Swatches palette for any publication, nor to objects with these colors applied. It also has no effect on the original library. You can reload removed libraries whenever it suits your purposes.

To remove a swatch library from the list of available Swatch Libraries, you must delete a file that instructs InDesign what libraries appear in the list.

1. First, be sure the InDesign application is closed.

   If you try to dispose of the file that holds library information while the application is running, you'll be warned that the file can't be deleted because it's in use.

2. Navigate to locate the file, InDesign SavedData, on your hard drive. It's inside the Adobe InDesign folder.

3. Trash this file and empty the trash.

When you open InDesign again, the InDesign Saved Data file rebuilds itself and shows only the original default listings.

InDesign Default Colors

By default, text is black, no matter what colors are displayed in the Tools palette boxes, but filling or stroking text with some other color is no more complicated than highlighting the text and selecting a color from the Swatches palette for the Fill box and/or the Stroke box.

Figure 9.17

Look to the lower-left corner of the Fill and Stroke boxes in the Tools palette to see the Default Fill and Stroke boxes.

In the Tools palette, at the left of the Fill and Stroke boxes, are two tiny boxes that also represent Fill and Stroke. These are the default color boxes. Straight out of the box, the defaults are Black for the stroke and White for the fill (see Figure 9.17).

As you work on a publication, changing the Fill and Stroke colors, you'll no doubt come to a moment when you want to activate the default colors again. Click on the default color to change the larger Fill and Stroke boxes to the default colors.

Temporary Default Colors

Many publications call for multiple objects with the same fill and stroke color. Changing the default colors lets you create these objects in rapid succession or intermittently, and automatically apply the same fill and stroke colors by activating the default colors.

To change default colors:

1. Choose Edit|Deselect All, to ensure that nothing in the publication is selected.

2. Click on a color in the Swatches palette.

3. Drag it to the Fill or the Stroke box in the Tools palette.

Colors displayed in the Tools palette boxes become temporary default colors, and they are available with just a click on the default boxes if you need them applied to subsequent objects. If you replace your new default colors in the Fill and Stroke color boxes of the Tools palette, they're still available, stored in the tiny Stroke and Fill boxes at the lower right of the large color boxes shown in Figure 9.17. Change defaults at a time when you have nothing selected. Just repeat the process with different color swatches, and the new default is ready to use.

Paper Color

If you're a converted PageMaker user, you're already familiar with the Paper color, but QuarkXPress users have no such choice. Paper is one of the default colors available in the InDesign Swatches palette that might puzzle you. It's a sort of magic trick.

The function of the Paper swatch is to give you an accurate preview of knocked-out portions of graphics. Edit the Paper color to match the paper stock you plan to use. Things filled or stroked with the Paper color will print no color at all. The Paper color simply is a way to more accurately assess your designs as you work.

Applying And Changing Color

InDesign has two variations of color, solid color and gradient. Of course, there's the option of no color. Apply these colors to text and objects created in InDesign from the Color, Swatches, or Tools palette. Currently displayed colors in the Tools palette boxes apply automatically to newly created objects, and they remain active until you change them. As I keep repeating (because it's important), it's always best to create colors and tints in the Colors palette, and add them to your Swatches palette, even though it's possible to apply color directly from the Colors palette.

To change colors you've already applied:

1. Select the object or text you want to change.

2. Check to be sure the color box you want the new color applied to, Fill or Stroke, is selected in the Tools palette, and click a different color in the Swatches palette for the Fill or the Stroke.

Note: If, by chance, you've set the Color palette to a percentage other than 100 percent for the stroke color displayed in the Tools palette before you restore default colors, say 25 percent, the restored default Black stroke will also be set to 25 percent. You must set the Color palette percentage of ink for restored default colors.

Note: InDesign colors can't be used for editing colors in imported graphics. The only exception to this is the ability to globally apply a single color to imported TIFF graphics, such as photographs.

QuarkXPress users accustomed to creating duotones on the fly are in for a disappointment, however. Globally applied colors affect the graphic content of a frame, but, even if you apply a color to the frame holding the graphic, the frame color doesn't show through.

Figure 9.18

Stroke and Fill boxes with question marks indicate that the fill and stroke of the objects you've selected differ.

Don't overlook that helpful little curved arrow to the right of the Tools Fill and Stroke boxes. It swaps the fill and stroke colors.

If you select multiple objects that have differing fill and stroke colors assigned, the Tools palette boxes display question marks (see Figure 9.18).

The question marks disappear as soon as you click on a color in the Swatches palette or on the default color boxes, and new color is applied to all of the selected objects.

Out-Of-Gamut Colors

In Chapter 8, gamuts were discussed because out-of-gamut warnings rely on CMS, but little was said about colors you create and how to be sure the colors will print accurately. To avert the possibility of creating or choosing colors that look great on screen, but print out completely differently, InDesign has an out-of-gamut warning in the Color palette. The out-of-gamut warning appears when you create a LAB or RGB color that won't work with your output device (see Figure 9.19).

Figure 9.19

This tiny out-of-gamut icon carries a big punch, and it warns you that the LAB or RGB color you're mixing is not going to work with your output device.

The out-of-gamut alarm appears in both the Color palette and the New Color Swatch dialog box (see Figure 9.20).

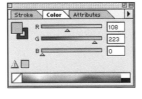
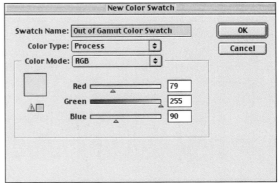

Figure 9.20

Out-of-gamut alarms show a color swatch to the right of the alarm with the nearest color that will work with your output device.

Figure 9.21

Any color set to RGB (Pumpkin) or LAB (Plum) is a candidate for being out of gamut.

If you want to use the in-gamut color, simply click on the color displayed to the right of the alarm icon. If you ignore an out-of-gamut alarm, there's no indication that the color is out of gamut in the Swatches palette. Your only tip-off might be the Color Type icon to the far right of the color name. Look closely at Figure 9.21. I intentionally named two of the colors with "o-o-gamut" appended to indicate that these both had out-of-gamut alarms before being added to the swatches.

Even publications designed for use on the Web give out-of-gamut alarms should you create a color that doesn't display correctly on any platform.

Gradients

There was a time in desktop publishing when blending more than two colors meant that you needed to create a gradient in Illustrator and import it to your document. Things have improved since those days. InDesign's gradients are every bit as powerful as Illustrator's. InDesign even lets you apply gradients to text without converting the text to outlines, so the text remains fully editable.

Gradients can consist of only process colors, only spot colors, or only named colors from the Swatches palette, or any combination of the three. A combination of color modes is always converted to CMYK at print time.

Each color in a gradient is assigned to a small square below the gradient ramp. Adobe calls these squares "stops," a term that is relevant only in the New Gradient Swatch dialog box, or in trying to explain how to create a gradient. Each stop is assigned one of the color modes or a named color from the Swatches palette.

Transition from one color to the next is controlled by a diamond above the gradient bar. By default, all gradients begin with two colors, and the transition point is directly between them at 50 percent. As you create a gradient, you determine whether the colors are laid down in a linear or a radial arrangement.

The easiest way to create a gradient is by using the Swatches palette.

1. Select New Gradient Swatch from the pop-up menu of the Swatches palette (see Figure 9.22).

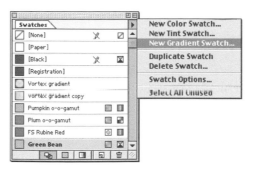

2. Enter a Swatch Name for the gradient.

3. Select the type of gradient, Linear or Radial.

4. Click on the first square to the left, below the gradient ramp, and select a Stop Color: CMYK, LAB, RGB, or Named Color.

Note: You must have CMS set up and activated to be warned of out-of-gamut colors. By default, every new publication has CMS turned off. To activate CMS for a document, select File|Color Settings| Document Color Settings, and click the Enable Color Management checkbox. Be sure you have a good sense of how CMS works, though. If you have little experience with CMS, and skipped Chapter 8, you'd better go back and read that now.

Figure 9.22
Choosing New Gradient Swatch from the Swatches palette assures that you'll be able to use a gradient repeatedly and maintain consistent color values in the gradient.

CMYK, LAB, and RGB have sliders for mixing a color, and a sample color swatch.

Named Color shows a scrolling list of all the colors in your Swatches palette. Choose a color from the list by clicking on the color you want.

This is the starting color for linear gradients (left to right), or the center color in a radial gradient.

5. Click on the stop at the right of the gradient ramp, and repeat Step 4 to set the ending or innermost color for the gradient.

   Add additional stops by clicking below the gradient ramp. Assign a color to each new stop.

6. Each new stop has a companion diamond above the ramp. Drag the diamond to set the transition point between two colors. Drag a stop to adjust the distance between transitions (see Figure 9.23).

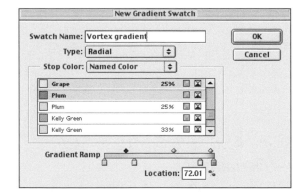

Figure 9.23
Establishing the colors, transition points, and type of gradient in the New Gradient Swatch dialog box is the first step to using the gradient stored in the Swatches palette.

Click on a stop to show a percentage figure in the Location box indicating how far along the gradient ramp that particular color is located. Click on a diamond to show another percentage figure indicating how far between stops the transition is located.

If you have Pantone swatches added to your Swatches palette, and want to use these in a gradient, you must click one of the gradient stops, and hold down the Alt or Option key as you click the color in the Swatches palette. What's more, you can apply gradients to strokes.

To remove a stop, drag it away from the gradient ramp, much as you delete a Tab stop in text. Colors and transitions in gradients can be edited as you construct the gradient or after they're stored in the Swatches palette. If you find a need for the same colors in a different configuration, select the gradient in the swatches and duplicate it using the Swatches palette pop-up, and then change the type.

Applying And Revising Gradients

Once a gradient is stored in the Swatches palette, it's ready to be applied. That's when the fun begins. Create an object or select a range of text, and apply the gradient from the swatches. Then use the Gradient tool to set the placement of the gradient in the text or object.

Where gradient colors fall is a matter of how you click and drag the Gradient tool. First, be sure the text or object is selected with either the Selection tool or the Direct Selection tool, and then switch to the Gradient tool. Drag the Gradient tool in any direction, up, down, from right to left, or left to right. Try clicking inside the selection and dragging to the outer edge, or vice versa. Click outside the bounds of your selection and drag across it to eliminate the display of one or more of the colors. You can even drag completely outside the selection. The variations are limitless, each producing its own special effect (see Figure 9.24).

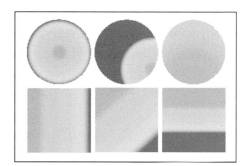

Figure 9.24
Gradients in the left shapes are located in the default position. The center and right objects' gradients are repositioned by dragging in various directions through and outside the shapes.

PROJECT Apply Colors And Gradients In The Boat Show Brochure

This project is the most simple one in this chapter. It involves adding some tint swatches to an existing set of swatches so you can create gradient swatches using the tints.

The file used is a spread from another brochure by APEX Communications, this one for the Newport, Rhode Island, International Boat Show. Fonts are not as big an issue in this project, but, if you prefer to view the file closer to the way it was designed, you may want to install or activate the fonts used: Clearface, Transport, Berkley, and Futura Condensed. These Mac screen fonts are available on the CD-ROM that comes with this book.

If you have the fonts in place, open the reference file, Boat cover.indd, located inside the Newport Boat Folder.

The first thing you might notice is that the text frames here and there throughout the spread have problems. I intentionally left these unedited to show you some of the things that don't translate perfectly when you convert a

QuarkXPress file to InDesign. You needn't be concerned with these right now, but you're welcome to tweak and adjust as necessary at a later time. Use the color InDesign Studio figure as your go-by for text placement.

I confess to having taken liberties with the original design of the brochure for this project. The final printed version has only solid color blocks, but gradients are certainly an option you might have employed.

Rather than drown you in verbiage, I'll see how well you do with just the essential specs. If you have a problem anywhere along the line, refer to earlier sections of this chapter. Every step of this project has been discussed in detail.

1. As your work file, open Boat1.indd. It is also located inside the Newport Boat Folder on this book's companion CD-ROM. You'll want to have the Layers, Swatches, and Color palettes open.

   When you have the work file open, you see that all of the layers are hidden and locked except the Bkgr Color Blocks layer. As you create and apply colors, you can show the other layers, but for now, leave them hidden.

2. Click on the various gray color blocks. One has Newport Warm Grey applied at 30%, but there's no tint swatch for that value, therefore you can't use 30% Newport Warm Grey in a gradient.

3. Click in the 30% Newport Warm Grey frame, and create a tint swatch.

4. Deselect All, and then select New Gradient Swatch from the Swatches pop-up.

5. In the New gradient Swatch dialog box, set the Swatch Name to Grey Gradient.

   Click the left stop and choose the following settings:

   - Type: Linear
   - Stop Color: Named Color
   - Newport Warm Grey

   Click the right stop and make these settings:

   - Stop Color: Named Color
   - Newport Warm Grey 30%

   Then close the New Gradient dialog box.

6. Use the Selection tool or the Direct Selection tool to click in the frame above the frame filled with Newport Warm Grey 30%.

7. Click the new gradient swatch, and use the Gradient tool to drag from the top edge of the frame to the bottom edge.

8. Deselect All and choose View|Hide Frame Edges to see how the gradient blends into the same color as the frame below it.

   Chances are very good that the gradient is banded on screen. This is not uncommon, but typically produces a smooth transition in the final printout.

Click the eye icon of all the layers in the Layers palette except the Guides from QuarkXPress layer to see the overall effect of the applied gradients in the layout. Continue creating and applying as many additional gradients as you feel you might want to use. You can always choose Select All Unused from the Swatches palette pop-up, and delete the selected swatches.

When you've had enough fun, and taken enough liberties with the layout design, save your work file, and print it, or close it. Remember, the file and all images in it are copyright protected.

Moving On

In the following chapter, you'll have an opportunity to learn how InDesign uses PDFs as a method of exporting publications. Additional export options, HTML, EPS, and PrePress, are also discussed. The key is InDesign's ability to adjust existing layouts, and you'll learn more about that, too.

10 REPURPOSE YOUR PUBLICATIONS

Make one publication serve several purposes by adjusting the layout or exporting it in a variety of formats or types.

Skills Covered In This Chapter

- Use Layout Adjustments to resize and repurpose publications

- Convert an InDesign publication to a PDF

- Export publications as EPS files

- Export publications as Prepress files

- Create Web pages from an existing publication

Layout Adjustment

Who knows what may prompt you to make such dramatic changes in a layout as the size of the page, the way it's oriented, or the margin and column widths, but it happens sometimes. Rather than tweak and fiddle for hours revising and repositioning what's already designed, let InDesign's clever feature, Layout Adjustment, give you a hand. You'll still need to tweak, but the time spent doing that is drastically reduced.

Layout Adjustments are like a "Mother, may I?" game. First you must tell InDesign what adjustments are permissible, and give the layout permission to adjust. That's done in the Layout Adjustment dialog box (see Figure 10.1).

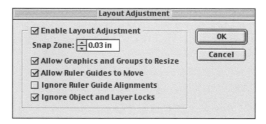

Figure 10.1

The Layout Adjustment dialog box sets the permissions that let you change the paper size, page orientation, margin, or column settings.

InDesign uses your Layout Adjustment settings to *approximate* the proportions you originally designed. Ruler guides, margins, and column guides may all be affected. For instance, InDesign adds or removes column guides to the right of existing columns if you change the number of columns on a page, and repositions frames if you change orientation.

After you decide what you want to happen and set up the layout adjustments, you then (if you want to adjust your layout) make adjustments using the Document Setup. It's not required that you make the adjustments, but you're ready to when you want to.

To open the Layout Adjustment dialog box, choose Layout|Layout Adjustment. Enable Layout Adjustments by clicking the checkbox, and then select what you want InDesign to control when you decide to repurpose or dramatically revise the layout.

THE IMPORTANCE OF GUIDES TO LAYOUT ADJUSTMENT

If you plan your layouts using guides to position every element on the page, you might want to remove some of the guides before doing a layout adjustment. One of the ways Layout Adjustment determines new positions and new sizes for objects is by scaling the margins and guide positions, and maintaining object alignment to the margins and guides. An adjusted layout will be more successful and give you less to correct if you assess and position guides wisely in the original layout.

Before starting an adjustment, with a keen eye to where your existing guides are set, look through the page or pages you plan to revise. Are guides running very close to objects other than the object originally aligned to the guides? Are any objects positioned without guides? The answers to these questions help you make the best choice in the Layout Adjustment dialog box to produce the best possible adjustments.

- *Snap Zone*—Set this measurement to tell InDesign how close to a guide, margin, or page perimeter an object must be in the adjusted layout before snapping to the guide, margin, or page perimeter. This requires a bit of thought if you haven't used guides consistently, or if guides proliferate in designing your publication. A setting that's too great will not keep the essence of your page intact, pulling objects into alignment with guides or margins intended for positioning different objects on the page. A setting that's too small may mean that objects you do want to snap to guides don't.

- *Allow Graphics And Groups To Resize*—This allows objects and groups to both scale and move during layout adjustment. If you don't choose this option, objects and groups simply move during the adjustment process. No scaling occurs.

- *Allow Ruler Guides To Move*—Unselected, this option leaves all ruler guides exactly where you placed them in the original layout. Occasionally, that is just what you want, if, say, you are happy with object placement, but want a bigger paper or page size. At other times, you should select this option to ensure that the relationship of objects is maintained.

- *Ignore Ruler Guide Alignments*—If, in your opinion, ruler guides aren't well placed to make the transition, select this choice. All the objects will still reposition in relationship to new page, margin, and column sizes, but they won't snap to any existing guides.

- *Ignore Object And Layer Locks*—This overrides any locking of objects or layers that are currently applied when you make a layout adjustment. Otherwise, locked objects and layers remain unchanged.

Note: Page columns and columns set in text frames behave differently during layout adjustment. Frame columns can resize proportionately only if you have not set Fixed Column Width in the Text Frame Options dialog box.

If you've done the projects in Chapter 9, you already have the correct fonts installed for working with the Skate brochure, but just in case, you'll need

Bauer Bodoni, Berkley, and Futura Condensed. PC users will need to continue using their system fonts.

PROJECT Resize Skate Brochure Cover To Be A Postcard

The original layout of the United States Figure Skating Association brochure was 4 inches wide by 9 inches tall (see Figure 10.2). Repurposing the cover to make a postcard could be quite a task without layout adjustments. To see the full-color version, flip to this book's color InDesign Studio.

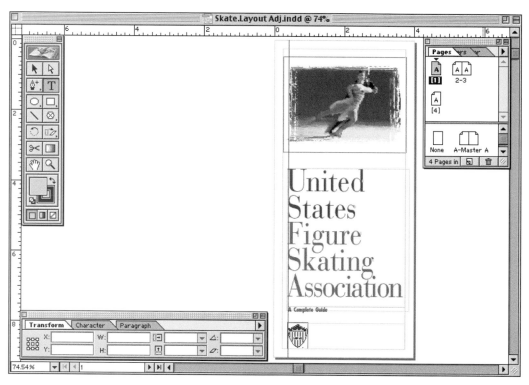

Figure 10.2
This is the Skate brochure publication cover that you'll turn into a postcard in this project.

Note: Unlike Export, which creates another file leaving the original intact, Layout Adjustment *overwrites* an existing file. With this in mind, you need to decide before starting to adjust a layout whether you want to save a copy of the current layout or overwrite it.

1. Open either the Windows or Macintosh version of the Skate.LayoutAdj.indd project file from the CD that comes with this book.

2. When the brochure is open, choose View|Fit Page In Window.

3. Look over each page to refresh your memory of how the publication is laid out, and then choose File|Save As, and name it Skate.Postcard.indd.

   Now you have two copies to compare the before and after adjustments.

4. Select Layout|Layout Adjustment, and click these instructions:

   • Enable Layout Adjustment: Selected

   • Snap Zone: 0.03 inches

- Allow Graphics And Groups To Resize: Selected

- Allow Ruler Guides To Move: Selected

- Ignore Ruler Guide Alignment: Deselected

- Ignore Object And Layer Locks: Selected

Then, click OK to close the Layout Adjustment dialog box.

5. Select File|Document Setup and change the settings to:

- Number Of Pages: 1

- Facing Pages: Deselected

- Page Size: Custom

- Width: 6 inches

- Height: 4.25 inches

- Orientation: Landscape

6. Click OK, and an Alert appears (see Figure 10.3).

Figure 10.3
This Alert opens immediately after you click OK in the Document Setup dialog box, so you can back out if you change your mind.

7. Click Yes in the Alert dialog box and wait a moment for InDesign to calculate the new scale and position of objects and text.

When all the adjustments are calculated, the postcard should look like Figure 10.4.

8. Save the postcard file, and make any further revisions that suit you, such as changing the color of text or nudging the photograph into a better position.

This layout adjustment works as a postcard, and saved hours of work that would otherwise be required to re-create the file in a different configuration. The text needs a different color applied to some of the words to improve legibility, but the relationship of text frames and graphic components is generally pleasing and retains its visual identity with the brochure and the USFSA.

If you have some time, continue to play with layout adjustment. Be sure to use copies of the Skate.LayoutAdj.indd file, and try different page sizes and orientation. Try adjusting all of the pages in the brochure file.

My experience with this feature tells me it's like the little girl who had a little curl right in the middle of her forehead. When it's good, it's very, very

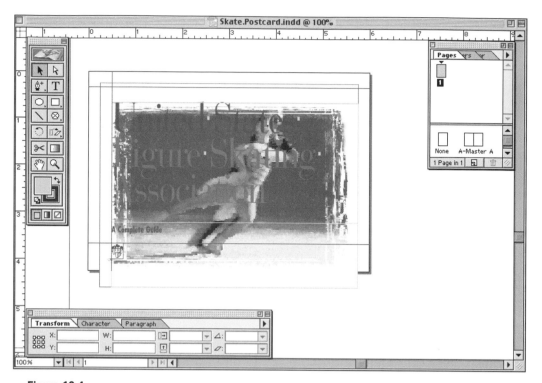

Figure 10.4

Clearly, the postcard is quite different from the original brochure cover.

good, but when it is bad, it is horrid. Only experimentation will tell you which result you'll achieve. Some adjustments will prove to be far less than successful, and others, like the postcard, will be perfectly acceptable and save time.

Export InDesign Publications

An odd sort of sequence occurs when you choose File|Export. Two successive dialog boxes must be dealt with, no matter what format or type you're exporting to. The first Export dialog box merely designates the format or type, and where the final export file is to be saved. At the lower right of the Export dialog box you select the format (Mac) or type (Windows) you want exported: Adobe PDF, EPS, HTML, or Prepress File (see Figure 10.5).

Look closely at the lower-right corner of the Export dialog box, and you'll see a Save button. Unlike other Save buttons, this one doesn't launch you into an automatic save of the export file; rather, it opens another dialog box with options appropriate to the format or type you choose in the Export dialog box.

The second dialog box has options specific to the format or type you select in the first dialog box. (I'll get into those options in the second dialog box shortly.) No matter which set of options you're viewing, the second dialog box always has a Cancel button, so, if you accidentally choose the wrong export format or type, you can bail out and start over.

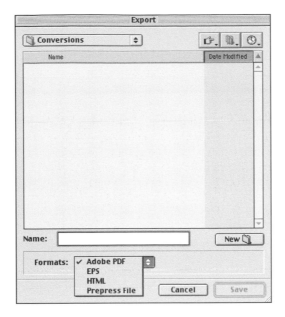

Figure 10.5
The pop-up menu in the Export dialog box lets you select the format or type for the exported publication.

PDF Ballyhoo

Now, I'm not here to write a PDF book or to explain all the ins and outs of Adobe Acrobat. (AGFA already has a PDF book that's nearly 200 pages long, and they hand it out at trade shows. If you're interested, go to the AGFA Web site and see if you can get a copy.) My job is to show you how PDF can make your InDesign publications more usable.

There's no denying that Portable Document Format (PDF) is today's strongest contender for Distribution Method Of Choice. Nearly everywhere on the Web you'll find PDFs for downloading or reading online. Print providers have embraced the format because of its overall reliability, its cross-platform consistency, and because it removes the necessity of having every version of every design program they're likely to print from. Designers revel in the knowledge that the integrity of their designs is maintained in PDFs, and that PDFs can be delivered just about everywhere, in print and on screen, to clients or service bureaus and print providers, with no further ado. With the proper plug-ins, PDFs can even be separated, have high-end trapping applied, and be rearranged using imposition software. Add to that the fact that InDesign PDFs can be printed on non-PostScript printers, and you have quite a revolutionary production tool.

The Nature Of PDFs

Some things are less than perfect. You may be frustrated by trying to print separation plates from a PDF. It helps immensely if you understand why PDFs print perfectly from InDesign when you choose a composite printout, but don't do well at all (without lots of intervention) when you choose separations. It's the very nature of PDFs to be composites, that is, a PDF is really a single graphic visualization of your file. To create separations from a composite file requires a plug-in or special software. (There's more about printing composites and separations in Chapter 11.)

Plug-ins are Adobe's panacea, and they're sure to produce more within a short time of the release of version 1 of InDesign—possibly even one to make separations from PDFs. At present, your best option for separating your own PDF is to use Distiller after the PDF is exported.

Export PDFs Directly From InDesign

Many print providers are ready and eager to receive PDF files for output. For one thing, PDFs are "platform-neutral," that is, any PC or Macintosh can read a PDF using Acrobat Reader. Keep in mind that InDesign's PDFs are saved in the same format as PDFs created by Acrobat 4, so you need Acrobat Reader 4 to view these files.

InDesign's PDF export produces a file that works with a variety of RIPs, as opposed to using Distiller, which requires a PostScript Printer Description (PPD) to describe a specific printer. That's another reason InDesign's PDFs are useful. Service bureaus have hundreds, maybe thousands of RIPs, and choosing just the right one could be a hassle.

Sending a PDF to a service bureau or print house doesn't mean you should bypass Preflight checks. A solid Preflight can save money, but more important, it helps ensure the fidelity of your final output. (For more information about Preflight, please refer to Chapter 11.)

PDFs have some similarities to EPS versions of your publications in that both become graphic representations of your pages. In multiple-page PDF publications, each page is saved as an independent graphic, which makes adding, moving, or inserting pages a simple matter.

As a starter, it's best to know what can't be done with PDFs in InDesign. InDesign publication files can't include these PDF features:

- Annotations
- Movies
- Sound
- Hyperlinks
- Form fields
- Bookmarks
- Thumbnails

These elements can be added after converting a publication. You then use Adobe Acrobat or third-party plug-ins (the ubiquitous plug-in solution) to add special elements.

InDesign PDFs offer these distinct advantages:

- *No learning curve*—Because you convert publications directly from within InDesign, it's not necessary to know how Acrobat works. If you can point and click, you can convert a publication to PDF.

- *Proof publications*—Because PDFs print to almost any desktop or network printer—inkjet, PostScript, color, or black and white—without requiring the native application, proofing in PDF format is ideal. PDFs travel well over the Internet. Email your clients proofs as either on-screen soft proofs or something they can print out at their end.

- *Print on demand*—Upload to a service provider who then can make basic edits in the PDF, and, using Adobe Acrobat, special software, or plug-ins, do the imposition, set trapping values, and create color separations. Here's another point. Whether your publication is long or short, you can print exactly as many copies as you have call for—from any available printer. This saves trees, time, and the stress of ordering extra professionally printed copies "just in case."

Export Options

All options you set for exports, including PDF export options, are application preferences, so, when you set or change options, these same options apply to all successive publications you export until you change the options again. Whether you leave the default PDF option in place or revise them to better suit specific publications, you need to know all the conversion options, and there are many. After you've read about the various decisions you must make, you'll have a chance to convert an InDesign publication to a PDF.

Know Your PDF Export Options

The Export PDF dialog box opens immediately after you close the File|Export dialog box. In the Export PDF dialog box, you identify Adobe PDF as the format or type, rename the exported file if you want to, specify where you want the exported file stored, and click Save (see Figure 10.6). Whatever PDF export options you set in this dialog box apply to all subsequent PDF exports. You can leave the default options in place, establish a preferred set of options, or change options with each PDF export.

> **Note:** Many of the options for PDFs are the same options available for other exports, so pay particular attention to these as you read through this section.

- *Subset Fonts Below*—This option is set in a threshold expressed as a percentage. The number you enter for Subset Fonts Below is the percentage of an entire set of font characters at which InDesign changes from embedding only the characters used to embedding the entire set. The percentage determines at what point InDesign is to include all the characters in a font, or only those characters used in your publication.

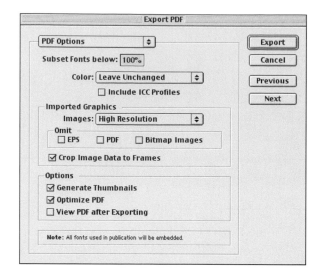

Figure 10.6
The Export PDF dialog box.

For instance, if you're exporting a newsletter, much of the content is likely to be set in a single font, therefore the number of characters used in the publication will surely exceed any percentage lower than 100 that you set here. At 100 percent, the entire character set for all fonts is embedded. Things like headlines, tables, or other text may use less than an entire character set. If you set the percentage at, say, 50 percent, the moment InDesign detects that half the characters from a font are used in the publication, the entire font is embedded.

As shipped, the default is 100 percent. You can lower that percentage and create a smaller file. The more font information embedded in your PDF, the larger the file.

- *Color*—This option determines the color mode in which all the colors—throughout your publication—are saved in the PDF version. PDFs don't usually take kindly to a mixture of, say RGB and CMYK, though you have the option to use multiple color types. Consider the destination of your PDF: on screen, composite, or separations. That's the most important concern in setting color options.

  - *Leave Unchanged*—This option is more frequently chosen for other formats of export than PDFs. If you have a reason to want a mixture of color spaces in your publication, choose this option. Colors throughout the publication remain in the color space you designated as you created, applied, and imported them.

  - *RGB*—Best selected for on-screen pieces, or transparencies. All colors in your publication are converted to RGB values in the PDF export. Know your destination before making this choice.

> **Note:** If you're planning to use a third-party plug-in to separate your PDFs, avoid using device-independent color, such as LAB or RGB. There are reports that these cause all pages to print on the black plate. Adobe is aware of this anomaly and may fix the situation before release, but chances are not until the next InDesign iteration.

- *CMYK*—This is the choice for printing separations. The resulting CMYK values may vary, however. If you enabled color management for the publication, you get calibrated color output. If you don't enable color management, all CMYK colors (not spot colors) use the InDesign RGB-to-CMYK conversion tables, and you get uncalibrated color.

- *Include ICC Profiles*—To use this option, you must have color management enabled for the publication. The profiles are used to translate color spaces—if the output device relies on this information. If it doesn't, nothing is lost by including the profiles.

> **Note:** Placing a PDF in a publication is exactly like placing any other graphic. Colors in PDFs you've placed in your publication remain unaffected by these color conversion options. That tidbit of information should run up a big red flag. Before importing a PDF, be sure you know the color space it uses. Otherwise you may find yourself returning to the original application that created the PDF to revise its colors to be compatible with the export format you choose. Also, before making any of these color choices, it's always best to consult your print provider.

Under Imported Graphics in the Export PDF dialog box, you face several choices that can profoundly affect your PDF and other exports.

- *Images*—These two options are so simple you might make a choice that doesn't suit your purposes because you're accustomed to a different way of working in publications during the design phase. Be sure to read the sidebar "PDF Planning." It relates directly to images and PDFs.

  - *High Resolution*—Use this option for exports you plan to print on high-resolution printers (1,220 dpi or higher or professional quality output devices).

  - *Low Resolution*—This option is suitable for PDFs that are going to low-resolution printers (300 to 600 dpi desktop printers), to be viewed only on screen, and for all HTML exports because they're always viewed on screen. The low-resolution image is 72 dpi. You can, however, combine the low-resolution option with Perform OPI Replacement for EPS or Prepress exports. (HTML, EPS, and Prepress exports are discussed very soon in this chapter, so keep this information in mind.)

PDF PLANNING

Knowing from the start of the design phase that you will save a PDF version of your publication gives you some other things to consider, such as the information included in graphic files placed in your publication. Photoshop files saved with DCS information (version 1 or 2) are good examples of PDF hitches you might encounter.

Using Acrobat, open a publication with a graphic that includes DCS information that was then saved in Adobe PDF format. All you see is the low-resolution preview of that image in the PDF. The high-resolution image is lost. That's because DCS is a color separation feature, and PDFs are composite files, so saving that information in a PDF with the hope of then creating separations of the PDF requires some twisting and turning.

First you must print separations of the InDesign publication before converting it, save the publication as a PostScript file, and then process it through Distiller to create separations of the PDF version of graphics saved with DCS information. Phew. It's far easier in that case to use a composite EPS or TIFF file in the first place.

- *Omit EPS, PDF, Bitmap Images*—Again, these choices are deceptively simple but can produce some surprising results. Your options eliminate the graphic proxy within your exported file, and they leave only the Open Press Interface (OPI) link information. The omitted proxy shows on screen as a gray box with an X in it, and, if your print provider doesn't have access to the high-resolution image the OPI links to, that's what you see in the printout as well.

- *Crop Image Data To Frames*—Activate this checkbox to convert only the portion of a graphic that is actually visible inside a frame. InDesign eliminates sending image information hidden outside the frame. This reduces file size, a huge concern if you expect folks to download your PDFs.

  If your graphic bleeds off the page, this is not a good option. The final output requires that extra information to create enough of the image to produce a suitable bleed. The extra information may also be needed if there's any chance the image needs to be repositioned after conversion to PDF.

- *Options*—Choices here determine what you see and what you get.

  - *Generate Thumbnails*—This creates a thumbnail image of each page. If you have chosen Reader's Spreads in the Pages And Page Marks panel of this dialog box, you get a thumbnail of each spread. (The Pages And Page Marks panel of the Export dialog box is discussed soon in this chapter.)

  - *Optimize PDF*—This reduces file size in a very clever way. If you understand how Web pages can display many instances of the same image, you'll get this immediately. On the Web, one image can be displayed many times on many pages of a site. But Optimize PDF handles more than just images. It locates and removes repeated instances of background text and images, and puts a "pointer" in their place. That pointer refers to the first instance for all successive repetitions. PDFs to be viewed over the Web or a network profit greatly from the reduced file size. Simply put, it takes less time to load the PDF on screen.

  - *View PDF After Exporting*—This immediately opens your converted PDF in the viewer you choose if the viewer is installed on your computer. Typically, that is Acrobat, and version 4 is the most accurate viewer for Adobe PDFs, although version 3 will display the file.

If you thought you were done with Export PDF options, think again. There are three more panels in this dialog box: Compression, Pages And Page Marks, and Security. Use the Previous or Next button to move to another panel. Or you can select the one you want from the pop-up menu at the top of the Export PDF dialog box (see Figure 10.7).

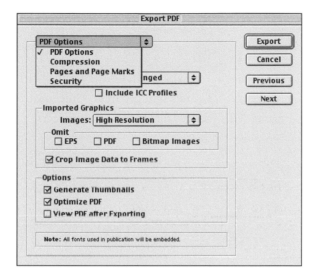

Figure 10.7
Select a different set of options using the pop-up menu of panel names in the Export PDF dialog box.

Compression

Sending any file over the Internet can be a time-consuming affair, but InDesign has features to reduce the time. One of those is the Compression panel of the PDF Export dialog box (see Figure 10.8). All the choices in this panel relate to ways of downsizing images and text. In the process, the PDF loses little or none of its clarity and details. Each section of the Compression panel in the Export PDF dialog box has a pop-up menu with the same

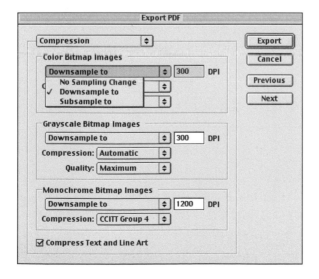

Figure 10.8
The Compression panel in the Export PDF dialog box.

choices for setting dpi. The top two sections have the same Compression and Quality choices in pop-up menus, and the bottom section has a unique set of choices in the Compression pop-up menu.

Downsampling and subsampling are means of reducing the amount of image data sent to a print device. To save printing time, reduce (never increase!) the dpi (dots per inch) to equal only what your output device can reproduce. The resampling process is accomplished by assessing the height and width of a bitmap image, and then determining the ratio of pixels in the image to the number of halftone dots the printer can produce.

- *Downsampling*—Replaces a sample area of the image with a color that is the average of all the colors in that area.

- *Subsampling*—Replaces the sample based on the color of the pixel dead center in the sample. Obviously, downsampling produces smoother transitions between colors, but it takes a bit longer to print. Because subsampling creates more abrupt color transitions, you don't want to use it for high-resolution printing. In on-screen PDFs, you might want to use this for graphics that have broad swaths of color.

So now that you've got that straight, how do you decide what dpi to use? The rule of thumb is 1.5 to 2 times the final output device's screen frequency. (Your print provider or printer documentation can help you with this.) InDesign ignores either resampling instruction if the original image is already less than 1.5 times the dpi value you specify.

If you leave the default Compression setting at Automatic, InDesign uses ZIP compression for text and line art. Color and grayscale bitmap images are compressed using ZIP or JPEG, and monochrome images are compressed with ZIP, CCITT (International Coordinating Committee for Telephony and Telegraphy) Group 3 or 4, or using Run Length compression. Each of these methods of compressions has its place. The lossless compressions lose no data, and lossy compression does lose some data. That's not always a bad thing.

- *ZIP*—A lossless compression good for large areas of flat color, black-and-white line drawings, and screen shots.

- *JPEG*—A lossy compression good for continuous tone images.

- *CCITT*—A lossless compression good for black-and-white drawings and 1-bit scans, such as faxes (Group 3) or most monochrome images (Group 4).

- *Run Length*—A lossless compression appropriate for images with large areas of solid black or white.

The Quality level determines how much data is preserved in lossy compressions. The default Quality setting is Maximum, but you can further reduce file size by lowering that to High, Medium, Low, or Minimum. In my experience with compressed graphics, I've often found that a quality level lower than maximum is perfectly acceptable. It takes some experimenting to determine which images suffer degradation at a lower level, however. You'll know as soon as you see a proof print or an on-screen image that is fuzzy or has noticeably fewer colors and more abrupt transitions between colors than the original.

The Compress Text And Line Art checkbox, when selected, applies ZIP compression to all text and line art in the PDF. Again, you reduce file size in this way, but without loss of any data used to print or display the text and line art.

Pages And Page Marks

In the Pages And Page Marks panel of the Export dialog box, you determine what pages of the original publication are exported, and what page marks to apply to the exported file. In addition, you see the checkbox for Reader's Spreads mentioned earlier when I talked about creating Thumbnails (see Figure 10.9). Options selected in the Pages And Page Marks panel of the Export PDF dialog box affect more than just the specific pages that are exported. They affect what's applied to those pages, as well.

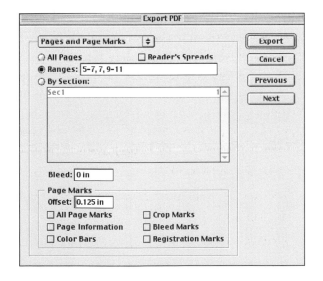

Figure 10.9
The Pages And Page Marks panel of the Export PDF dialog box.

- *Reader's Spreads*—Activating Reader's Spreads tells InDesign to export spreads as a single graphic to be printed on a single sheet of paper.

- *All Pages*—The default in this panel is to export All Pages, but you can export a range of pages if you prefer.

- *Ranges*—A Range can be consecutive pages, such as 5–7; or individual pages separated by commas, such as 5, 7; or a combination of each, such as 5, 7, 9–11. If you've defined sections in your publication, you can also export just the sections you select from the list under By Section.

- *Bleed*—The bleed is stated in inches or fractions of inches, and it tells InDesign how far beyond the perimeter of the publication page your bleeds extend. You need this measurement to correctly position page marks you want printed so as to avoid printing the page marks on top of your bleeds.

- *Page Marks, Offset*—Set the distance from the edge of the page (not how far from the bleeds) that page marks should be placed. Then choose the page marks you want included in your exported file.

Security

You'll recall that I said the Export options are application preferences. Well, I should have said that all but Security settings are saved with the application. If you want a secure PDF, you must click the Use Security Features checkbox in the Security panel (see Figure 10.10), and set a password that can have up to 32 characters, total, no spaces. You only have to set a password if you want to control access to the file. The other security features can be set whether or not you use a password.

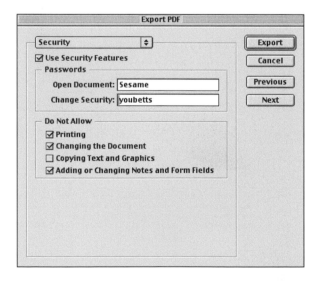

Figure 10.10

Set these Security options on a document-by-document basis.

Why are there two passwords? Because one is used to open the document, and the Change Security password is for gaining access to the security settings in order to change or remove them.

With or without passwords in place and Use Security Features activated, you can pick and choose among the features. Each is self-explanatory. Activate only those things you *don't* want others to do.

Now that you have an overview of the way InDesign's PDF export conversions work, how about trying it yourself? The next project is to convert the Pikes Peak International Raceway newsletter to a PDF for distribution from a Web site. The file used in this project is a shortened version of the newsletter. The original QuarkXPress file that I converted for this book has a total of eight pages. Rather than convert the newsletter to a series of Web pages, a downloadable PDF that can be viewed either online or downloaded for reading offline is more considerate of your viewers' time, and often more efficient than scrolling through pages on screen.

The files that you need for this project are on the CD-ROM that comes with this book. You don't need to copy the InDesign publication to your hard drive unless you feel you can work faster by doing so. To open the newsletter file for conversion, open either the Windows or Macintosh version of the Race.Convert.indd project file.

Note: The Open Document and Change Security passwords should be different to avoid the possibility of someone with viewing access to the document making unwanted changes in your security settings. As with all passwords, make a note of the ones you enter in the Security panel, and store the note in a safe place where only you can refer to it. You'll need the Open Document to view your PDF, and your Change Security password if you decide to change the Security settings.

PROJECT Convert Raceway Newsletter To Online PDF

In working with this publication (see Figure 10.11), it became evident that viewing it on screen was something that some subscribers would prefer. Converting it to PDF was a good solution.

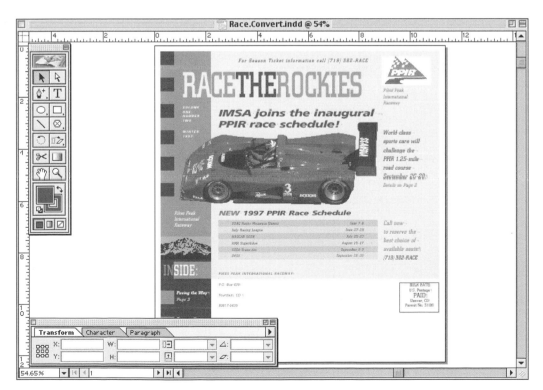

Figure 10.11
The original publication cover.

With the Race.Convert.indd publication file open, follow these steps.

1. Choose File|Export.

2. In the Export dialog box, select a place to store your exported PDF, then make these settings:

   - Name: Race.pdf

   - Format or Type: Adobe PDF

3. Click the Save button in the Export dialog box.

4. In the Export PDF dialog box that opens, select the following:

   PDF Options

   - Subset Below: 100%

   - Color: RGB

   - Include ICC Profiles: Deselected

   - Imported Graphics

   - Images: Low Resolution

   Omit: Deselect all

   Options

   - Generate Thumbnails: Deselected

   - Optimize PDF: Select

   - View PDF After Exporting: Select

5. Use the pop-up menu at the top of the Export PDF dialog box to select Compression.

6. In the Compression panel, set:

   Color Bitmap Images

   - Downsample: 100 DPI

   - Compression: Automatic

   - Quality: High

   Grayscale Bitmap Images

   - Downsample: 100 DPI

   - Compression: Automatic

   - Quality: High

Monochrome Bitmap Images

- Downsample: 100 DPI

- Compression: CCIT Group 4

Compress Text And Line Art: Selected

7. Use the pop-up menu to select the Pages And Page Marks panel, and check to be sure All Pages is selected. Nothing else needs to be set in this panel.

8. Use the pop-up menu to select the Security panel, and make these settings:

Use Security Features: Selected

Passwords

- Open Document: Leave blank

- Change Security: Enter your personal password for access to change these settings

Do Not Allow

- Printing: Selected

 The original InDesign file is set up for a paper size of 11.375 inches by 12.25 inches. This works well on rolls of newsprint paper, but it doesn't work well for sheets of paper used by desktop printers.

- Changing The Document: Selected

- Copying Text And Graphics: Deselected

- Adding Or Changing Notes And Form Fields: Selected

9. Click the Export button, sit back, and let InDesign do its stuff. It takes a moment.

When the conversion is complete, the new PDF should open in Acrobat Reader (see Figure 10.12). The original InDesign newsletter file is a little over 1MB. The total file size of the PDF conversion hits around the 250K mark. (Grayed-out text is due to the magnification size, not loss of text.)

If you want to practice more, feel free to convert the newsletter (or any other of the project files) to PDFs for different destinations, such as sending to a service bureau for printing, or to a print provider for separation. Refer to the earlier options discussion for the appropriate choices.

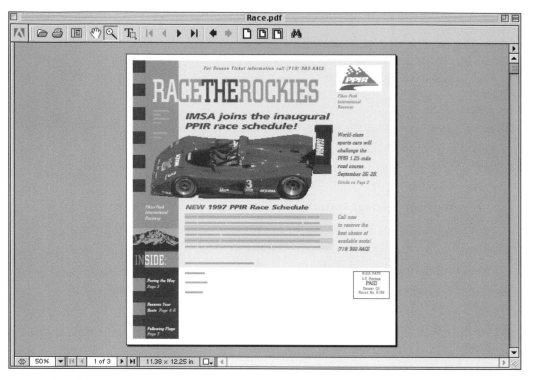

Figure 10.12

The converted InDesign newsletter opens in Acrobat Reader.

EPS Export Options

InDesign's EPS export feature is specifically made for taking to a prepress application such as Presswise or Trapwise. As you no doubt know from experience, an EPS file is a sure way to keep your design intact. Nobody can monkey around with an EPS file (unless they're so committed to freedom-of-revision that they invested in additional software). It's cast in stone. This can be a good thing, if you're absolutely certain that everything in your publication is exactly as you want it.

Before exporting an EPS version of your InDesign publication, you need to have some specific information in hand about the printer that will reproduce your EPS. For instance:

- Does your target output device require ASCII or Binary data?

- Is the output going to a Level 1, 2, or 3 PostScript printer? (There is an option to save the EPS in a format compatible with all three.)

- What kinds of fonts have you used (PostScript or TrueType), and what kinds of fonts does the output device recognize? This helps you decide which choice to make when it comes to embedding fonts. If you've used TrueType fonts, will the output device recognize their newly applied PostScript names? If you embed subsets, you get a smaller file because only the characters used are included in the EPS. Embedding a complete character set for fonts includes all characters from every font used. If you embed none, the InDesign EPS file includes only a link to the fonts you've used, and so all the fonts must be downloaded to the print device. That slows things down a lot, but the file size is smaller.

- It isn't a good idea to have a mixture of RGB and CMYK images in your publication, but sometimes, it happens. Be aware that all graphics are changed to a single format throughout the EPS. Is this going to work for you in the exported file? Do you need the EPS saved in a particular color space for the final printing? For instance, transparencies work best when colors are in the RGB color space, and separations require CMYK. Do you want a grayscale version of your color publication, or is there no color used in the file, so a grayscale EPS would be fine?

- Do you want the imported images to be high or low resolution in the EPS? Depending on the resolution of your output device, you could choose either.

- Will this EPS version need to omit graphics saved in specific formats, EPS, PDF, or bitmap images?

- Do some or all of the graphics in your publication have OPI comments saved in them? If they do, do you want to have OPI replacement during the conversion?

With the answers to these questions in hand, you can safely proceed with a conversion. Preparing to convert takes more time than the actual conversion. There are only two panels to set up, the EPS panel and the Pages panel (see Figure 10.13).

Figure 10.13

The EPS Options panel on the left determines how the elements of your InDesign publication are saved in the conversion, and the Pages panel of the Export EPS dialog box on the right determines which pages in your publication are exported.

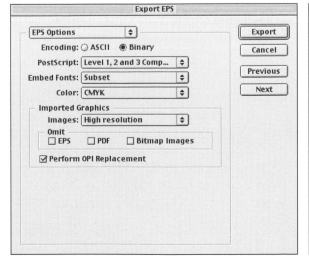

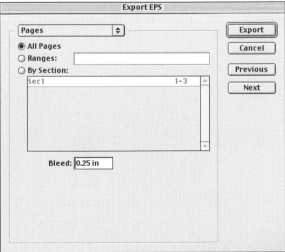

Note: Be sure to select the export format. Merely typing in the correct extension (.eps, .pdf, .sep, .htm, or .html) isn't enough to tell InDesign what format you want.

Exporting an EPS creates single-page files, even if the InDesign publication is laid out in spreads. The steps for exporting an EPS version of your InDesign publication are few and straightforward.

1. With the InDesign file open, choose File|Export.

2. Select the Format or Type, EPS, and determine where you want the exported file saved, then click Save.

3. In the EPS Options panel, select:

   - Encoding: ASCII or Binary

   - PostScript: Level 1, 2, And 3 Compatible, Level 2, or Level 3

   - Embed Fonts: Subset, Complete, or None

   - Color: CMYK, Gray, RGB, or Device Independent

   - Images: High Resolution or Low Resolution

   - Omit: EPS, PDF, Bitmap Images

   - Perform OPI Replacement

4. Select the Pages panel from the pop-up menu at the top of the panel, and set:

   - All pages, Ranges, or By Section, and select the sections from those listed

   - Bleed: Enter a dimension

5. Click the Export button, and it's done.

Remember, the options you set are application-specific, so the options remain in place for all subsequent EPS conversions until you change them. Then those new options remain in place until changed. As always, consult your print provider or user's manual for the output device before setting up export options for your InDesign publication conversions to EPS.

Prepress Export Options

In many respects, a prepress file is the same as an EPS export. It's a PostScript file, but also includes additional PostScript data that prepress applications use for trapping, and imposition, to mention but two things. As a matter of fact, the Export Prepress Options panel is identical to the Export EPS Options, but with several additional choices in the Pages And Page Marks panel. You'll be happy to see that Reader's Spreads are supported in Prepress exports (see Figure 10.14).

Two more observable differences between standard EPS exports and Prepress exports are the file extension (.sep) and file size. The extra PostScript information in a Prepress file added about 1MB to the conversion of an InDesign

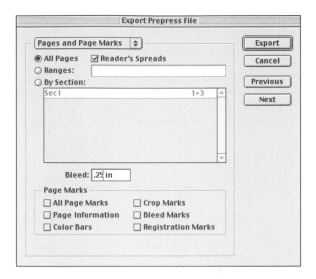

Figure 10.14

The prepress Pages And Page Marks panel is identical to the PDF Pages And Page Marks panel, except for the title bar of the dialog box.

file I exported as both an EPS and a Prepress file. The EPS was a little over 10MB, and the Prepress file was 11.5MB.

Prepress files can be printed to specific inkjet printers. The list is not distributed by Adobe at the time of this writing. Information about InDesign compatibility with specific models of inkjet printers should be obtained directly from the manufacturer.

This much I can assure you. If you use a Mac, you must have a PostScript printer, but not necessarily a high-end PostScript printer. A PostScript inkjet will do. There are utilities out there now that allow Macintosh non-PostScript printers to behave as if they were PostScript printers. And the soon-to-be-released Adobe PressReady will make producing proof prints from some models of non-PostScript printers a breeze (see the sidebar "PressReady Can Do").

Desktop printing a Prepress file in Windows can be done on either a PostScript or a non-PostScript printer. Naturally, the output quality of your printer dictates the quality of the proof print. On both Macintosh and Windows, the real determinate is whether the printer has a driver that is compatible with InDesign.

To create a Prepress file from an open InDesign publication, follow these steps.

1. Select File|Export.

2. Select File Format or Type: Prepress File.

3. Click the Save button to open the Export Prepress File dialog box. Remember, this only tells InDesign the file name, format, and where to save the new file.

PRESSREADY CAN DO

Adobe is marching toward the goal of providing every tool you need for working with and preparing publications. PressReady will be another arrow in that quiver. This is information I gleaned in an interview with one of the Adobe PressReady team members.

Many designers would far rather select colors, design the layout, and leave the rest to someone else. Printer setup, PPDs, all those technical demands are not for them. Well, PressReady, used in conjunction with InDesign's color management, is for them.

PressReady lets designers view full-color comps of their work printed to select inkjet printers without requiring PostScript or complicated software RIPs. There's no need to own a PostScript output device, or to pay for the use of one at a service bureau, just to view designs during the creative process. After a brief setup to tell PressReady which inkjet device you're using, PressReady handles the under-the-hood settings.

The only things you need to do in InDesign are: Be sure CMS is enabled, and select the exact same printer for Separations and Composite printer destinations as the printer you assign in the PressReady control panel. From there on, you don't even have to launch PressReady. Simply choose Print to get a good, representative color comp. PressReady closes automatically after the print is run.

PressReady supports select inkjet models, including the following:

• Canon Bubblejet 800

• Epson Stylus Color 800, 850, 1520, 3000

• HP DeskJet 895Cse, 2000C, 1120C

When you purchase PressReady, Adobe gives you a free, 18-month subscription to Internet Update Program, which lets you know the moment new printer drivers are added to the list of those already supported. You can access this update information via the Adobe Web site. It's there for you 24 hours a day, seven days a week. Registered owners of PressReady can download whatever they need. Locate the most up-to-date list of supported printers and drivers at Adobe's PressReady Web site, www.adobe.com/prodindex/pressready/printers.html.

PressReady is also another way to create PDFs of documents when, heaven forbid, you're not using InDesign. Use PressReady with any application that designers use—InDesign, Illustrator, Photoshop, even the competition's desktop layout application.

4. In the Prepress Options, select the options needed for this particular export. (Those options were discussed in the Export PDF section of this chapter.)

5. Use the pop-up menu to choose Pages And Page Marks. Define which pages and page marks you want included in your Prepress file.

   Be sure to set the bleed distance if your publication has bleeds extending off the perimeter of any publication pages. Remember, the page marks need to know how far bleeds extend beyond the page perimeter to position the page marks so they don't overprint bleeds.

6. Click the Export button, and it happens.

You can now run a proof print, send the Prepress file to a service bureau, or send the file to a print house for separations and printing, according to the options you've chosen. Always ask your print provider to guide you in setting up the Prepress options to meet their specific output devices. Some print providers use high-end trapping and imposition software that will override any options you set in your Prepress file. Some do not. That's why you need to communicate with your print provider.

PROJECT Export To A Prepress File

This is a simple, self-directed project. To test drive the Prepress export, you can use any publication, including the Race.Convert.indd file you already converted to PDF. Refer to Steps 1–6 in the "Prepress Export Options" and to the "Export Options" section of this chapter if you need to refresh your memory.

HTML Export Options

HTML options differ from print exports because these files need to meet a set of conventions established for the Web. Among other things, file naming must be based on the Unix convention (eight characters plus an extension), and you should limit colors to 216 colors in order to display correctly on any platform.

If you've never created a Web page from the ground up, that is, writing the HTML tags and preparing the graphics for the pages, there are some things you need to know before converting a publication. These points help you understand why and how an InDesign publication converted to HTML looks different in some respects from the original file.

- *Text attributes*—Not everything you can do in print translates to a Web page. Text, for instance, has attribute limitations on the Web. Web text can display specific fonts, but the viewer must have those fonts installed. The size, leading, underline, strike-through, alignment, indents, and space before or after paragraphs can be replicated in HTML. However, some text in your publication may be converted to a graphic, which means it is no longer editable. Some things, such as tracking, kerning, paragraph rules, justification, hyphenation, and no-break text settings, are lost in the translation unless InDesign converts text with these attributes to a graphic.

- *Text flow*—Not all browsers display HTML exactly the same. Each browser has slightly different capabilities. InDesign conforms to the World Wide Web Consortium standard for Cascading Style Sheets, and browsers version 4 or higher of Netscape Navigator/Communicator or Internet Explorer should display your text similarly cross-platform. Line breaks will vary based on the options you choose, the size of the original publication, the size of the screen the HTML version is viewed on, and, in some cases, the browser preferences a user establishes.

Note: If you design a publication, knowing from the outset that it will be used as an HTML file, you can use browser-safe colors as you design. To add the Web library of colors to your Swatches, choose Window|Swatch Libraries|Web, and select the colors you want to use from the library. Then, use the pop-up menu attached to the library to Add To Swatches. Otherwise, you may find that colors shift during conversion.

- *Graphic conversion*—All of the graphics in the original publication are converted to GIF or JPEG format. Some text frame attributes and embedded graphics, including all those graphics created directly in InDesign, are converted to GIF or JPEG based upon the need for transparency in the Web versions.

- *Item placement*—Positioning of objects on your original pages can be maintained to a greater or lesser extent based on your choice of options for Positioning. Again, the version of browser used to view your pages has a great deal to do with what is seen. Version 4 or higher is the best bet, but even then, some objects are repositioned during conversion.

With these caveats in mind, your best bet is to try a conversion and preview it in a browser before uploading it to the world.

The first part of the job of exporting to HTML is identical to all the other exports.

1. Select File|Export.

2. Choose the Format or Type, HTML, and name your file according to Unix convention (eight characters plus .htm or html, no special characters in the first eight except an underline to indicate a space).

3. Set the place you want the conversion stored, and click Save to open the Export HTML options dialog box (see Figure 10.15).

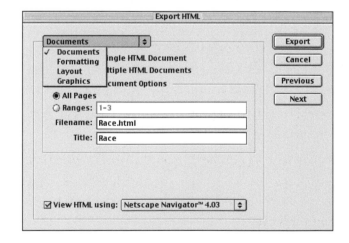

Figure 10.15

You have four panels of options to set before completing your HTML export: Documents, Formatting, Layout, and Graphics.

4. In the Documents panel, select the option that suits your export needs best:

- *Export As, Single HTML Document*—This converts all pages of your publication into one Web page. Each publication page is divided from succeeding pages by a horizontal rule. That may be perfect for a one- or two-page layout, but may create an excessively long single Web page if your original publication has many pages. Most folks hate to scroll through long pages on the Web.

To spare the scrolling frustrations, you might want to select Multiple HTML Documents for long publications. According to your choice of Single HTML Document or Multiple HTML Documents, the lower portion of this panel changes. Single HTML Document Options are shown in Figure 10.16.

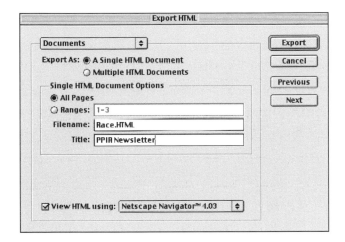

Figure 10.16
Notice in particular the title entered for this single HTML page.

- *All Pages*—This one is obvious. All publication pages are converted.

- *Ranges*—Select and identify specific pages to export and convert into a single HTML page.

- *Filename*—You can change the name of the exported pages in this text box. This change appears within the HTML code, not in the name of the file.

- *Title*—This is a very important text box. The words you enter here appear in the title bar of the Web page when it is displayed on a browser. You can use real words, spaces, and special characters here.

- *View HTML Using*—The pop-up menu here lists all the browsers you have loaded on your computer. Select the one you want to use to preview the converted pages.

- *Multiple HTML Documents*—All the pages exported have links, and a navigational bar (discussed later in these options) to access

Note: If you have Web page coding background, and you have a Web text editor, such as BBEdit (or any application that displays text-only documents, even Notepad or SimpleText), you can edit the HTML code after conversion. Be advised, though, that this takes real expertise and is not for the novice.

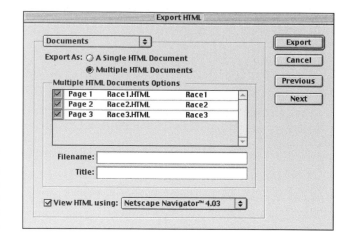

Figure 10.17
The Multiple HTML Documents options also allow you to change the default file name and/or title for each of the publication pages you're exporting.

those links. To rename each exported page, highlight it in the list and enter a new file name and/or title (see Figure 10.17).

- Deselect any publication pages you want omitted from the Web conversion.

- To enter a file name different from the default file name, or a title for any of the pages (one that appears in the title bar of the browser window) you're exporting, select the page from the list first, then enter the name changes.

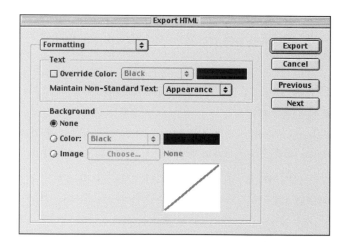

Figure 10.18
The Export HTML Formatting panel.

Note: If you export a publication with Type|Show Hidden Characters activated, all text converted to graphics includes the hidden characters.

5. Use the pop-up menu to select the Formatting panel (see Figure 10.18).

- *Override Color*—Choose this to apply a new text color from the list of browser-safe colors to all of the text in your publication. All text except, that is, text that is converted to a graphic, and that is determined by the next option.

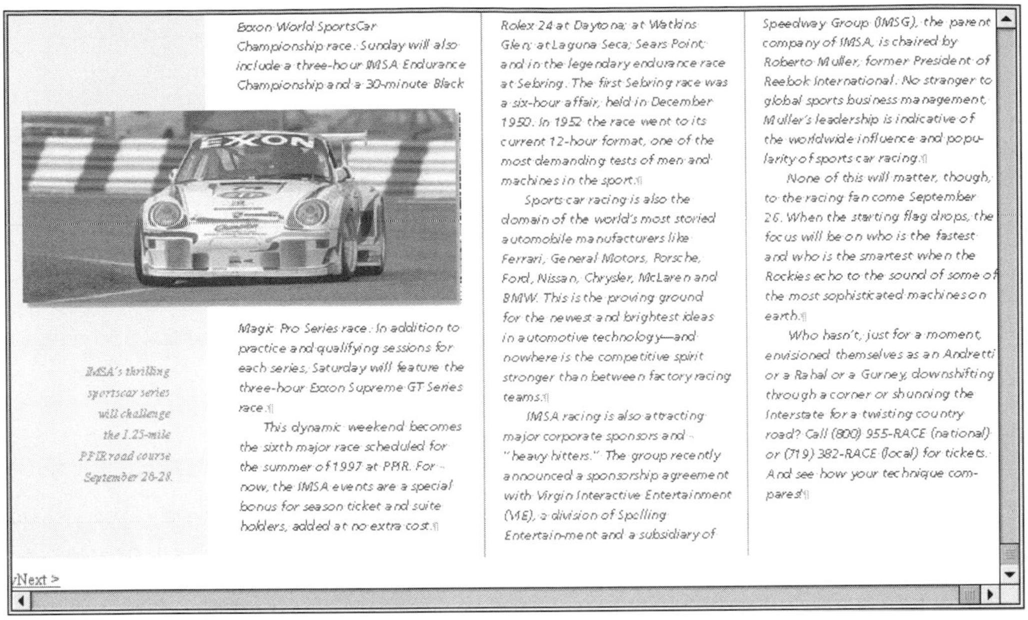
Exxon World SportsCar Championship race. Sunday will also include a three-hour IMSA Endurance Championship and a 30-minute Black
EXXON
Magic Pro Series race. In addition to practice and qualifying sessions for each series, Saturday will feature the three-hour Exxon Supreme GT Series race.
This dynamic weekend becomes the sixth major race scheduled for the summer of 1997 at PPIR. For now, the IMSA events are a special bonus for season ticket and suite holders, added at no extra cost.
IMSA's thrilling sportscar series will challenge the 1.25-mile PPIR road course September 26-28.
Rolex 24 at Daytona; at Watkins Glen; at Laguna Seca; Sears Point; and in the legendary endurance race at Sebring. The first Sebring race was a six-hour affair, held in December 1950. In 1952 the race went to its current 12-hour format, one of the most demanding tests of men and machines in the sport.
Sports car racing is also the domain of the world's most storied automobile manufacturers like Ferrari, General Motors, Porsche, Ford, Nissan, Chrysler, McLaren and BMW. This is the proving ground for the newest and brightest ideas in automotive technology—and nowhere is the competitive spirit stronger than between factory racing teams.
IMSA racing is also attracting major corporate sponsors and "heavy hitters." The group recently announced a sponsorship agreement with Virgin Interactive Entertainment (VIE), a division of Spelling Entertain-ment and a subsidiary of
Speedway Group (IMSG), the parent company of IMSA, is chaired by Roberto Muller, former President of Reebok International. No stranger to global sports business management, Muller's leadership is indicative of the worldwide influence and popularity of sports car racing.
None of this will matter, though, to the racing fan come September 26. When the starting flag drops, the focus will be on who is the fastest and who is the smartest when the Rockies echo to the sound of some of the most sophisticated machines on earth.
Who hasn't, just for a moment, envisioned themselves as an Andretti or a Rahal or a Gurney, downshifting through a corner or shunning the Interstate for a twisting country road? Call (800) 955-RACE (national) or (719) 382-RACE (local) for tickets. And see how your technique compares!
Next >

Figure 10.19

These columns of text were converted to a graphic and have the hidden characters in the Web page, because they weren't hidden in the publication. Text below and to the left of the car photo is editable text and shows no hidden characters.

- *Maintain Non-Standard Text*—If you choose this option, the text attributes changed to graphics (GIF) are: baseline shift, ligatures, Old Style, tracking and kerning, paragraph rules, justification, hyphenation, and no-break settings applied in your original publication. Also, you must make one further choice to affect the text.
  - *Appearance*—This maintains the look of the text as it appears in the publication, but renders it uneditable because it becomes a graphic.
  - *Editability*—Editable means that the text could be revised in the HTML code. Be aware that Editability removes any additional formatting attributes you may have applied, such as rotating (see Figure 10.19).
- *Background*—Many Web pages have fancy backgrounds, and you can apply one to your publication pages, if that suits your needs and taste.
  - *None*—This leaves the background of all your exported HTML pages as they appear in the original publication.
  - *Color*—Apply a browser-safe color to all the exported pages by choosing from those listed in the pop-up menu of choices. The color you choose is applied to all exported pages.
  - *Image*—Choose an image for the background of all your exported pages. Only images saved as JPEG or GIF can be assigned as a background image.

Be aware that the size of the image you choose has a definite effect on your background, because the image is automatically tiled. A very small image will be repeated more frequently than a large image (see Figure 10.20).

6. Select the Layout panel from the pop-up menu and set the following options (see Figure 10.21):

   • *Positioning*—It's a matter of experimentation. Try one. If you don't like the result, you can always ditch the converted file and reconvert with different options.

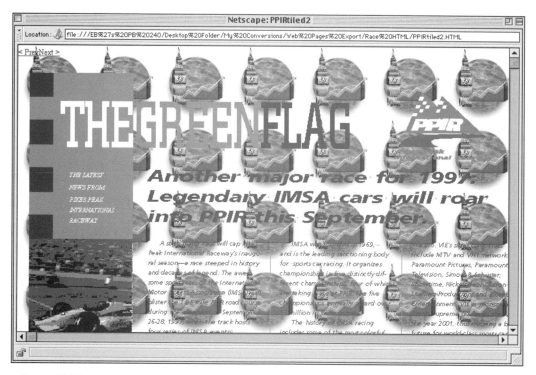

Figure 10.20

Avoid images that might make text on your pages difficult or impossible to read. Contrast between background and text is the key.

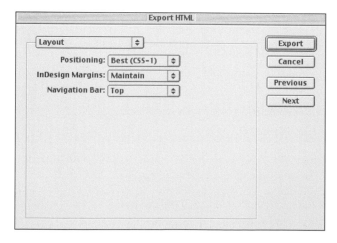

Figure 10.21

The Export HTML Layout panel has only three options.

- *Best CSS-1*—This choice attempts to replicate your original placement of objects according to the Cascading Style Sheet conventions.

- *None*—Choose this to ignore your placement of objects, and let InDesign place objects for you on the HTML pages. This may be a better choice than you think.

- *InDesign Margins*—Only you know whether the margins in your publication are critical to your Web page conversion.

  - *Maintain*—If your margins are dear to you, and you want to keep them as designed after the conversion, make this choice.

  - *None*—This uses the viewers' browser default margins for your exported pages.

- *Navigation Bar*—The navigation bar in InDesign conversion is not the usual banner or button sort of navigational device (see Figure 10.22).

Figure 10.22
InDesign's navigation bar is simply words, <PrevNext>, linking pages so that viewers can move through the pages.

- Position the navigation bar with any of three options.

  - *Top*—If your pages are short, this is a good option.

  - *Bottom*—If you prefer to have viewers see the content of your pages before moving to the next or previous page, choose this option.

  - *Both*—This gives your viewers a choice. They can zip right to the next page from the top of any page, or read the content and proceed to the next or previous page after reading. This is a particularly thoughtful choice if your pages tend to be long.

7. Choose the Graphics panel from the pop-up menu and set the following options (see Figure 10.23):

  - *Save Images As*—You can force all graphics to be saved as either GIF or JPEG, or let InDesign make the decisions.

    - *Automatic*—InDesign assesses each graphic and determines whether it is better suited to GIF (good for line art and broad swaths of flat color), or JPEG (good for continuous tone images).

Note: In some conversions the navigation bar will overprint the page content. There is no way of knowing whether that will happen until after you've converted the publication and previewed it on a browser. If you find that your choice of navigation bar placement doesn't work, you have to reconvert the publication with the navigation bar set to another option. Just discarding a single page that has a poorly placed navigation bar and reconverting that page loses the linking that existed in the multiple page conversion.

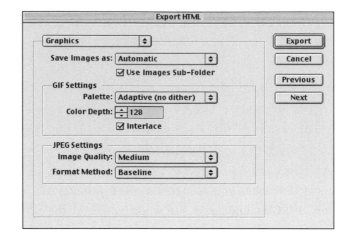

Figure 10.23
Graphics options in the Export HTML dialog box are critical to the quality of your images displayed in Web pages.

- *GIF*—Forces all images, continuous tone and line art, to be GIFs. This can be quite acceptable in some cases, and definitely makes smaller image files that load more quickly. In some cases, file size reduction can cause color shifts because of the GIF color palette maximum of 256 colors.

- *JPEG*—This forces all graphics, even simple line art, to JPEG format. The display quality is sometimes higher, but the download/display time can be lengthy.

- *Use Images Sub-Folder*—This creates an additional folder to hold your converted graphics. Believe me, this is a good idea. If the publication you're converting is image-heavy, and particularly if you plan to change any of the graphics at a later time, you won't have graphics mixed up with HTML pages.

- *GIF Settings*—These options determine the way your GIFs are saved.

  - *Adaptive (No Dither)*—Dithering is mixing tiny bits of colors to simulate colors other than those available in the 216 Web palette.

  - *Web*—This applies only the Web-safe colors (216) drawn from the Windows and Macintosh system colors.

  - *Exact*—This creates a palette based on only the colors used in a graphic. If any graphic has more than 256 colors, you are alerted that the exact palette can't be used.

  - *System (Win)*—If you know that your converted pages will be viewed on a single platform, this option allows you to draw from the system palette in the Windows operating system.

- *System (Mac)*—Again, this is best used only if you are certain the converted pages will always be viewed on a Macintosh. Some rather unattractive results can occur if the pages are viewed on a different platform.

- *Color Depth*—This option is available only if you've chosen either Adaptive or Exact. In the spinner, specify the number of colors for each GIF created during the conversion. The maximum is 256, but a lower number results in a smaller file size for the GIF. To make an educated decision, you need to assess the graphics that will be converted to GIFs, and decide just where you think the breaking point is. Choosing too low a number can make for ugly graphics. Too high a number adds unnecessary bulk to the graphic files.

- *Interlace*—Those graphics that twinkle onto the screen in a random appearance of pixels are interlaced graphics. The effect was created to hold viewers' attention while downloading larger graphics. Small graphic files don't need to be interlaced.

- *JPEG Settings*—These options apply to continuous tone images, such as photographs.

- *Image Quality*—Low, Medium, High, and Maximum are your choices. The only advice I can offer here is, "Let trial and error be your guide." Low produces the smallest file size, and Maximum the largest file size. Depending on the quality you demand, it's quite possible to have acceptable JPEGs at any setting. For instance, a map that is continuous tone may look fine set to Low, but a client's garment photograph could do great disservice to the product at anything but Maximum.

- *Format Method*—This sets how quickly JPEG images begin to appear on the Web page.

  - *Baseline*—The entire JPEG must download before appearing on the Web page. This works fine for small JPEGs, but not so fine for larger JPEG files.

  - *Progressive*—Similar to interlacing GIFs, this displays the JPEG as a fuzzy image at first with increasing clarity as the download is completed. Like interlacing, it holds the viewer's attention, and often averts the "click...next" syndrome found in so many Web cruisers.

HTML Export Errors

Occasionally you'll encounter an error as the export process rolls on. A warning appears to let you know the sort of error that cropped up, but not where it occurred. The Warning dialog box shown in Figure 10.24 opened as I exported a publication. The only solution was to scrutinize each page to determine what was omitted.

Figure 10.24

The Warning dialog box appears only if there has been an omission during the export process, and it behooves you to be very familiar with the file to identify the omitted items.

> One or more objects failed to export due to an unknown error. Please check the HTML file.
>
> OK

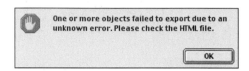
Convert Files To HTML

This is another self-directed project. Using the previously discussed export options for HTML, try converting either or both of the files you've already worked with, Skate.Convert.indd or Race.Convert.indd, to HTML. You'll find several surprises after conversion. For instance, in the conversion I did, the cover of the Skate brochure landed in an unexpected position. If you choose to convert the Raceway newsletter, you'll see that the majority of the text in the newsletter is converted to graphics, and the editable text at the far lower right on the last page of the Race newsletter has odd line breaks.

1. Try different options, making a pencil and paper note as you select options in each panel of the Export HTML options dialog box.

2. Compare the results of each export in your browser. This takes some time, so turn up the music, and get ready to examine every page carefully.

3. Make a list of options that don't work well and why. That way, when you approach a paying job, you'll spend much less time fiddling to get just the right result.

Moving On

In the final chapter, you address printing concerns and features that InDesign offers. You'll learn about In-RIP, the newest way to handle trapping in the desktop publishing world, investigate the Print dialog box, and gain insights into all the printing options available.

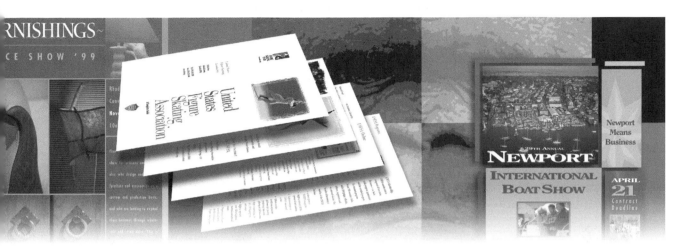

PUTTING YOUR PUBLICATION TO BED

11

Every print job differs, but InDesign has many interesting print features to help you proof and print your publications.

Skills Covered In This Chapter

- Set up In-RIP trapping for compatible printers

- Discover InDesign's PostScript Printer Descriptions (PPDs), Adobe PostScript, and Virtual Printers

- Review all the options in InDesign's specialized Print dialog box

- See how InDesign's Preflight feature can reduce printing problems

- Learn how to Package a publication for hand-off

Communicating With Your Output Provider

This may seem like an obvious statement, but if you plan to output your publication to a professional print house or to a service bureau, talk to your print representative before you even start designing a new publication. As you may have discovered, not all things the mind conceives can be made visual, at least not by all output providers. With your ideas in the formative stage, you'll stand a far better chance of achieving the results you want if you're aware of any limitations imposed on your design by the equipment used to output your publication. Different providers have different equipment, and you may have to search for just the right one to meet your lavish ideas.

Be sure to ask for the appropriate PostScript Printer Descriptions (PPDs) from your provider. (These are discussed in greater detail later in this chapter.) Ask if there are any settings or special ways of handling imported graphics that will smooth the way to output. Many providers have guidelines to make handing off your file as problem-free as possible. This saves you time, aggravation, and, above all, money.

People in the print industry may perform feats of magic, but they're not clairvoyant, and only you know exactly the results you want at output. Different service bureaus and print providers often have different requirements for what seems like the same output. Never assume you know what they want. Your best defense is a good offense, and it's anything but offensive to ask a lot of questions, seek help, and make certain that you're present (or, at least, accessible) for the printing of your work.

Subtle bribery (chocolates or doughnuts for the pressman and print rep) can make a big difference in the attention given your job. Weigh your hourly rate against the cost of misprints and reruns, and you're sure to see that the investment is worthwhile.

InDesign Trapping

Trapping, the printing instructions applied to contiguous inks so as to prevent gaps between the inks, is critical to the quality of your final printed output. Throughout your years as a graphic designer, you've no doubt heard again and again: "Trapping is best left to the experts." "Let the print folks do that." "It's a black art." "It's either pay me now or pay me later, but don't mess with trapping."

Well, just to be sure you don't overstep your skill level, InDesign provides only two methods of adjusting trapping. You can set individual objects to Overprint Fill or Overprint Stroke in the Attributes palette (see Figure 11.1).

Figure 11.1
Trapping choices in the Attributes palette are applied only to selected objects.

Choosing Overprint Fill or Overprint Stroke slightly enlarges the ink span of frames, type, and paragraph rules for PostScript Level 2 or higher printers. Either of these options applied to an object overrides any automatic trapping set by InDesign.

Trapping With In-RIP

Adobe In-RIP Trapping is a means of automatically creating high-quality, professional trapping values that are recognized by the Raster Image Processors (RIPs) of output devices compatible with In-RIP. In-RIP is a function of the Adobe PostScript 3 page-description language, so that dictates whether a printer is compatible or not. Both colors created and applied within InDesign and colors imported from other programs are trapped by In-RIP in text and graphics throughout your publication.

According to Adobe, In-RIP technology offers "a number of benefits—including better quality and performance." That's undeniable, as you'll learn the first time you actually apply and print a publication with In-RIP settings. Print the same publication from a different device, and you'll really see.

To activate In-RIP's options, you need to have Adobe PostScript printer driver 8.6 (Mac OS), 4.3 (Windows 98), or 5.1 (Windows NT) installed. These are included on the InDesign installation CD-ROM. You also must install and select an In-RIP compatible PPD (PostScript Level 3 Printer Description) through the Adobe PS driver. (The Adobe PS driver is on the InDesign installation CD-ROM, and it's installed automatically with InDesign.) With these installed, you don't even need to have the selected PostScript printer hooked up to your computer. Just activate In-RIP in the Trapping panel of the Print dialog box (see Figure 11.2).

The catch here is that In-RIP actually performs the trapping only with "supported PostScript 3 devices that have the In-RIP option." If you or your print provider don't have the proper printer and use the proper RIPs (there are thousands of RIPs out there), you're out of luck. My favorite print rep assures me that it won't take long for manufacturers to develop the necessary RIPs and make them available to all.

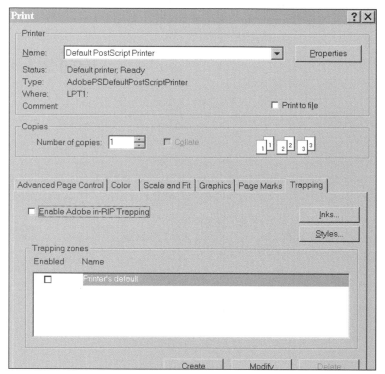

Figure 11.2
The Print dialog box option
Enable Adobe In-RIP Trapping
on Mac and PC.

Note: One solution to personalized trapping that Adobe speaks of is a plug-in. They're working on that and will make it available—someday—for those who need host-based trapping. We can hope that the plug-in is available at release time, but to date, it's still in development. You can also use a specialized trapping program (such as TrapWise).

For In-RIP-compatible PostScript Level 3 printers, you can make modifications to the In-RIP default trapping in the Print dialog box. If your print provider has no In-RIP compatible devices, or prefers to use his own trapping software, In-RIP can always be turned off before the press run.

Don't let the absence of high-end trapping give you second thoughts about InDesign, though. Some graphics applications, such as Illustrator, give you trapping options not available to InDesign. If specialized trapping is an issue in some of your graphics, set the trapping specs in the graphics application. Those trapping values are imported to InDesign when you place the graphic.

When you, as the designer of a publication, are able to set trapping, plenty of pitfalls present themselves. You may already know that resizing graphics imported with trapping values (never the best way of working) could, in some other DTP applications, require that you or your print provider reset the trapping. When, as in other DTP applications, you need to set trapping for colors that are close in value, you sometimes need to change your monitor to grayscale to compare the values and determine which color is darker, or you can convert the colors to HLS (Hue, Lightness, and Saturation) to determine comparative color values. That's a lot to ask, and unless you're expert in trapping to every output device you're ever likely to use, it's risky business.

In-RIP takes care of those adjustments. And therein lies the heart of the matter. In-RIP traps automatically based on information you provide as to the output device. It recognizes the different trapping requirements for solid, contiguous colors, and continuous tone colors in relationship with solid colors and other continuous tone colors. There's no chance you'll make a muddle of trapping, so there's no chance of running up expenses to correct your erroneous trapping. Activate In-RIP, select the In-RIP compatible driver for the printer you will use, and let the trapping begin.

Printing

InDesign's documentation has a remarkably concise overview of each kind of printing output. Rather than bore you with information you already have, I suggest you flip to the printing chapter of the documentation if you've misplaced a certain definition or piece of basic printing information, or if you want more information about printer drivers and PPDs chances are good that it's there.

PostScript Printer Descriptions (PPDs)

Every PostScript printer should have a PPD associated with it. The PPD communicates information about the printer to InDesign, such as the fonts resident in the printer. It also relays what paper sizes the printer can handle, screen frequency, and resolution capabilities.

Installing the proper PPD before you spend time setting printing parameters is a must. "Proper" is not always the PPD that was installed when you installed the printer driver. Each new PPD applied to a printer creates what amounts to an additional printer, though; in fact, it's the same printer with different instructions attached to it. If you don't know what the proper PPD is for the printer you're targeting, you need to ask your print provider, or contact the print device manufacturer. Chances are good that your print provider will talk you through installing and setting up a PPD.

Because PPDs are nothing more than files full of instructions, they can be stored anywhere on your hard drive or network. Documentation that comes with your printer should guide you through the installation process. Again, the InDesign documentation is very helpful, too, and it covers both Mac and PC instructions for installing and using PPDs.

Virtual Printer And Adobe PS Printer Driver

On the install CD for InDesign, there is the option to install Adobe's updated printer driver (8.6 for the Macintosh, 4.3 for Windows, or 5.1 for Windows NT). If you don't already have this update, do it. It's required by InDesign. Along with the installation, you get a folder with a Virtual Printer ReadMe file. By all means, take a moment to read this carefully. It's helpful, and explains the ins and outs of using the Virtual Printer to generate PostScript files for a printer you aren't connected to (see Figure 11.3).

Figure 11.3
The ReadMe files contain valuable information about using the Virtual Printer and Adobe PS printer (8.6), and, as a bonus, Watermark information.

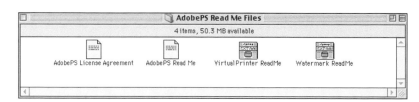

Every print job designated as going to the Virtual Printer also needs to have assigned to it the correct PPD for the real printer that will eventually do the print job. Mac users select the Virtual Printer in the Page Setup dialog box and assign a PPD. Win users need to use the printer setup on the InDesign CD to install the Virtual Printer and select a PPD you have for it during the installation. After each installation with a PPD, an additional icon appears in the Windows Print dialog box.

Selecting Virtual Printer in the Print dialog box saves your publication to a file on your hard drive. That file can be transported elsewhere, or printed at a later date when you are connected to the proper printer (see Figure 11.4).

Figure 11.4
At the left is the PostScript file generated when you select to print to the Virtual Printer.

Print Dialog Box

InDesign implements a broad array of print options through a special Print dialog box that expands on the usual Print dialog box. The appearance of Mac and PC print dialog boxes differs slightly; the Mac uses different panels selected from a pop-up menu in the Print dialog box to display options, whereas the PC uses tabs in the Print dialog box. However, all the same options are available to both platforms. Some of the Mac and PC print options are accessed in places other than the Print dialog box, though. As I go through the Mac Print dialog box panels, I'll tell you if the two platforms diverge, and where to find the same choices on either platform.

To make things easier to understand, you may want to open one of your InDesign publications, and choose File|Print.

Advanced Page Control

Both the Mac and PC have these controls in the Print dialog box. You can choose to print All Pages, a range of pages, or only certain predefined sections of your publication (see Figure 11.5).

Note: As with all page layout programs, there is no print preview choice for printing because the entire document viewed at 100 percent with guides, text threads, and frame edges hidden is your print preview.

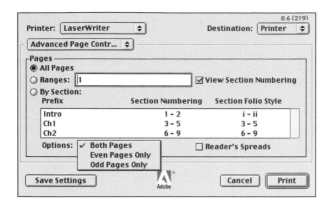

Figure 11.5
Advanced Page Control options in the Print dialog box determine what part of your publication is sent to the printer.

Use a hyphen to separate multiple pages (1–5) and a comma to separate ranges or individual pages. No matter whether you opt to print all pages, a range, or a section in your publication, in facing-page publications, you can also further define whether to print Both Pages (both odd- and even-numbered pages), Even Pages Only, or Odd Pages Only.

General

This panel of the Mac Print dialog box lets you choose the number of copies, whether to collate or print in reverse order, and what paper source to use, Cassette or Manual. On a PC, these options appear in the upper portion of the Print dialog box, but there is no option for printing in reverse order (see Figure 11.6).

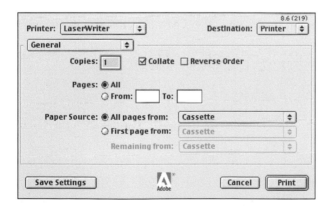

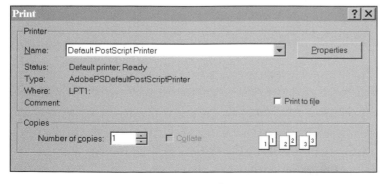

Figure 11.6
The figure on the top shows the General pane of the Mac Print dialog box. On the bottom is the upper half of the Windows Print dialog box.

Color

This panel applies to composites and to color separations, so Cyan, Magenta, Yellow, and Black always appear in the list of colors. In addition, any spot colors used anywhere throughout the publication also appear (see Figure 11.7).

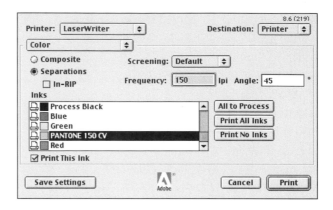

Figure 11.7

Look closely at this Color panel of the Print dialog box and you'll see a checkbox for activating In-RIP trapping and an option to print a Composite proof.

If you activate In-RIP in the Color panel, several things are required: a PostScript Level 3 printer, or certain PostScript Level 2 printers that support In-RIP separations, must be installed; the proper PPD must be installed; and a couple of test prints must be run to determine that the In-RIP defaults suit you. The manufacturer, your printer's documentation, or your print provider can help you decide if In-RIP trapping is suitable for your publication.

Be sure to ask your print provider if they want a composite file optimized for In-RIP. That could make it easier for them to set up trapping, separations, and OPI (Open Press Interface) replacements (cutting your costs), or it could be simply overridden, in which case your time is better spent designing.

By default, the optimal line screen and resolution for the PPD you have chosen is displayed in the Color panel. If you're reading this information and, at the same time, have the Color panel open, click on several of the colors listed under Inks, and notice that the frequency and angle values change.

As resolution increases, so too can the line screen values increase. Keep in mind that line screens and the resolution capability of your output device should correlate. In other words, setting a high line screen value for a printer capable of only low-resolution output doesn't give you a better print. It actually reduces the quality of the output.

It's possible to separate every color used in a publication, including spot colors, by clicking the All To Process button. You can also keep a spot color unseparated if you highlight the ink and deselect Print This Ink. In that case, instead of the four plates made when you click the All To Process button, you'll have five plates, one each for CMY and K, and one for the spot color.

WHY CREATE COMPOSITE PROOF PRINTS?

The world of digital print is less and less segmented. Designers carry many burdens that were previously left to printers. Clients are becoming more and more demanding as they perceive that digital publication production is cheaper because it's easier than traditional methods. In the early years of DTP, print houses often bore the added expense of repairing poorly built files just to keep their clients. Now, to place the responsibility for the final "print-ability" of files where it justly belongs—in the hands of the person who designed and built the file—many service bureaus and print providers request that a comp accompany the electronic file. If there is no comp, your consent is implicit, and you'll be charged for any repairs required to get your separated file to print correctly. This is a very good argument for running composite prints.

You can produce comps from certain models of color inkjet printers that have InDesign-compatible profiles, from dye-sublimation printers, or color laser printers.

You've been at this computer design business long enough to know that proofing a document on screen is a simple matter. Everything looks great. With color management, it even looks darned close to the way it will print, but actually getting the file to print is another matter.

A composite print, rather than using four or more plates to create colors, is a one-pass print that simulates the final CMYK output. You can print comps for proofing your work at any point during the designing of a publication. Each composite page layout corresponds exactly to each document page layout. How closely the printed comp corresponds to final separation printing is determined by the capabilities of your composite printer.

There are two options for producing composite prints: convert the file to PDF format and print it, or print a composite directly from within InDesign by selecting Composite on the Color panel or tab of the Print dialog box.

When you're ready to hand off the publication, you should run both a composite and separation printout of your publication, even if they are done only in black and white. The composite gives you an overview of the design. The separations tell you if everything is printing on the correct plate. Give these proofing printouts to your print provider when you deliver the electronic file. You'll not only be thanked, you'll save press charges.

Scale And Fit

Scale and Fit is primarily for producing printouts of publications whose size exceeds your desktop printer's paper handling capabilities. Though you may be able to scale a printout in other applications using your printer's options, this panel or tab, not the printer driver dialog box, is the only place you should use to scale the printout of InDesign publications (see Figure 11.8).

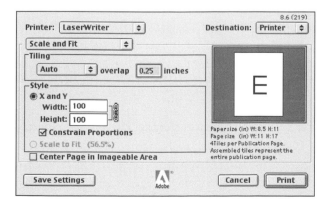

Figure 11.8

Set up tiling of oversize publications in the Scale and Fit panel or tab of the Print dialog box.

- *Tiling*—Most of the time you'll set Tiling to Auto, but the option for tiling manually is available. If you opt to tile manually, you must enter the amount of overlap you want.

- *Constrain Proportions*—It's hard for me to imagine why you'd deselect Constrain Proportions, but you can, and then you set the Width to Height ratio yourself.

If you want to reduce the printout of an oversize publication to fit each page of the publication on a single sheet of paper, InDesign has already calculated the reduced percentage that your print will produce. The reduction appears in parentheses beside the Scale To Fit option. When you choose Scale To Fit, Center Page In Imageable Area is automatically selected. If your particular printer produces off-center printouts due to the paper grabber feeding more of each sheet along the leading edge of each page printed, you will need to compensate for that by deselecting Center Page In Imageable Area.

Graphics

This panel or tab controls how graphics print. If you want images to print, make a selection from the Send Image Data pop-up menu in the Graphics panel or tab (see Figure 11.9).

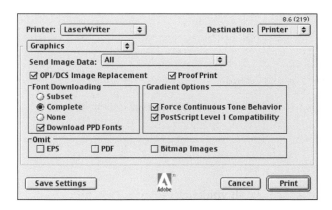

Figure 11.9

The Graphics panel or tab in the Print dialog box determines what graphic information is sent to the printer and allows you to turn off specific types of graphics (or all graphics if you choose Proof Print).

- *All*—Makes for a big chunk of data to churn through your printer, and it's best used at final output. It may just be overkill if all you want is a good, clean print of hi-resolution graphics from your desktop printer.

- *Optimize Subsampling*—Sends only enough data to your printer to get the best printout the printer is capable of. Optimize Subsampling, in conjunction with the frequency set in the Colors panel or tab, controls how much data is sent to the printer.

- *Low Resolution*—Reduces printing time by sending the screen resolution (72 dots per inch) of graphic data for the bitmap images in your publication. Low Resolution works in conjunction with OPI/DCS Image

Replacement. (DCS stands for Desktop Color Separators.) It does not affect any placed EPS files, though. You can also use the Low Resolution option when you just want to look at the layout of a page.

Click the OPI/DCS Image Replacement checkbox to cause images with these comments or instructions to replace low-resolution, for-position-only (FPO) images with the high-resolution version of the image as it is sent to the printer. If all you're doing is a low-resolution printout, naturally, you'll want to deselect this option. By default, all graphics created in InDesign include OPI instructions.

If you're more interested in proofing a printout of text and overall page geometry, click the Proof Print checkbox. When this checkbox is selected, no graphics print. They're all replaced with a placeholder graphic frame in the printout.

The Font Downloading options determine what font information is sent to the printer.

- *Subset*—Is the default and sends only the characters that appear on each page as the page prints.

- *Complete*—Downloads all the fonts used in your publication for each page as it prints.

- *None*—Is used when all the fonts used in a publication are fonts resident in your printer.

Other Graphics panel options include:

- *Force Continuous Tone Behavior*—If your publication has gradients, choose the way you want these to print. Selecting Force Continuous Tone Behavior gives the nicest transitions with the least amount of banding in gradients.

- *PostScript Level 1 Compatibility*—If you're targeting a PostScript Level 1 printer, gradients are handled slightly differently, so be sure to select PostScript Level 1 Compatibility.

- *Omit*—In the Graphics panel or tab, you see that it's possible to print include or exclude graphics saved in certain formats. Selecting all of these—EPS, PDF, and Bitmap Images—has essentially the same effect as selecting Proof Print. None of the graphics print. By including some types of graphics while omitting others, you might be able to track down the source of printing errors (a topic discussed later in this chapter), or to speed up printing.

Page Marks

At this point in your career, you surely have experience with page marks (sometimes called printer's marks). These apply only to publications being outsourced to a print house or service bureau, not to desktop printouts. A print house uses the marks to align the separations, to calibrate their device, measure dot density, and for trimming the publication. InDesign provides all the page marks required by high-end publications (see Figure 11.10).

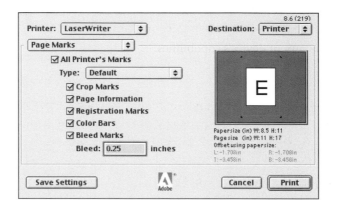

Figure 11.10

Opt to include or exclude any of the Page Marks in this panel or on this tab of your Print dialog box.

Naturally, when you choose any of these Page Marks, your paper stock needs to be large enough to accommodate the marks in addition to your publication pages and any bleeds you've designed. To see how this relationship stacks up, glance at the preview to the right on the Page Marks panel. Below the preview are measurements telling you the Papersize and the Pagesize. These measurements tell you whether your paper stock is sufficiently large to include the page marks you've chosen, and also tell you and print personnel what size paper stock is required to fit each page on a single sheet.

The option All Printer's Marks is self-explanatory. InDesign's default values for each page mark are applied automatically when you select this. You might want to customize or omit some of the page marks. In that case, select each mark individually.

- *Crop Marks*—Adds double hairlines at each corner of the publication pages for aligning the paper cutting machine blades. They can also be used to align the separation plates.

- *Page Information*—Prints the name of the file, the number of each page, today's date and time, and the color separation plate name at the lower left on each page or separation film.

- *Registration Marks*—Looks like a small crosshair target, and are used for aligning the separation plates. If you have both crop marks and registration marks, there is that much less chance of misregistration, though registration marks are usually enough for most print houses.

- *Color Bars*—Includes samples of the CMYK inks and a rank of grayscale ink. The color bars are used to adjust a printing device's ink density for your specific publication's run.

- *Bleed Marks*—Indicates how much beyond the page perimeter is imaged on each plate to ensure that the bleeds are, in fact, running beyond the cropped area of the page so that no paper stock shows along the edge after publication pages are cropped. Below the bleed marks option, you can specify how far bleeds should extend, from 1/8th of an inch up to a full inch. This distance is determined in part by the dimensions of your publication and the output device's capabilities.

> **Note:** If you save your publication in Prepress format (discussed in Chapter 10), you may find that a post-processing application (such as Adobe PressReady) can apply application-specific bleed specs that may vary from your setting in the Page Marks panel.

Trapping

I've already exhausted my stream of warnings about trapping earlier in this chapter, and discussed In-RIP at length, so it remains here only to look over the trapping options in the Print dialog box. Settings in the Trapping panel of the Print dialog box modify the In-RIP default settings. Even if you never intend to set trapping, familiarity with the breadth of these options gives you insights to the power of InDesign In-RIP trapping (see Figure 11.11).

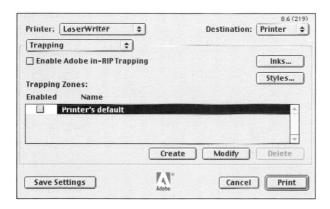

Figure 11.11

As the starting point for establishing complex trapping parameters for In-RIP, the Trapping panel gives access to additional panels.

- *Styles*—Are global and can be applied to any publication, or any zone defined within a publication. (Zones are discussed next in this section.) Set up trapping specification styles, using the Styles button on the Trapping panel (see Figure 11.12), and apply them to selected pages of a publication.

  Set up trapping styles for print devices you use frequently, or for special kinds of publications (such as annual reports), or for specific color combinations (such as overlapping spot colors). With a trapping style defined, all you need to do when you set up In-RIP trapping is click the Styles button and choose the style from the Trapping Styles dialog box (see Figure 11.13). Because trapping styles are application settings, every style you create is available to all publications.

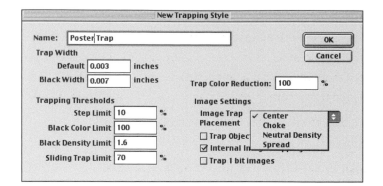

Figure 11.12
Set up and name a new trapping style by clicking the Styles button on Trapping panel or tab.

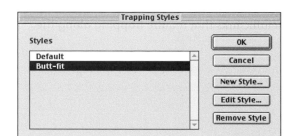

Figure 11.13
Each trapping style you create and save is listed in the Trapping Styles dialog box.

- *Trapping Zones*—Are local and they define specific pages and areas of pages within a publication where you want to apply a trapping style. One advantage to trapping zones is that you can speed up printing on pages that have no abutting colors by defining them as a zone and turning off In-RIP trapping.

- *Inks*—Allows you to define individual ink types, the neutral density, and the order in which the ink prints (see Figure 11.14).

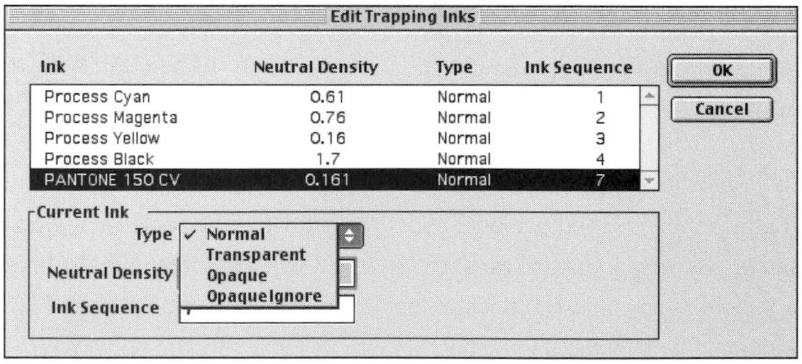

Figure 11.14
To edit the trapping of special inks, such as metallic ink or varnishes, use the Inks button on the Trapping panel to open the Edit Trapping Inks dialog box.

Select the ink from the list of inks used in the publication, and then choose the type from the pop-up menu, enter its neutral density, and the sequence (some folks call this "printing order").

- *Ink Sequence*—Is wonderfully useful, especially with opaque inks stacked on top of each other, if your output device supports sequencing. It determines the order in which you want the ink to print. The last ink in the sequential order is instructed not to spread, but still produces a good trap to other inks. Be sure to consult your print rep or the manufacturer of the device before relying on this option.

  - *Normal*—Covers most process and spot colors.

  - *Transparent*—Is used to be certain that underlying colors are trapped.

  - *Opaque*—Is right for metallic inks that require trapping along the edges.

  - *Opaque Ignore*—Eliminates trapping the ink altogether, both along the edges and to underlying inks. It's used for inks that don't blend well when trapped to other inks.

PostScript Settings

PostScript settings are the point at which things diverge between the Mac and PC Print dialog box. On a Mac, there is a panel listed for PostScript Settings. The PC version of InDesign doesn't have a PostScript Settings tab in the Print dialog box.

Setting Printer Options

On a Mac, in order to use the PostScript Settings panel, establish the print driver and PPD specifications before you open the Print dialog box. You do that within InDesign. Choose File|Page Setup. Select a printer and activate the options applicable to your publication.

For Windows, use the Start menu to select Settings|Printers and right-click the printer icon you are using, and set the options.

Error Handling

For error handling, too, the Mac and PC differ slightly. The Mac error handling is accessed in the Print dialog box by selecting Error Handling from the pop-up menu of panels. On the panel, select those options you want for the publication.

On a PC, select Start|Settings|Printers and highlight (or right-click) the appropriate printer icon, and select Properties, and click the PostScript tab. Select Print PostScript Error Information. That's it.

Note: Before you get to this point in setting up Print parameters, both Mac and PC users must have the proper printer driver installed (these are on the InDesign application CD-ROM), and you must have the proper PPD installed and selected. If you're outsourcing your printing, you may want to ask your provider to supply you with the correct PPD, and, if necessary, talk you through installing it and setting up any required PostScript Settings.

SAVE A PUBLICATION AS A POSTSCRIPT FILE

You no doubt know that saving a publication in PostScript format removes the necessity for having InDesign installed on the computer that is sending printing information to a PostScript output device. As I mentioned in Chapter 10, you can save a publication in prepress PostScript format with the extension .sep, or in standard PostScript format with the extension .ps.

If you work on a network, or plan to deliver files on external media, save the PostScript version of your publication to your hard drive to avert the possibility of creating a corrupted file caused by the time it takes to transfer data to an external storage medium or network.

To save your publication as a PostScript file, on a Mac, choose File from the Destination pop-up menu on the Print dialog box. Destination shows no matter which panel is selected. After all this is done on a PC, click the Print To File checkbox in the Print dialog box.

On a PC, open the Print dialog box using File|Print, and then click the Properties button in the upper-right corner of the Print dialog box. The Properties dialog box has a PostScript tab. Select that and choose the appropriate options for the printer you're targeting and your publication.

Layout

Determining the way your publication is placed on the paper stock is done differently on a Mac than on a PC. The Mac uses the Layout panel of the Print dialog box and the PC uses the Properties screen of the Printer settings, which you can access by choosing Start|Settings|Printers, then right-clicking the printer icon, and selecting Properties. Click the Paper tab in the Properties dialog box and set the options you want (see Figure 11.15).

Printing Errors

Highly complex objects, gradients, masks, compound paths, patterns, and multiple grouped objects—any and all of these can cause printing errors. Fonts can cause problems, too. (No derisive laughing!) Though ATM resolves missing font issues much of the time, some devices, such as a Lambda printer, won't print fonts with forced attributes. For instance, a plain font made to appear italic by using the Character palette or a keystroke to apply italic is guaranteed to make a printing error on some printers.

The easy answer is, "Don't use these elements, and don't force fonts to be what they aren't designed to be." But that's not always possible. The font issue can be resolved only by installing and using the proper font face, but some other hitches might be resolved by checking the settings in the Print dialog box.

By far the most common printing errors are caused by graphics. If you encounter printing problems you can't resolve by changing Print dialog box options (turn off EPS, PDF, and Bitmap Images in the Graphics panel), watch the print progress bar to identify a renegade graphic. The name of each graphic file being processed and printed appears below the progress bar. When you've pinpointed the problem file, place that graphic on a

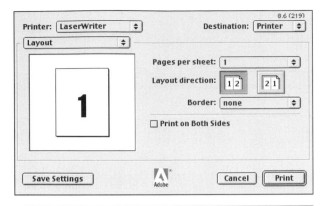

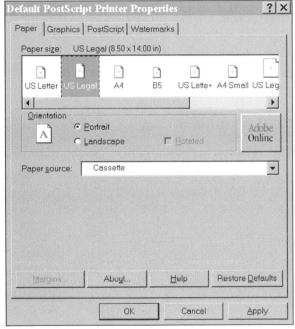

Figure 11.15

Mac options (top) for pages per sheet, direction, border, and whether to print on both sides are chosen in the Layout panel of the Print dialog box. The PC Print dialog box (bottom) has no Layout panel, so some of these settings, such as page orientation, are found in the Paper tab of the Printer Properties screen.

nonprinting layer. Run another test print, and, if all goes well, you can be sure that the graphic file needs replacing.

If that doesn't work, move all the graphics to a nonprinting layer, and return each graphic, one at a time, to its original layer. Run a test print after each addition. Continue moving the graphics from the nonprinting layer to a printing layer, and making additional test prints with each transfer until you find the files that need replacing. It's rather like tracking down a troublesome system extension on a Mac. No fun at all! But it works.

Cover Page And Background Printing

These last two panels listed in the pop-up menu of the Mac Print dialog box allow you to include a cover page that prints before the publication prints, or after, or to select None and avoid the whole issue. Background Printing, a Mac-only option, can be activated only if you have activated the system

Extension that enables background printing. Presuming you can do background printing, you can set a priority for the printing file, the time of day to send the spooled data to the printer, or you can spool the data, but suspend printing until you decide when you want it printed.

Because background printing dramatically slows down print time and processing on other work you may be doing simultaneously and consumes huge amounts of hard disk space for complex files, you probably will leave this option disabled. Patiently waiting for a publication to print is far less annoying than watching your computer strain to perform even simple tasks while also sending print data down the tubes.

A final reminder about the Print options you've chosen in the various panels or tabs: You can save these as a set, name the set, and reuse them quickly any time. The settings are application-wide, and so they apply to all publications you print. Keep in mind, however, that you can save only one set of print options.

Preflight To Prevent Oversights

Until InDesign, preflight checking was a matter of buying a separate piece of software or relying on reports created as you gather all the components of a publication for handoff. Neither PageMaker nor QuarkXPress includes a full-blown, built-in preflight capability. InDesign does, and it's both easy to use and thorough.

Note: If you have Composite selected in the Color screen of the Print dialog box, the Preflight report can give erroneous information about colors used in publications translated from QuarkXPress.

Typically, you perform a preflight check just before packaging a publication for handoff to a service bureau or print provider (there's more about packaging later in this chapter). With InDesign, you can run a preflight check at any time, even before you've established the print parameters. Check to see if everything you think is in the publication *is*, in fact, there—if all the fonts are what you think they are, if any colors are set to the incorrect type, if you have spot and process versions of the same color, if all the links are still intact. These picky little things can trip up output. In a collaborative work environment where many people work on the same publication file, or for in-house printing that doesn't need to be packaged, this preflight check can be a real lifesaver.

Choose File|Preflight and watch the progress bars as InDesign checks fonts, links and images, colors and inks, and print settings. When the check is complete, the Preflight report screen opens. Use the pop-up menu to view each panel of the Preflight screen (see Figure 11.16).

InDesign lets you save the Preflight report to a file. All the information shown in the Preflight screen is included in the report. You might want to use the date and time in naming your report, and make printouts to hand around at production meetings or go over with your print rep so everyone

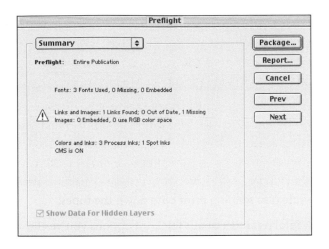

Figure 11.16

In the Summary screen of this Preflight report, there is one missing image. The pop-up menu lets you review the fonts, links and images, colors and inks, and print settings in your publication.

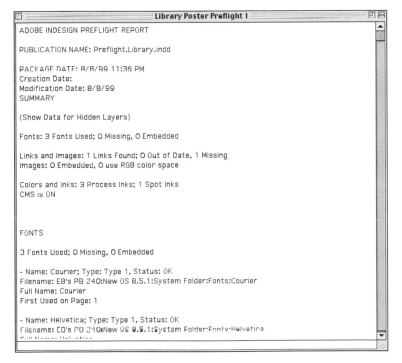

Figure 11.17

Saved Preflight reports contain a wealth of information about your publication, including all the information on the Preflight panes, and, in addition, creation and modification dates, lines per inch (lpi) settings for each color, and all of your current print settings.

knows the current status of the publication. Click the Report button in the Preflight report screen, name the report, and store it wherever you like (see Figure 11.17).

Macintosh Preflight reports are saved in SimpleText format that can't be imported to a new InDesign document (as can QuarkXPress Collect For Output reports). Preflight reports also can't be edited in SimpleText or unlocked by resaving! Windows Preflight reports are saved as Notepad (.txt) documents, and they have the same limitations. But, hey, a report is for information, not editing or art. There's no reason to edit a preflight report.

After looking over the preflight report, if you're ready to gather up all the things needed to print your publication, click the Package button. That starts the process discussed in the next section of this chapter.

Package

In addition to assembling in one place everything needed to print a publication, Package is a great way to archive your work. When you choose Package from the File menu, or click the Package button in the Preflight screen, InDesign scoots about your hard drive to gather up copies of all the components needed to print your publication. Yes, International Color Consortium (ICC) profiles are included, and even the fonts! There is an alert about the fonts, though (see Figure 11.18).

Figure 11.18
As InDesign bundles up your fonts for printing, you are sternly reminded of your responsibility to respect copyright by a Font Alert dialog box.

If, in the haste to meet your deadline, you forget to do a preflight check, InDesign automatically compares the latest preflight data with the current state of the publication. If things have changed in your publication since the last preflight check, you're advised in a dialog box, and the instructions document contains the correct updated information (see Figure 11.19).

The Continue button in the Instructions window proceeds to the next step in packaging your publication (see Figure 11.20).

When all is done, you have a folder that contains everything you requested to be copied for final output (see Figure 11.21).

A Word About All Print Jobs

NEVER MAKE ASSUMPTIONS

Always consult your print provider before setting final output print parameters.

As you know, every print job has a world full of options. Some print folks I know say (with no shame) that designers should concentrate on designing and leave printing to the people who are experts in printing. That makes a lot of sense. Most of us have tried, at one time or another, to give ourselves a haircut, and you know the consequence of that. Each print house has different equipment with different setup requirements. The people who use this equipment day in and day out know best how to get the results you want from their equipment. In some cases, all the trapping and print setup you do is overridden. Mind you, it can't hurt to do the setup, or to adjust trapping, or apply overprint, but unless you really have some expertise and know the quirks of your target output device, you may be using your time unwisely.

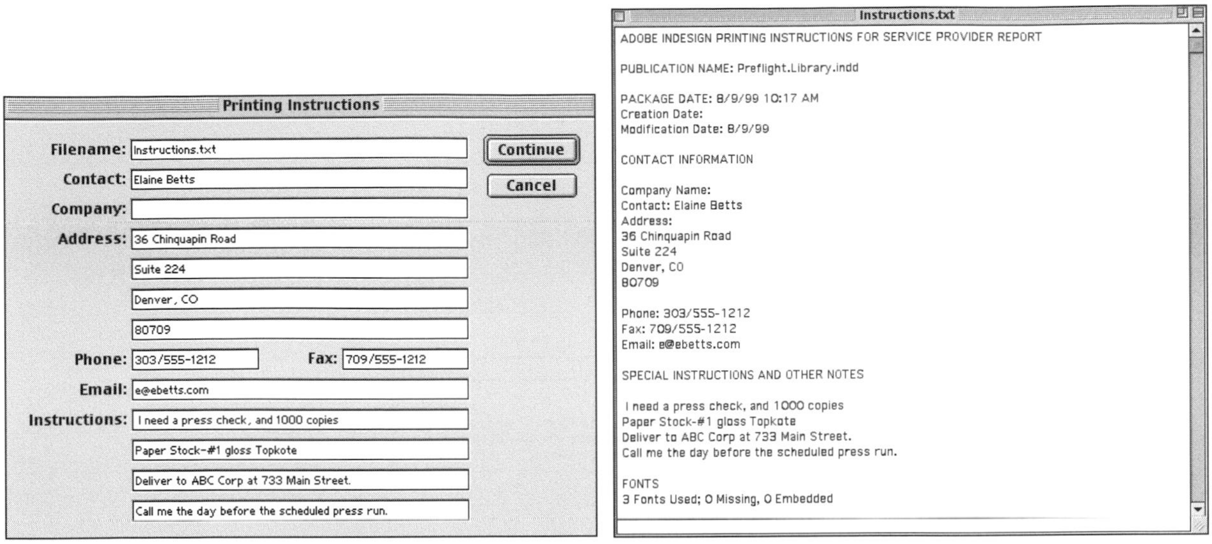

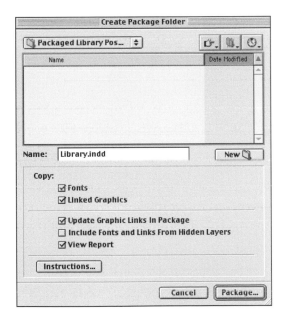

Figure 11.19

The figure on the top left shows the Instructions dialog box where you enter personal information and instructions to the print provider. The figure on the top right shows that same information as it appears in the print report, which also includes information about your publication and print settings that the person doing your print job uses to set up your job.

Figure 11.20

Create a new package folder to hold the things needed for your print job, and select those things you want copied to the package folder.

Figure 11.21

In this package folder is a copy of all the fonts used throughout the publication, your instruction document, the original InDesign publication, and all linked graphic and text files.

Photo Processing Lab Printing

Printing with photographic techniques is a slightly different ballgame from printing from a web press or other such device. Granted, some photo processing work is done on paper, but the printing devices used for photographic output use different techniques and have special requirements.

All papers handle color differently, including the various photographic papers. Some photographic materials inherently limit the gamut of colors you can use in your publications. For instance, C-print, Mural, D-flex, and Duratrans materials have difficulty with reds, oranges, and some shades of green, and fluorescent colors are sure to be less than you hope for in these outputs, if you get anything even close. Fluorescent colors, you see, depend on reflection of light from the surface applied inks, and these outputs, being photographic, use projected light to imprint the images on media. Inks are CMYK. Light is RGB. And therein lies the basis for certain color deviations.

Printers' inks are blended according to weight of inks applied to a medium (10 percent black, 40 percent magenta, and so on). Even color matching systems don't guarantee a perfect match. Keep in mind that color matching swatches can deviate from one book of swatches to another, though the variance is controlled. Speak to someone at Pantone, for instance, and you'll learn that they expect a variance of plus or minus 5 percent, and, in some cases, a considerably larger margin for error is acceptable in both their swatch books and your output. Yellow, for instance, can vary as much as 10 percent from the color sample and still be acceptable because the human eye doesn't perceive the deviation as precisely in yellows as it does in, say, grays, which are perceptible when the variance is more than 5 percent.

Your best solution is good planning from the outset of your publication. If you're certain of the destination device, design within the appropriate color space and gamut of the device. Multipurpose publications may require color space adjustments before transitioning from one device or medium to another. For instance, a web press piece designed in the CMYK color space and converted to RGB for a Web page will have little difficulty, because the RGB gamut is larger than CMYK, but reverse that order, and you're headed for color disappointments and color shifts in the printed piece.

Colors selected from a matching system are more limited than the CMYK gamut of colors. Especially for publications headed for both print and photographic output devices, using color matching swatches is more consistent, and aids your service bureau. It gives them a reliable comparison color to target, whereas CMYK colors that you create give them nothing more than the on-screen colors to judge by, and, as you know so well by now, every monitor displays color differently, even with Adobe's Color Management System (CMS) enabled.

Although color inkjet printers are four color devices, they handle laying down color quite differently from a separation printer. Web presses rely on successive application of ink dots of a single color (a plate) in relationship to other colors (screen angle) on a global, page-wide basis. Inkjet printers lay down inks on a linear basis, with each pass across the page printing the ink color assigned to each pixel. Because all printed media must have a receptive coating to accept the dye-based inks, the base material and coating determine both resolution and possible gamut. For instance, the same file printed on a coated paper will look different when printed on canvas or synthetic silk, white film, or photo gloss paper.

Some designers and service bureaus feel that the Pantone Solid To Process book gives the closest approximation of inkjet output, but there will always be variations of color from any output device, based on media, coatings, and even surrounding colors.

Table 11.1 shows specifications for optimum output to photographic media. There are general rules that apply to all output:

- *Scans*—Place scans in InDesign at 100 pixels per inch (ppi) or more and scaled to 100 percent to avoid interpolation at output time. The time spent preparing good scans is more than saved when you hand off your file to a service bureau or print provider, and that means money saved.

- *Fonts*—Use either Adobe PostScript or TrueType fonts throughout your publication, not some of each. Provide all screen and printer fonts for output, including those embedded in EPS art.

- *Continuous tone art*—Use EPS or TIFF format, sized and cropped appropriately before placing in your publication.

- *Vector art*—Use PMS colors at 100 percent, rather than choosing a PMS color and adjusting the ink weight, for example, to 50 percent.

- *Links*—Update all links before submitting file for printing.

- *Printouts*—Supply a hard copy printout (black and white will do) of the file with any notes you feel necessary to ensure good communication with output technicians.

Table 11.1   Handoff specs for photo processing output.

Device	Output	Preparations	File Size	Caveats
LAMBDA	A laser beam process done in the RGB color space suitable for large format photographic output, such as trade show booths, retail display, and paneled pieces. The output is PostScript on any traditional photographic material that comes in roll stock. It produces good resolution RBG output such as C-prints, Duraflex, Duratrans. Maximum size: 48" x 48" paper size.	RGB color space only. Scans must be 200 ppi, and not exceed 30,000 pixels in any one dimension. (A low-resolution scan produces a low-resolution output.) For best results, flatten all TIFFs, and remove channels and paths from Photoshop documents before placing them. Check all graphics at 1:1 ratio (minimum) for artifacts such as scratches, dirt, watermarks, and so on.	Not available.	Never mix color spaces within the publication. Use no image compression. For most accurate color, avoid using PMS uncoated colors.
Inkjet Less costly because CMYK, on a huge variety of substrates, such as gloss or semi-matte paper, clear film, canvas, removable vinyl, white film, synthetic silk, gold or silver matte paper, vinyl scrim, watercolor paper.	8 color—adds light and medium magenta and cyan to the usual CMYK, thus increasing the gamut.	Use the RGB color space. This allows better simulation of true RGB values.	Original scans determine the end result. Graphic file size at 100 ppi: 20" x 24"=13.7MB 24" x 30"=20.6MB 30" x 40"=34.3MB 40" x 50"=57.2MB 50" x 60"=85.8MB 70" x 80"=160.2MB 80" x 90"=206MB	Check for graphic artifacts (dirt, scratches, watermarks, and so forth).
Inkjet	4 color—CMYK.	Use the CMYK color space. For graphics select UCR (Under Color Replacement) at 90 percent black ink limit, and 275 percent total ink limit.	Add 25 percent to the RGB file sizes when using this CMYK output.	
35mm slides	Output size is 1.375" x .875".	Document setup size: 11"x 7.33", including background color. This is the correct proportion for slides.	Not available.	No bleeds. Leave a 0.5" margin around each page to ensure that slide mounts don't cover your work. Scans should be 150 to 200 ppi for best results. Do not set trapping values because this output doesn't rely on inks.

Moving On

This book's companion CD-ROM includes a PDF file filled with helpful information about scripting, and ways that scripting can be of use to you to increase your efficiency and alleviate drudgery. Both AppleScript and VB (Visual Basic) scripting are covered, and you'll have a chance to examine and create simple scripts that gently guide you into the world of scripting.

INDEX

If you like this book, you'll love these...

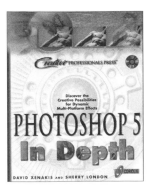

PHOTOSHOP 5 IN DEPTH
David Xenakis and Sherry London
ISBN: 1-57610-293-9 • $59.99
1,028 pages with CD-ROM

New techniques every designer should know for today's print, multimedia, and Web. Xenakis and London provide the most lucid and complete volume of its type, a practical how-to that never loses the designer's perspective of Photoshop as a key program in the production process.

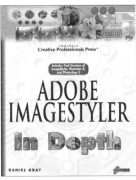

ADOBE IMAGESTYLER IN DEPTH
Daniel Gray
ISBN: 1-57610-410-9 • $39.99
400 pages with CD-ROM

Stop pushing those pixels around and supercharge your Web graphics with Adobe ImageStyler! You'll learn the ins and outs of ImageStyler in an easy-to-read, hands-on manner. *Adobe ImageStyler In Depth* dives into the program's features and goes far beyond the program's documentation to help you take your designs to the next level.

ILLUSTRATOR 8 F/X AND DESIGN
Sherry London and T. Michael Clark
ISBN: 1-57610-408-7 • $49.99
500 pages with CD-ROM

Take an exciting journey into the world of Illustrator graphics. Harness the power of Adobe Illustrator 8's new features: Brushes, Gradient Mesh objects, the Pencil tool, and the Photo Crosshatch filter. And then practice these techniques while completing real-world projects such as creating packaging, ads, brochures, and more.

CORELDRAW 9 F/X AND DESIGN
Shane Hunt
ISBN: 1-57610-514-8 • $49.99
400 pages with CD-ROM

Pick and choose the effects and techniques you want to emulate—from traditional to avant-garde, retro to techno, clean to chaos—all perfect for use in everyday design tasks. Load files off the companion CD-ROM—or use your own artwork—and walk through simple, step-by-step tutorials to get immediate satisfaction.

WHAT'S ON THE CD-ROM

The *Adobe InDesign f/x and Design* companion CD-ROM contains files required to complete projects in this book, including:

- *InDesign files*—These publication files are used in projects.
- *Fonts*—The Macintosh screen font files needed to properly display project publications are included.
- *Images*—The graphic files required to complete projects and properly display publications are included.
- *AppleScripts*—Macintosh AppleScripts for learning scripting and scripts for your immediate use with InDesign are included.
- *VB Scripts*—PC Visual Basic Scripts for learning scripting and scripts for your immediate use with InDesign are included.

System Requirements

Software

Macintosh

- Adobe InDesign 1 or higher is required
- Mac OS 8.5 or later
- A Web browser version 4 or higher is needed to view publications exported to HTML
- Adobe Acrobat Reader is needed to view publications exported in PDF format

PC

- Adobe InDesign 1 or higher is required
- Windows 98, Windows NT 4 Workstation with Service Pack 3, or later
- A Web browser version 4 or higher is needed to view publications exported to HTML
- Adobe Acrobat Reader is needed to view publications exported in PDF format

Hardware

Macintosh

- PowerPC 603e processor or greater (PowerPC G3 processor recommended)
- At least 48MB of RAM (64MB or more of RAM is recommended)
- A hard disk with at least 120MB of free space
- A CD-ROM drive
- Monitor resolution of 800 by 600 pixels
- Adobe PostScript Level 2 (or higher) printer

PC

- Pentium II Intel processor (Pentium II 300Mhz or faster Intel processor recommended)
- At least 48MB of RAM (64MB or more of RAM is recommended)
- A hard disk with at least 75MB of free space
- A CD-ROM drive
- High resolution monitor (24-bit Super VGA or greater) with video display card
- Adobe PostScript Level 2 (or higher) printer